# POST-GROWTH PLANNING

This book draws on a wide range of conceptual and empirical materials to identify and examine planning and policy approaches that move beyond the imperative of perpetual economic growth. It sketches out a path towards planning theories and practices that can break the cyclical process of urban expansion, crises, and recovery that negatively affect ecosystems and human lives.

To reduce the dramatic social and environmental impact of urbanization, this book offers both a critique of growth-led urban development and a prefiguration of ecologically regenerative and socially just ways of organizing cities and regions. It uncovers emerging possibilities for post-growth planning in the fields of collective housing, mobility, urban commoning, ecological land-use, urban–rural symbiosis, and alternative planning worldviews. It provides a toolkit of concepts and real-life examples for urban scholars, urbanists, activists, architects, and designers seeking to make cities prosper within planetary boundaries.

This book speaks to both experts and beginners in post-growth thinking. It concludes with a manifesto and glossary of key terms for urban scholars, students, and practitioners.

**Federico Savini** is associate professor in environmental planning, institutions, and politics at the University of Amsterdam, Center for Urban Studies. His research focuses on the interaction between regulations, politics, and urban transformations. As a degrowth scholar and activist, he studies, and experiments with, how cities can reduce their material footprint across different sectors, from housing commons to regenerative metabolism, from waste reuse to energy infrastructures. His most recent publications are "Towards an urban degrowth" (in *Environment and Planning A*, 2021) and the book *Planning and Knowledge: How New Forms of Technocracy Are Shaping Contemporary Cities* (2019, with Mike Raco). He is co-initiator of the housing cooperative de Nieuwe Meent in Amsterdam.

**António Ferreira** is deeply concerned with the environmental, social, and economic crisis the world is currently facing, and what that crisis means for our children and future generations. He hopes to contribute to addressing this crisis through the development of a deeper and ethically informed understanding of the world around us. He works as a Principal Researcher at CITTA: Research Centre for Territory, Transports and Environment, University of Porto, Portugal. His research interests cover a variety of themes, namely urban and transport policy, worldview theory, emotions in planning, and planning education.

**Kim Carlotta von Schönfeld** is a research fellow at the Centre for Transdisciplinary Research on Culture, Space and Memory at the University of Porto, Portugal. She is an interdisciplinarily oriented academic, critically but constructively bridging the fields of urban and regional planning, mobility, geography, governance, post-growth economics, psychology, critical innovation studies, international development, futuring, and third cultures. Her PhD thesis – defended at Wageningen University in 2021 – explored the benefits and drawbacks of social learning in co-creative planning processes, engaging a psychology-based lens. She holds a BSc in Human Geography and Planning and a Research Master's in Urban Studies from the University of Amsterdam, The Netherlands.

# POST-GROWTH PLANNING

Cities Beyond the Market Economy

*Edited by Federico Savini, António Ferreira,
and Kim Carlotta von Schönfeld*

NEW YORK AND LONDON

Cover image: L'anello; permanent landscape installation by Mauro Staccioli, Volterra, 2009.
Courtesy of Archivio Mauro Staccioli, Florence. Photo: Enrico Savini, 2017

First published 2022
by Routledge
605 Third Avenue, New York, NY 10158

and by Routledge
4 Park Square, Milton Park, Abingdon, Oxon, OX14 4RN

*Routledge is an imprint of the Taylor & Francis Group, an informa business*

© 2022 selection and editorial matter, Federico Savini, António Ferreira, and Kim Carlotta von Schönfeld; individual chapters, the contributors

The right of Federico Savini, António Ferreira, and Kim Carlotta von Schönfeld to be identified as the authors of the editorial material, and of the authors for their individual chapters, has been asserted in accordance with sections 77 and 78 of the Copyright, Designs and Patents Act 1988.

All rights reserved. No part of this book may be reprinted or reproduced or utilised in any form or by any electronic, mechanical, or other means, now known or hereafter invented, including photocopying and recording, or in any information storage or retrieval system, without permission in writing from the publishers.

*Trademark notice*: Product or corporate names may be trademarks or registered trademarks, and are used only for identification and explanation without intent to infringe.

*Library of Congress Cataloging-in-Publication Data*
Names: Savini, Federico, editor. | Ferreira, António (Environmentalist) editor. | Schönfeld, Kim Carlotta von, editor.
Title: Post-growth planning : cities beyond the market economy / edited by Federico Savini, António Ferreira, and Kim Carlotta von Schönfeld.
Description: New York, NY : Routledge, 2022. |
Includes bibliographical references and index. |
Identifiers: LCCN 2021055979 (print) | LCCN 2021055980 (ebook) |
ISBN 9780367751012 (hardback) | ISBN 9780367751005 (paperback) |
ISBN 9781003160984 (ebook)
Subjects: LCSH: City planning–Environmental aspects. |
Land use–Environmental aspects. | Rural development–Environmental aspects. |
Housing–Environmental aspects. | Community development–Environmental aspects. |
Sociology, Urban.
Classification: LCC HT166 .P6447 2022 (print) |
LCC HT166 (ebook) | DDC 307.1/16–dc23/eng/20220209
LC record available at https://lccn.loc.gov/2021055979
LC ebook record available at https://lccn.loc.gov/2021055980

ISBN: 9780367751012 (hbk)
ISBN: 9780367751005 (pbk)
ISBN: 9781003160984 (ebk)

DOI: 10.4324/9781003160984

Typeset in Bembo
by Newgen Publishing UK

# CONTENTS

List of Illustrations                                                        viii
List of Contributors                                                           ix
Acknowledgements                                                               xv
Foreword: Post-Growth and the Ontology of "Not Yet"                          xvii
Simin Davoudi

**PART 1**
**Beginning**                                                                   1

1  Uncoupling planning and economic growth: towards
   post-growth urban principles: an introduction                                3
   *Federico Savini, António Ferreira and Kim Carlotta von Schönfeld*

2  When greening is not degrowth: cost-shifting insights                       19
   *Marta Conde, Giacomo D'Alisa and Filka Sekulova*

**PART 2**
**Dwelling**                                                                   33

3  Housing commons as a degrowth planning practice: learning
   from Amsterdam's de Nieuwe Meent                                            35
   *Federico Savini and Daan Bossuyt*

4  Dwelling beyond growth: negotiating the state, mutualism
   and commons                                                                 49
   *Anitra Nelson and Paul Chatterton*

## PART 3
## Moving 63

5 Individual well-being beyond mobility growth? 65
  *Luca Bertolini and Anna Nikolaeva*

6 Beyond the rule of growth in the transport sector: towards
  "clumsy mobility solutions"? 80
  *António Ferreira and Kim Carlotta von Schönfeld*

## PART 4
## Governing 95

7 The city as a commons: diffused governance for social and
  ecological reproduction 97
  *Massimo De Angelis*

8 Hacking the legal: the commons between the governance
  paradigm and inspirations drawn from the "living history"
  of collective land use 112
  *Giuseppe Micciarelli*

## PART 5
## Regulating 127

9 Planning beyond the backwash of a growth node: old and new
  thinking in Cambridgeshire, England and Skåne, Sweden 129
  *Yvonne Rydin*

10 Planning law and post-growth transformation 143
   *Jin Xue*

## PART 6
## Nurturing 157

11 Nurturing the post-growth city: bringing the rural back in 159
   *Julia Spanier and Giuseppe Feola*

12 Towards a post-growth food system: the community as a
   cornerstone? Lessons from two Amsterdam community-led
   food initiatives 173
   *Beatriz Pineda Revilla and Sarah Essbai*

**PART 7**
# Being   187

13  Becoming a post-growth planner: inner obstacles to
    changing roles                                                  189
    *Christian Lamker and Viola Schulze Dieckhoff*

14  Once upon a planet: planning for transition from ego-driven
    to eco-driven economies                                         203
    *Leonie Sandercock*

**PART 8**
# Envisioning   217

15  A manifesto for post-growth planning                            219

16  A glossary of and for post-growth planning                      221

*Index*                                                             *227*

# ILLUSTRATIONS

## Figures

| | | |
|---|---|---:|
| 3.1 | The management architecture of de Nieuwe Meent (source: de Nieuwe Meent) | 44 |
| 6.1 | A typology of worldviews for transport planning (source: authors) | 88 |
| 7.1 | Diagrammatic representation of a VSM (source: Lowe, Espinosa, and Yearworth, 2020: 1015) | 105 |
| 7.2 | Relationship between scale and (re)productive functions (source: author) | 107 |
| 9.1 | A schematic illustration of the limited backwash of local economic growth (source: author) | 130 |
| 12.1 | Top: view of one of the fields cultivated by Pluk! CSA. Bottom: display of a portion of the weekly Pluk! CSA harvest with a map of the harvesting locations in the background (source: photographs Pluk! CSA Groenten van West) | 182 |

## Tables

| | | |
|---|---|---:|
| 5.1 | Characterization of localism and stagnancy (source: Ferreira et al., 2017) | 67 |
| 10.1 | Post-growth grounds for planning law (source: author) | 147 |
| 13.1 | Nine positions adopted by planners on post-growth planning debates (source: authors) | 194 |

## Box

| | | |
|---|---|---:|
| 6.1 | Economic appraisal of new transport infrastructure | 84 |

# CONTRIBUTORS

**Luca Bertolini** is Professor of Urban and Regional Planning at the University of Amsterdam. His research and teaching focus on the integration of transport and urban planning for humane, sustainable, and just cities, concepts, and practices to enable transformative urban and mobility change, and ways of enhancing collaboration across different academic disciplines and between academia and society.

**Daan Bossuyt** is a Postdoctoral Fellow at the University of Amsterdam, Center for Urban Studies. His PhD research dealt with the institutional dynamics of self-build and cooperative housing in The Netherlands and Brazil.

**Paul Chatterton** is a writer, researcher, and campaigner. Professor of Urban Futures, School of Geography, University of Leeds (UK), his work focuses on radical visions of sustainable cities beyond growth. Paul is an activist-scholar who supports numerous civic interventions. He is a co-founder and resident of the award-winning low-impact housing cooperative Lilac. He helped set up Leeds Community Homes to promote community-led housing. Recent books include *Low Impact Living* (2015), *Do it Yourself: A Handbook for Changing our World* (2007), and *Unlocking Sustainable Cities* (2018). He co-founded the public charity "Antipode" dedicated to research and scholarship in radical geography.

**Marta Conde** is a political ecologist exploring the expansion of extractive industries. She has linked this research to science and activism interactions, the environmental justice movement, and degrowth. She is currently Marie Curie Fellow at the Institute of Environmental Science and Technology (ICTA) at the Universitat Autònoma de Barcelona and the CSRM Institute at University of Queensland, Australia. She is a founding member and President of the organization Research & Degrowth.

**Giacomo D'Alisa** is a political ecologist and ecological economist with interdisciplinary skills. He works as a Research Fellow at the Centre for Social Studies at the University of Coimbra, Portugal, granted with the Portuguese Foundation for Science and Technology (FCT) Post-Doc Fellowship for a six-year project on the commons. He is one of the founding members of Research and Degrowth Barcelona.

**Simin Davoudi** is Professor of Environmental Policy and Planning at Newcastle University. She is Director of the Global Urban Research Unit (GURU) and Co-Director of the Centre for Researching Cities at Newcastle University, UK. She is past President of the Association of European Schools of Planning (AESOP) and elected Fellow of the Royal Town Planning Institute, the Academy of Social Sciences, and the Royal Society of the Arts. Simin has served as an expert and advisor for the UK government, European Commission, and several research councils. She has held visiting professorships at the universities of Amsterdam, Nijmegen, BTH, Virginia Tech, RMIT, and Tampere. Her research and publications cover the socio-spatial and political aspects of urban planning, environmental governance, climate change, resilience, and imaginaries. Recent books include *Hope under Neoliberal Austerity* (2021), *The Routledge Companion to Environmental Planning* (2019, Routledge), and *The Resilience Machine* (2018, Routledge).

**Massimo De Angelis** is Emeritus Professor at the University of East London. He has been working and writing on commons and social change for about two decades. His latest book, published in 2017, was *Omnia Sunt Communia: On the Commons and the Transformation to Postcapitalism*.

**Sarah Essbai** is an independent researcher and holds a Master of Architecture from the École Nationale d'Architecture (Rabat, Morocco) and a Master of Urban and Regional Planning from Ball State University (Indiana, United States). She is a Fulbright alumna and contributed in that capacity to community-based projects in Indiana, United States, tackling local community issues such as affordable housing and ageing communities. She is a founding member of the Amsterdam-based Community Supported Agriculture initiative "Pluk! Groenten van West" and is interested in self-organizing communities, social design, and urban food security.

**Giuseppe Feola** is Associate Professor of Social Change for Sustainability at the Copernicus Institute of Sustainable Development at Utrecht University. He conducts research on socioecological change in modern societies, with primary empirical foci on agri-food systems and grassroots actors such as the civil society and social movements. His current research critically examines the prospects of societal transformation towards forms of society and economy that aim at the well-being of all and sustain the ecological basis of life. He holds a PhD from the Department of Geography, University of Zurich.

List of Contributors  **xi**

**Christian Lamker** is Assistant Professor in Sustainable Transformation and Regional Planning at the University of Groningen (Netherlands). His research and teaching within the Department of Spatial Planning and Environment focus on roles in planning, post-growth planning, regional planning, and leadership in sustainable transformation. He has studied and worked on spatial planning in Dortmund, Aachen, Auckland, Detroit, and Melbourne. He coordinates the Master programme Society, Sustainability and Planning (SSP) in Groningen.

**Giuseppe Micciarelli** is a political philosopher and legal sociologist (University of Salerno). He is the author of numerous essays and articles for international journals on the themes of democracy in transformation, institutional theory, global governance, and social movements. His latest book is titled *Commoning. Beni comuni urbani come nuove istituzioni. Materiali per una teoria dell'autorganizzazione* [*Commoning. Urban Commons as New Institutions. Materials for a Theory of Self-Organization*] (2nd edn, 2021). His research on the commons and democratization focuses on the creation and implementation of new participatory institutions, at both a local and a transnational scale. In July 2019, he was awarded the Elinor Ostrom Award, the most prestigious award in the field of the defence and management of the commons. He supports numerous groups, networks, associations, and local administrations to implement models of participatory democracy. He is President of the Permanent Citizen Observatory on the Commons, participatory democracy, and fundamental rights of the city of Naples.

**Anitra Nelson** is Associate Professor, Honorary Principal Fellow at the Melbourne Sustainable Society Institute, University of Melbourne (Melbourne, Australia). She is an activist-scholar with special interests in post-capitalism and non-monetary economies, in collectively establishing and maintaining caring local-to-global communities, and in living in environmentally sustainable ways. Anitra is author of *Small is Necessary: Shared Living on a Shared Planet* (2018), co-author of *Exploring Degrowth: A Critical Guide* (2020), and co-editor of *Food for Degrowth: Perspectives and Practices* (2021), *Housing for Degrowth: Principles, Models, Challenges and Opportunities* (2018), and *Life Without Money: Building Fair and Sustainable Economies* (2011).

**Anna Nikolaeva** is an Assistant Professor in Urban Mobility Futures at the University of Amsterdam. Her research focuses on the relationship between cities and mobilities, more specifically on the governance of transitions to sustainable and inclusive mobility and the role of technology in urban mobility futures.

**Beatriz Pineda Revilla** is a Senior Researcher and Lecturer at the Amsterdam University of Applied Sciences. Her current research and teaching focus on the governance of the energy transition, specifically looking at how to improve citizen participation processes to increase energy awareness and affect behavioural change. She holds a PhD in Sociology and Urban Planning from the University of Amsterdam and an MSc in Urban Studies from the same university. She also has a

Master of Architecture with a specialization in Urban and Regional Planning from the University of Navarra and practised for several years as an urban designer before starting her academic career.

**Yvonne Rydin** is Professor of Planning, Environment and Public Policy in the Bartlett School of Planning, University College London. She specializes in governance for sustainability, ranging across a variety of policy domains including green space management, air quality management, community energy, and renewable energy. She is the author of *The Purpose of Planning* (2011) and *The Future of Planning: Beyond Growth-Dependence* (2013). Her current research is on planning for low-growth areas, looking for a new model of local economic development and spatial planning that can promote well-being in these contexts. She also has a central concern with the role of theory in planning research and her most recent book is *Theory for Planning Research* (2021).

**Leonie Sandercock** is a Professor in the School of Community & Regional Planning at the University of British Columbia where she co-created, with the Musqueam Nation, the Indigenous Community Planning program. Her practice has focused on using the medium of film as a catalyst for dialogue, healing, community development, and cultural revitalization with Indigenous communities, most recently with the Haida Nation and the Inuit film collective, Isuma, on the first Haida-language feature film, *Edge of the Knife*. Leonie received an Honorary Doctorate for lifetime contribution to planning scholarship from Roskilde University in Denmark in 2012. She is also the recipient of the Davidoff award for best book on the theme of social justice and planning (*Cosmopolis 2: Mongrel Cities of the 21st Century*, 2003), and the Distinguished Planning Educator award from the Association of Collegiate Schools of Planning for her contribution to planning scholarship and education.

**Viola Schulze Dieckhoff** is a Researcher at the School of Spatial Planning, Department of Spatial Planning and Planning Theory at the Technical University Dortmund. Transformative action and planning practices, post-growth planning, and the future of planning currently are the guiding topics of her teaching, research, and networks. She has studied and worked in Dortmund, Berlin, Erfurt, Halle (Saale), and Surfers Paradise (Australia).

**Filka Sekulova** is an ecological economist and social scientist working at the Institute of Environmental Science and Technology (ICTA) at the Universitat Autònoma de Barcelona. Her field of research centres around the thematics of degrowth, well-being, justice, community-based initiatives, and green amenities. She is one of the founders of the academic think-tank Research and Degrowth.

**Julia Spanier** is a PhD candidate at the Copernicus Institute of Sustainable Development at Utrecht University. She investigates the unmaking of capitalism in agricultural grassroots initiatives, locating her research at the intersection of rural and urban geography. She holds an MSc in Nature, Society and Environmental Governance from the University of Oxford. In addition to her academic work, she is engaged in the Civil Society and Indigenous Peoples' Mechanism for relations with the UN Committee on World Food Security.

**Jin Xue** is Associate Professor in urban and regional planning and is currently working at the Department of Urban and Regional Planning, Norwegian University of Life Sciences. Xue's research interests are in urban and housing sustainable development, the interface between environmental and social sustainability in urban regions, the relationship between degrowth and urban development and planning, urban futures based on scenario planning, and critical realism. Particularly, she has engaged actively with the frontier of international post-growth debates to explore alternative urban development and planning paradigms.

# ACKNOWLEDGEMENTS

This book emerged from a common sense of urgency. Three years ago, we recognized that a post-growth imaginary would offer much-needed direction in attempts to address worsening social and ecological problems in cities all over the world. Yet at that time we could not find any indication of such an imaginary within the existing planning literature. We only came across a scattered constellation of inspiring but isolated studies, providing a few signposts towards a post-growth urban reality. This motivated us to connect this constellation and systematize it into a more cohesive view of post-growth planning theory and practice.

To this end, we first organized a special session on post-growth planning at the Annual Conference of the Association of European Schools of Planning (AESOP) in 2019. Somewhat unexpectedly, the session attracted an impressive crowd of people. Once all of the available chairs were occupied, they started sitting on the tables as well. Their enthusiasm for the topic was obvious and contagious. Here we would like to express our gratitude to all who participated in that remarkable session, for this initial spark of energy emboldened us to embark on a longer editorial process.

We were fortunate enough to find a wonderful set of authors willing to write the chapters that form this edited book. The first drafts of the chapters were presented and discussed during a seminar conducted online in fall 2019. There, the contributors all gave each other feedback and engaged in hearty discussions about what a post-growth planning theory and practice might actually entail. The insights gathered during these discussions were eventually curated by the editors as a manifesto, included at the end of the volume. We would like to thank the authors for their hard work, excellent ideas, extraordinary energy, and mutual respect. Without you, this book would not exist.

It would have been much more difficult, if not impossible, to fulfil all of our hopes for the book without the support given by Paulo Pinho at CITTA: Research

Centre for Territory, Transports, and Environment at the University of Porto; Luca Bertolini, Maria Kaika, and Jules Klinkhamer at the Centre for Urban Studies (CUS) at the University of Amsterdam; and Kathryn Schell at Routledge. We wish to express our special gratitude for their confidence in our early attempts to move this project forward, as well as the funds offered by CITTA and the CUS to support our activities. A special thanks goes to Simon Ferdinand for editing the English of some of the chapters.

This book takes the first steps of a path towards a post-growth planning theory and practice. It cannot fully capture the diverse and geographically dispersed landscape of existing post-growth urban practices worldwide. Yet we hope that it will encourage its readers to continue searching for these practices and imagining how planning can foster post-growth values. Hopefully, it will inspire both those who are already convinced of the urgency of post-growth thinking and those who might still be sceptical as to whether this approach has value for planning. As editors and contributors, we would be more than happy to be contacted for further discussion and critique.

This work was financially supported by Base Funding UIDB/04427/2020 of CITTA: Research Centre for Territory, Transports and Environment funded by national funds through the FCT/MCTES (PIDDAC); and by a seed grant of the Center for Urban Studies of the University of Amsterdam.

The Editors
Federico Savini, António Ferreira, and Kim Carlotta von Schönfeld

# FOREWORD

## Post-Growth and the Ontology of "Not Yet"

*Simin Davoudi*

> Hard times are coming, when we will be wanting the voices of writers who can see alternatives to how we live now and can see through our fear-stricken society and its obsessive technologies to other ways of being, and even imagine some real grounds for hope.
>
> *(Le Guin, 2014: np)*

These are the words of Ursula K. Le Guin, a renowned speculative fiction writer, in a speech given after receiving the Medal for Distinguished Contribution to American Letters from the National Book Awards in 2014. Today, when hard times are getting harder due to the spiraling crises of a global pandemic, growing inequalities, and climate breakdown, we need, more than ever, to *see* capitalist social and economic relations not as how things are, but as how they have been made to be, and how they might be unmade. Negation is the first step. We need to question the taken-for-granted assumption that the given "reality" is the *objective* reality, and that any alternatives are "unreal", fanciful and no more than daydreaming. This requires exposing the positivist and "ossified concept of reality" which, according to Bloch (1988: 196), forecloses the possibility of alternatives and denies the ontology of "Not-Yet". It requires unraveling the politics of reality-fixing and the power relations involved; asking what and whose reality counts.

We are told that "there is no alternative" to capitalism's relentless pursuit of growth. That exponential economic expansion is the only "real" path to prosperity. That instrumental rationality is the most effective way to achieve it. And that neoliberal political ideology is the most reliable guarantor of freedom. These taken-for-granted assumptions, dressed up as realities, have colonized our social imaginaries to the extent that it is easier to imagine the end of the world than to contemplate the end of capitalism and neoliberalism. Any dissenting views are "deemed to be the act of lunatics, idealists and revolutionaries" (Jackson, 2009: 14). That is why Latouche

(2009: 95) urges us to begin any solutions for social and ecological problems with a "decolonization of the imaginary".

The concepts of "post-growth" and "de-growth" seek to do just that. They invoke a series of emerging political economic imaginaries which seek to unsettle the hegemony of "growth" as inevitable, and problematize the proclamation that "good life" can only be premised on ceaseless capital accumulation. Post-growth offers a counter-imaginary to that of pro-growth by highlighting and questioning the ramifications of the exponential pressures that the fossil-fueled unbridled accumulation is placing on the earth and on our social and individual well-being. It promotes more sustainable ways of life. Whereas pro-growth puts the emphasis on quantity, post-growth insists on quality. The latter is not about "less", but about "different":"different activities, different forms and uses of energy, different relations, different gender roles, different allocations of time between paid and non-paid work and different relations with the non-human world" (D'Alisa et al., 2015: 4).

Two influential advocates of post-growth, Tim Jackson (2009; 2021) and Kate Soper (2020), have put forward powerful accounts of how we might prosper without perpetual growth, and how life would look without relentless capitalist production and consumption. Both criticize hedonistic lifestyles of affluent consumers but, whereas Jackson rejects them outright, Soper seeks to replace them with a different form of hedonism, one in which putting limits on consumption does not work against human desire and pleasure, but rather works within its grain. Both scholars challenge the illusory notion of "green growth" and the fallacy of capitalist systems to deliver environmentally benign growth. *Post-Growth Planning* builds on these lines of argument and examines what they mean when applied to spatial (and more specifically urban) planning. Instead of limiting the discussions to mere critiques of planning theory and practice, the book provides multiple examples of post-growth practices in the fields of local food production, co-operative housing, active travel, and urban commons, to name just a few. By doing so, the authors offer a glimpse of post-growth socio-spatial imaginaries and, as such, "real grounds for hope" (Le Guin, 2014: np). But what kind of hope?

In his *magnum opus*, *The Principle of Hope*, Ernst Bloch, a humanist Marxist, makes a distinction between abstract hope, which is "fraudulent" and a "booty for swindlers", and concrete hope which is "genuine" and arises from "informed discontent" with the present (Bloch, 1988: 56). The former is wishful thinking, whereas the latter is willful action (Levitas, 1990). Abstract hope relocates the present to a postponed future and, hence, perpetuates the status quo. Concrete hope brings the future into the present (Wrangel, 2014) as the basis for action. Abstract hope is "fantastic and compensatory", whereas concrete hope is "anticipatory" (Levitas, 1990: 15). It is praxis-oriented, encouraging us to step out of the present, "rather than remain hopeful in it" (Wrangel, 2014: 194).

There is no shortage of both "abstract" and "concrete" hope in the history of planning. We can find examples of both in the early-twentieth-century utopian urban visions (such as garden city, radiant city, functional city) and in the more recent eco-topian and techno-topian urban visions (such as eco city, smart city).

However, as Peter Hall, a great "futurist historian" of planning (Davoudi, 2014: 252), suggests, there is a distinction between those who are "good at understanding what was happening in the world [...] and harnessing these trends", and those who just let their "flight of fancies rove" (Hall, 1983: 191). Using Bloch's categories of hope, we can call the former willful planning that leaves its mark on the urban landscape for better or for worse, and the latter wishful planning that gets "passed into limbo" (Hall, 1983: 191).

As Davoudi and Ormerod (2021: 319) argue, although concrete "hope is harder to find, because it is the hidden and invisible drive behind socio-political change", it is nevertheless present in the multitude of practices that are happening in the fissures and cracks of the existing political economic "realities". These practices need to be extracted, made visible, and circulated. That is what the authors of *Post-Growth Planning* seek to do. They make visible those actions that are performed in the interstices of everyday lives. Those that are played out in streets, in neighborhoods, across the urban–rural spaces, and in urban commons. These multiple forms of collective actions are challenging the normalization of growth-centric socio-spatial imaginaries. They do so by engaging with another reality: the "Not-Yet" reality. What energizes these struggles is a concrete hope which is mobilized by the prefigurative power of post-growth imaginaries.

However, as Bloch (1988: 16–17) reminds us, "Hope is not confidence. If it could not be disappointable, it would not be hope. That is part of it. [...] Hope is surrounded by dangers." This is an important insight about what concrete hope is. It is not a promise of a pre-determined or pre-defined end-state, but a mobilizing force that drives the struggle towards prefigured futures. Thus, "post-growth" initiatives and practices should not be seen as blueprints for a no-growth, non-capitalist future (being), but as prefiguration of alternatives in a non-linear process of transformation (becoming) which is riddled with tensions and contradictions and has uncertain outcomes. Spatial planning is an integral part of this relational process, but its efficacy depends on whether or not it is capable of stepping out of pro-growth imaginaries that have been embedded in and perpetuated by its institutions. The examples presented in this book offer hopeful possibilities. They show that despite the hegemony of neoliberal imaginaries, there are myriad planning practices and processes that successfully navigate power relations and break up rigid institutional structures to bring about change. These examples provide a glimmer of "hope in the dark" (Solnit, 2004).

## References

Bloch, E. (1988 [1957]) *The Principle of Hope*, Volume 1. Boston, MA: MIT Press.
D'Alisa, G., Demaria, F. and Kallis, G. (eds) (2015) *Degrowth: A Vocabulary for a New Era*. New York: Routledge.
Davoudi, S. (2014) Urban futures. In M. Tewdwr-Jones, N. Phelps and R. Freestone (eds) *The Planning Imagination: Peter Hall and the Study of Urban and Regional Planning*. Marcham, UK: Alexandrine Press: 252–266.

Davoudi, S. and Ormerod, E. (2021) Hope at the time of pandemic. *Town Planning Review*, 92(3): 317–322.

Hall, P. (1983) Utopian thoughts: a framework for social, economic and physical planning. In P. Alexander and R. Gill (eds) *Utopias*. London: Duckworth.

Jackson, T. (2009) *Prosperity without Growth; Economics for a Finite Planet*. New York: Earthscan.

Jackson, T. (2021) *Post Growth: Life after Capitalism*. London: Wiley.

Latouche, S. (2009) *Farewell to Growth*. Cambridge: Polity Press.

Le Guin, U. (2014) Speech at the American National Book Awards, available at www.ursulakleguin.com/nbf-medal.

Levitas, R. (1990) Educated hope: Ernst Bloch on abstract and concrete Utopia. *Utopian Studies*, 1(2): 13–26.

Solnit, R. (2004) *Hope in the Dark: Untold Histories, Wild Possibilities*. New York: Nation Books.

Soper, K. (2020) *Post-Growth Living*. London: Verso Books.

Wrangel, A. (2014) Hope in a time of catastrophe? Resilience and the future in bare life. *Resilience: International Policies, Practices and Discourses*, 2(3): 183–194.

# PART 1
# Beginning

# 1
# UNCOUPLING PLANNING AND ECONOMIC GROWTH: TOWARDS POST-GROWTH URBAN PRINCIPLES

An introduction

*Federico Savini, António Ferreira and Kim Carlotta von Schönfeld*

## 1. Introduction

In contemporary capitalism, global increases in wealth and urbanisation are structurally coupled. The migration of large groups of people from rural to urban areas has become an index of developing economies' GDP growth rate. In late-industrial countries, megaregions are becoming powerhouses of industrial development and dense concentrations of jobs for large volumes of transnational migrant labour. In early-industrial countries, urban regions have become the hubs of socio-cultural and financial innovation (Scott, 2019). The servers sustaining the platform economy are situated in cities; financial circuits prosper from real-estate transactions; commodity markets respond to cities' fluctuating demand for batteries, photovoltaic panels, and turbines, to mention only a few examples.

Cities, then, have long been and remain growth machines (Molotch, 1976), the sites at which economic growth alliances are compelled to fuel national and global economies. If investments in urban amenities increase, national economies grow. If those investments stall, national economies fall into recession. Given cities' economic centrality, it is unsurprising that they are widely seen as being both sites of economic innovation and the spaces in which its negative consequences can be addressed most effectively. Cities have been praised as a triumph of humanity's capacity to find innovative solutions to contemporary socio-ecological challenges (Glaeser, 2011). Indeed, they have become laboratories in which new economic alliances and tools are prototyped. Energy-efficient housing; compact urban living; shared e-mobility systems; circular production; and digital consumption are increasingly understood as the pathways along which urban economies will grow in the future. Developments in these areas, it is hoped, will also help to prevent planetary socio-ecological collapse. This celebratory attitude towards urban economic growth and its putatively positive effects, however, obscures a much more complex and less optimistic socio-economic picture.

DOI: 10.4324/9781003160984-2

Urbanisation is a prime source of environmental degradation. Cities' ecological footprints – which are five to ten times higher than any sustainable threshold – are just one among many indexes that testify to urban lifestyles' massive impact on the environment (Baabou et al., 2017). Despite this, the celebration of the economic performance of cities and the 'immaterial' platform economy has made urbanists virtually blind to the extractive practices that sustain mainstream urbanisms. The neo-colonial approach to urbanisation sees areas of material extraction and production as functionally subordinate to the wealth of urbanised areas; rural areas are managed as 'supply' for urban economies, progressively eroding their ecological viability, biodiversity, and indigenous cultures. Undeveloped areas have become little more than sites for obtaining sand to produce concrete, rare materials for electronic equipment, and animal proteins to feed humans. These extractive practices have disseminated zoonotic diseases such as COVID-19 and are likely to continue doing so increasingly rapidly, with ever-more ominous impacts (UNEP, 2020).

This extractivist logic comes at dramatic costs for poorer populations both within and beyond urban areas. In urban economies, the quest to make land productive has become an essential means of fuelling economic growth. It has institutionalised an entrepreneurial approach to urban governance that makes governments constantly pursue economically valuable urban functions to the detriment of those that do not produce quantifiable economic outputs (Peck, 2016). Today, the provision of essential urban features and public services – public spaces such as green areas or playgrounds, as well as healthcare and social housing – rests on the incessant increase of the value of land and real estate. According to this logic, within current planning frameworks it is inevitable that cities pursue maximum land productivity. If they relinquish this aim, then they run the risk of failing to provide essential services for the well-being of their inhabitants.

The need for land productivity reproduces an urban geometry that devalues (or rather commodifies) history, standardising place identities that are embodied in indigenous communities and their urban fabrics. It compels neighbourhoods to specialise economically through place branding and expel activities and social groups that do not reproduce the advertised identity (Zukin, 1993). The hyper-diversity of contemporary urban areas glosses over the pauperisation, standardisation, and degradation of large housing estates and the socio-ecological neglect experienced at the urban fringes. On the one hand, the pursuit of economic productivity has complexified relations and activities in dense urban areas. On the other, however, it has simplified both natural ecosystems and social relations by exclusively maintaining economically quantifiable functions – to destructive effect. The pursuit of economic productivity standardises patterns of consumption and production; narrows the scope of creativity and innovation; increases the need for long-distance mobility for work and shopping; and produces peculiar forms of loneliness and stress-induced diseases (Okkels et al., 2017; von Schönfeld and Ferreira, 2021).

Under these conditions, planning (and planners) play a crucial role. Planning has provided the conditions for boosting urban economic productivity and has effectively lubricated the urban mechanisms that generate economic growth (Savini, 2021). Planners managed to develop and mobilise a large number of instruments to enhance places' ability to compete for and attract investments. To do so, planners have nurtured private actors' profit-seeking aspirations while endorsing private-led experiments in all sectors of city governance. In many countries, public governments have proactively fostered private initiative through large-scale public investments in city branding, infrastructural planning, cultural facilities, and ecosystem services. These developments are rooted in a longstanding historical trajectory that has conceptualised planning as a practice of 'growth management' (Grant, 2017). Urban planning policy has been, and remains, fundamentally geared to coupling ambitions for increased economic growth with socio-ecological improvements. Throughout its history, planning has succeeded in tightening the knot between economic and socio-ecological targets. In recent years, it has developed numerous instruments and approaches for tightening it still further, from citizen participation to co-production (Purcell, 2009). The link between growth and planning is so strong today that it is hardly possible for planners, governments, and their constituencies to question economic growth as the *sine qua non* condition of urban well-being.

Disentangling planning from this growth-dependent paradigm remains a key contemporary challenge. Although cities with long traditions of social-democratic public planning have succeeded in redistributing the wealth generated by urban growth, it has become almost self-evident that this paradigm undermines planning's ability to address contemporary socio-ecological challenges. Urban economic growth is inevitably connected to the ecological damage increasingly wrought by urbanisation and the degradation of living conditions among poorer social groups. Attempts to decouple urban growth from its socio-ecological impacts have been ineffective, for their realisation ultimately depends on new economic output – thus perpetuating the actual source of the damage (Xue, 2015).

If it is to contribute effectively to a system that pursues prosperity within ecological limits in a socially fair way, planning must be emancipated from the imperative for economic growth. This volume establishes stepping-stones towards that emancipation by exploring post-growth planning theories and practices. In so doing, it develops a critique of the predominance of economic growth and market logics in planning institutions and toolkits. As we proceed to illustrate, planners can draw on an increasingly large body of literature from environmental economics, environmental geography, and political ecology to develop this critique. Nevertheless, given urban areas' significant role in shaping economic conditions, planning research and practices also need to contribute to establishing a new economic logic, which goes beyond the growth imperative. To do so, planners must learn from the multiplicity of contemporary urban practices that prefigure and enact alternative urban futures. This logic needs to provide a realistic but utopian vision of urban prosperity, based on the principle of post-growth urbanisation. It also needs to be backed up by a matching toolkit of planning instruments. This vision must decouple socio-ecological prosperity from the imperative for economic growth and put socio-ecological justice at the forefront of planning practices. In practical terms, this agenda raises two important questions: what would a post-growth logic involve and how can it inform alternative ways of planning urban areas?

## 2. What is post-growth? A brief outline of an emerging field

Engaging effectively on prefigurative post-growth planning theories and practices requires looking at key debates in post-growth thinking outside the discipline of planning. Accordingly, we now plunge into some of the fundamentals of this field.

Advocates of post-growth thinking tend to agree upon the necessity to abandon – or at least treat very sceptically – the mainstream use of aggregate indicators of wealth such as GDP. They do not consider such indicators sufficiently valid to serve as constructive measures by which public policymakers can assess human prosperity and development (Jackson, 2017; Raworth, 2017; Kallis, 2018). For example, the use of GDP growth as an indicator of public policy success has been associated with the risk of promoting 'uneconomic growth' (Daly, 1999). This corresponds to a damaging situation in which the environmental, social, and even economic costs of maintaining continuous GDP growth exceed the benefits of doing so.

A fundamental claim of post-growth thinking is that aggregate econometric indicators (such as GDP) motivate policies that exploit everything that such indicators can quantify, and destroy everything that they cannot. As a result, not converting altruistic social relations into commodified services, which can be effectively counted as contributions to GDP, is considered a sign of underdevelopment; not fully exploiting natural areas so as to produce environmental resources is perceived as inefficient; and lastly, not converting money itself into a financial product to be traded for profit in global markets is considered a missed opportunity. According to this paradoxically circular belief system, economies need to be more efficient in order to grow, efficiency results from commodification, and commodification equals growth. It has led policymakers uncritically to promote strategies that downgrade and threaten social relations, the environment, and the economy itself (Fraser, 2014).

Although post-growth thinkers generally agree on this critique, there is as yet no consensus on what a post-growth society might entail and what exactly would define it (Cosme et al., 2017). This can be seen, for example, in debates over how this field should be named (Drews and Antal, 2016). In some cases, it is referred to using terms that explicitly but critically employ the notion of *growth*, including the slogans *post-growth*, *degrowth*, and *agrowth*. In other cases, the field is signalled by way of aspirational economic visions, such as *green economics* or *steady-state economics*. In still other cases, it is referred to through concrete proposals for alternatives and evocations of aspirational values. These include, for example, terms such as *buen vivir* or *the good life*.

The diverse, multi-disciplinary character of post-growth thought is also evident in the dilemma as to whether it should maintain or reject economic language and ways of thinking (Ferreira and von Schönfeld, 2020). Indeed, some post-growth advocates argue that societies must move beyond 'economism' (Latouche, 2012), that is, the subjugation of the human mind to the superordinate notion that anything and everything (from subjects to objects, places to relations) can and should be materialistically managed as capital. These advocates stress the need to decolonise the social imaginary by expunging it of economism – a process that could enable societies to pursue more diverse, inspired, and democratic paths to prosperous futures. The critique of growth-oriented colonisation involves all aspects of society, from the ways in which individuals think about their well-being and lives, to how education works in areas as diverse as biology, engineering, the humanities, and urban planning. For these reasons, post-growth thinkers have proposed an alternative vocabulary to understand contemporary societies, freed from the straitjacket of liberal economic thought (D'Alisa et al., 2015). This vocabulary refrains from a simplistic and rationalist representation of relations both within societies and between humans and ecosystems (Raworth, 2017).

There is no clear consensus among the multiplicity of post-growth thinkers, however, as to whether a post-growth society would inevitably result from escaping economism altogether or, instead, might emerge from a more humanistically and ecologically inflected use of existing economic concepts, tools, legal frameworks, and state institutions. Regardless, proponents of both views argue that pro-growth economic thinking must lose its prominence in policymaking and democratic politics regain a leading role. As Raworth (2017) puts it, it is important to remain agnostic about growth so as to open up possibilities of deceleration, regeneration, and redistribution. By altering policymaking's economic premises, it becomes possible to engage with real-life strategies beyond growth.

For this volume, we have invited each team of contributing authors to enrol the terms and strands of thought that they consider most appropriate for conveying their message. As editors, we have deliberately chosen to use the term post-growth to stress that paths towards a new planning paradigm are evolving and remain open-ended. All contributions and their authors are united by a common motivation: that of critically debating alternative ways of organising socio-economic relations, beyond the ruthless principles of growth-oriented economic thinking. These principles include individual responsibility and freedom of enterprise; efficiency and competition; market-based designs and market expansion. In opposition to such principles, it may be desirable for alternative ways of organising socio-economic relations to aim to promote a move away from individualist materialism and instead promote conviviality and meaningful social relations of reciprocity. In so doing, the goal should be to reduce human activities' detrimental environmental impacts and reshape collective decisions so that they no longer serve the imperatives to accumulate wealth for the benefit of the few (Cosme et al., 2017).

Defining post-growth thinking along these lines might lead some readers to be uncertain about how it differs from classical left-wing politics. Both are deeply concerned with social justice, redistribution, and other humanitarian values. Post-growth thinking, however, strongly emphasises the need to avoid trespassing on ecological planetary limits and promotes ecological regeneration. It explicitly sets out to address the fundamental questions of both social and ecological justice

(Meadows and Meadows, 1972; Daly, 2005; Alexander, 2012; Kallis, 2011). Today, the key limit confronting human societies is no longer the difficulty of extracting resources from ecosystems and processing them to satisfy our needs and aspirations. Instead, we live in unprecedented circumstances, in which the planet has become fundamentally incapable of regenerating itself fast enough due to the rapidity and magnitude of human extractive and polluting activities. The social challenges of our times are not only about redistributing wealth and achieving social justice. They require addressing social and ecological problems through coherent and synergistic solutions. The value of a post-growth approach lies in how it connects social and ecological questions, claiming that we need to adjust patterns of human activity to the crucial ecological metabolisms on which human societies depend, while also keeping social justice in mind. To do so, it is necessary to integrate the notion of limiting growth into public policy. The core challenge of post-growth thinking, therefore, is that of injecting a sense of limits into how societies and places function, and people live. This inevitably takes us back to planning.

## 3. Towards post-growth planning theories and practices

Even before the term was coined, post-growth planning activism existed in the form of urban movements resisting the expansion of airports, highways, industrial food production, and aggressive real-estate development. The post-growth urban activism of the 1970s and '80s included a constellation of interventions, strategies, and policies ranging from cycling advocacy to squatting, slow food production, street markets, cooperatives, and self-managed public spaces. The post-growth imaginary at stake in these movements was later captured by a body of scholarship that widely recognised cities' potential role in re-appropriating individuals' time and devising new ways of life based on principles of solidarity and well-being (Gorz, 1991). Indeed, early post-growth thinkers envisioned urban settlements with the village atmosphere of southern European towns and celebrated the Mediterranean utopia of free time, family ties, identity, and cohabitation in rural towns (Latouche, 2009, 2014).

An imaginary for post-growth planning needs to be much richer than this if it wishes to address major socio-ecological problems experienced today both in urban areas and beyond. Yet given urban movements' remarkable role in post-growth initiatives, it is surprising to see how little planning theory has engaged with post-growth insights. Aside from a few recent exceptions (e.g. Brokow-Loga and Eckardt, 2020; Ferreira and von Schönfeld, 2020; Rydin, 2013; Savini, 2021; Xue, 2021), planners have yet to outline the key features of a form of urbanisation that does not depend on economic growth. Despite this scarcity of thought on post-growth planning, a transition towards a post-growth economy will inevitably require support from planning. As a project that has deep ramifications at all levels of society (from economics to welfare, human well-being to biodiversity), a post-growth agenda requires careful planning if it is to be achieved in a way that avoids dramatic social and ecological costs. Planning needs approaches that can both prefigure and institutionalise post-growth principles in cities. Without such approaches, it is likely that post-growth planning practices will remain fragmented (Alexander and Gleeson, 2018) and thus fail to place a mark on the ideology of perpetual economic growth.

In setting out to define post-growth planning approaches, with which urban processes should we start? Both this and the following chapter provide a point of departure for this agenda by setting out two conditions that must be in place in order to answer that question. In this introduction, we argue that prefiguring a post-growth approach requires that planners address the relationship between practices of urban living and mobility on the one hand, and the governing institutions and planning regulations that shape those practices on the other. We argue that this ultimately entails reconsidering the planner's professional ethic by adopting alternative views of their role in society. The chapter by Conde, D'Alisa, and Sekulova proposes that such a transformation first requires a critical recognition of the effects of 'cost shifting' between urban development's environmental and social impacts. The minimum condition for moving towards a post-growth practice, they argue, is the recognition that planning interventions have social and ecological costs that go far beyond the jurisdiction of planning.

Building on existing work on urban post-growth, we now describe six areas of planning interventions that are specifically addressed in this volume.

## 3.1 Dwelling

Housing presents significant opportunities for a post-growth urban transformation, for residential real-estate is a principal commodity in financialised capitalism (Nelson and Schneider, 2018). As the 2008 economic crisis brought starkly into focus, housing has become a central socio-economic pillar upon which the infrastructure of financialised capitalism and debt-economy rests. Post-growth urban activism envisages forms of co-living, co-ownership, and eco-housing that present palpable alternatives to individualist approaches to housing. Collective ownership, self-regulation, and self-building are pivotal to these proposals, for they question individual homeownership and link community cohabitation with a culture of sufficiency and care. Such projects are built around the principle that housing is not a commodity, but a practice through which to experiment with self-sufficiency, caregiving, sharing space, and living together (Chatterton, 2016). Post-growth initiatives also understand de-commodified and cooperative housing as a testing ground for ecological practices of production and consumption. Eco-housing, when de-commodified and self-organised, gives rise to real-life instances of how food, waste, and energy management can be coupled with community democracy (Pickerill, 2016).

This volume critically analyses the productive tension between these practices of ecological and collective housing and existing planning institutions. The contributions look at the internal challenges of collectively organising cooperative housing provision in the context of intentional commoning communities. Moreover, they show these practices' potential for changing their institutional environments.

Savini and Bossuyt (Chapter 3) dissect the institutional arrangement of a housing collective in Amsterdam, which is inspired by principles of reduction, sharing, conviviality, and democracy. Radical cooperative housing, they demonstrate, entails a complex institutional set-up with a distributed and disputable system of ownership rights. It is essential that housing cooperatives maintain democracy, they claim, if such initiatives are to avoid being co-opted by market logics. Nelson and Chatterton (Chapter 4) observe two different models of eco-collaborative housing: the Lilac in Leeds, United Kingdom and the Kalkbreite and Kraftwerk1 in Zürich, Switzerland. By comparing these two approaches, they show how a way of life beyond growth works through mutual networks of cooperation and by enacting the principles of commoning. Ultimately, these practices affect the planning institutions of the State. Both of these chapters advocate a post-growth configuration of planning, which facilitates the commoning of housing as an essential resource for well-being.

## 3.2 Moving

Mobility plays a controversial role in contemporary planning. Transport systems have been and are still being expanded according to the assumption that improving mobility allows individuals to reach an increasing number of social contacts, jobs, services, and goods. Through this unchecked assumption, mobility – and particularly car-based mobility – has become deeply intertwined with the values of societal progress, individual freedom, and self-expression (Urry, 2004). Legitimated by such values, large investments in mobility systems are seen as tools to boost land development through public spending. Promoting dependence on mobility, however, has unacceptable environmental costs (Urry, 2008) and can easily devolve into a situation in which individuals travel more to access less (Ferreira et al., 2012). Furthermore, transport infrastructures not only have massive ecological costs, but also deeply impact human health (Khreis et al., 2016).

A post-growth approach to transport planning needs to devise mobility systems that are able to promote mobility justice, human health, and ecological sustainability. This entails a trans-disciplinary approach, which targets the relationship between mobility and well-being, and envisions a reduction of the overall demand for mobility in city-regions. Following this line of reasoning, in Chapter 5 Bertolini and Nikolaeva reflect on the COVID-19 pandemic's disruptive effects on the mobility choices made by people based in various countries. They critically analyse how individuals have adapted their patterns of mobility in response to the constraints of lockdowns and remote working. Their analysis offers important clues about the challenges and opportunities of implementing a post-growth approach to mobility. In Chapter 6, Ferreira and von Schönfeld explore possibilities for establishing post-growth transport planning processes. They criticise the social and ecological risks of growth-centric, innovation-based, and efficiency-oriented decision-making paradigms that are typically applied to transport. As an alternative to these logics, they call for an approach to transport planning that is 'clumsy' in that it appreciates the merits of different, potentially conflicting worldviews as sources of insight and creative alternatives for future mobilities. Accordingly, their chapter has implications for post-growth governance.

## 3.3 Governing

Post-growth planning needs post-growth institutions. As part of socio-spatial redistribution processes, planning has produced a multiplicity of planning agencies, some public, others private, and still others hybrid. The apparatus formed by these agencies has serious limits in terms of accountability and transparency, as well as its adaptability to specific needs and economic circumstances (Scott, 1998). The push to stimulate investment in urban land has led to technocratic planning agencies, which rely heavily on contractual relations and standardised models (Raco and Savini, 2019).

Within post-growth thinking, the emergence of new forms of cooperative eco-living is seen as a germ of an unprecedented restructuring of the State and its socio-cultural roots (D'Alisa and Kallis, 2020). Post-growth thinkers heavily rely on the notion of commoning to identify new State forms that might be able to govern urban complexity in a way that is more inclusive and participatory. They recognise that the democratisation of the State through these commoning practices demands both centralising and decentralising forces (Xue, 2018). In a global–local tension, local urban practices of collective self-organisation develop new State institutions and gather political legitimacy for radical divestment and redistribution programmes.

This book addresses difficult ways in which local commoning practices coexist with stable forms of post-growth urban governance. De Angelis argues that post-growth urban governance needs to be diffused so as to be tailored around everyday practices of social reproduction instead of accumulation (Chapter 7). These practices guarantee that urban dwellers have access to essential services and cast cities as territories of care and solidarity. In his chapter, De Angelis addresses the difficult task of formulating planning in such a way that it is able to organise a diffuse form of governance that still ensures that different practices of care are coordinated. Here, the State is identified as a system of 'holons' with a range of functional organisations that are to be built from the bottom up.

In Chapter 8, Micciarelli argues for a tactical re-functioning of the neoliberal State that pushes it towards logics of commoning. He defines this as a 'hacking' planning method: a proactive legal intervention undertaken by cooperative networks with the aim of altering the profile of both public and private law. His insights suggest that post-growth planners should not use legal frameworks in a strictly defensive manner (e.g. to maintain environmental standards). Rather, they might be applied creatively as a means of generating new land tenures beyond the public and private distinction.

## 3.4 Regulating

The repertoire of planning instruments that are used to govern spatial development has become increasingly rich. As such, it often surpasses legal boundaries between public and private. Planning regulations remain the most impactful instruments when it comes to organising economic investment as well as offsetting its socio-ecological costs. Examples include compensation measures; betterment fees; value-capturing mechanisms; (collective) benefits agreements; charges; required urban standards; land redistribution mechanisms; and much more besides. The successful functioning of these instruments, however, is bound to perpetual urban development. They regulate urban growth, but their positive social effects largely depend on the prerequisite that the economic value of urban land increases (Rydin, 2013; Savini, 2019).

A post-growth planning approach needs to carefully address those instruments' pitfalls and rethink the political priorities that shape their use. This does not mean abandoning these instruments, which would only throw the baby out with the bathwater. Overall, the toolkit of post-growth economics is likely to include a revised version of many of these planning tools. Tentative examples of these reworked instruments can be seen in public land management projects in Switzerland (Gerber and Gerber, 2017) and green preservation and rewilding initiatives, amongst other projects (Kallis et al., 2020). Similarly, a post-growth planning toolkit must be able to fulfil the ambition of maintaining well-being through reduction.

This book provides two insightful examples of regulatory instruments that might enable a post-growth transition. In Chapter 9, Rydin dissects the limits of regional economic development strategies in the two regions of Cambridgeshire (eastern England) and Skåne in Malmö (southern Sweden). She shows that strategies promoting the economic growth of core cities do not trickle down to cities on the fringe. These strategies are motivated by corporate aspirations to increase the economic gains derived from urban development. Fringe cities end up being locked into an economic dependency that erodes their indigenous economies. As an alternative to such strategies, Rydin advocates community land trusts and regulations that stimulate autonomous development in these localities.

Xue hones in on the key problem of the relationship between an ideology of growth and the legal planning system (Chapter 10). By looking closely at Norway's 2008 Building and Planning Act, she shows how neoliberal planning reforms have privileged governance processes and networks rather than outcomes and regulations. In so doing, these reforms have weakened the laws' guiding role in setting limits to development. She calls instead for a planning law that has a clear ontology of limits, focuses on substantive results (namely reductions), institutes property rights as a social function, and reorganises hierarchies.

## 3.5 Nurturing

Contemporary cities tend to have an antagonistic relationship with nature. This is expressed in a variety of ways, ranging from the encroachment of urban sprawl on otherwise arable land, to the destruction of environmental resources to sustain urban lifestyles characterised by conspicuous consumption and waste production (Kaika et al., 2006; Tzaninis et al., 2020). Such lifestyles are becoming increasingly problematic for human health (as manifested in high rates of anxiety, depression, and obesity), as they are for environmental sustainability. Most urban dwellers have lost a sense of the interdependency amongst their consumption patterns, the industrial–agricultural system that sustains them, their personal health, and the ecosystem they inhabit. This begs the question of how rekindling old and forging new connections between the natural and the urban can address the environmental and social challenges of our times (Gerber, 2020).

Allowing for the emergence of post-growth planning practices requires questioning the rural/urban/industrial divides that have produced zoned urban development. This requires exploring 'urban symbiotic practices' (Kallis et al., 2012), that is, ways of organising space in which urban and rural areas are mutually sustained. Cities should not be organised exclusively as sites of consumption and cognitive production (as envisioned by advocates of the 'knowledge economy') but as sites of social and biological reproduction too. To achieve this, planning needs to put the socio-ecological prosperity of urban habitats – rather than their economic position – at the centre of its practice (Savini, 2021). This might be delivered through planning for regional food systems, which would produce food locally, and circular waste and water systems, which would sustain regional agriculture. These practices have the potential to establish a regenerative relation between cities and their ecosystems (Cattaneo and Gavaldà, 2010).

In their contribution to this volume, Spanier and Feola tackle this challenge from a regional perspective (Chapter 11). They point at the excessive optimism in urban and transition studies concerning cities' role in achieving social well-being and regenerating ecologies. They claim that planners should abandon the obsolete rural/urban/natural trichotomy and instead think in terms of territories that include a variety of ways of using space. Looking at the example of the Territorios Campesinos Agroalimentarios in Colombia, they show that a strategy of re-centring territories' agro-ecological qualities might rebalance the asymmetry of power between urban and rural environments.

In Chapter 12, Pineda-Revilla and Essbai approach the urban/rural divide within urban areas. Looking at two cases of community-led food initiatives in the Amsterdam region, they question whether and how these initiatives might institute a post-growth food system. In so doing, they celebrate the social and political value of prosumption practices, which allow consumers to produce and manage their food. Through these practices, urban inhabitants can regain consciousness of their relationship to rural lifestyles while also helping establish a more systemic, long-term change. The creation of hubs within cities, in which these prosumption practices can take place, is essential.

## 3.6 Being

Post-growth approaches to planning will inevitably require the planning profession to adopt a new ethic. Above all, it needs to unpick planners' belief in the idea that urban economies must continuously grow for cities to prosper. This intellectual shift has the potential to stimulate the creation of a radically different repertoire of approaches in planning, inspired by creativity, discovery, moderation, and ecological consciousness (Sandercock, 2004). All of this being said, questioning economic growth remains taboo amongst contemporary planners. In planning schools, students are typically trained to solve problems exclusively within the narrow confines of the pro-growth logic. In practice, planners find themselves locked into protocols that lack space for critical reflection on pro-growth, mainstream approaches. In both public and private agencies, professional planners are far from agnostic about economic growth and even further from promoting post-growth strategies as real ways of achieving socio-ecological justice than ever before. To develop an approach that sees the pursuit of well-being within ecological limits as its central purpose, planning needs a professional ethic that questions the imperative of pro-growth economic efficiency in urban policymaking.

Post-growth worldviews, particularly those framed under the heading of degrowth, often praise indigenous political ecologies that conceive the meaning of human life in terms of a symbiotic relationship with nature and ethic of well-being (Kothari et al., 2014). These worldviews recognise that in abandoning an economistic and rationalist view on society, it is useful to revalue ethics that foreground relationality and mutual care, as well as the maintenance and healing of nature.

These worldviews' implications for planning (particularly in early-industrial countries) remain entirely open to question. This book explores possible avenues of thought and action for addressing this key issue. In Chapter 13, Lamker and Schulze-Dieckhoff analyse planning professionals' inner selves, especially when they are confronted with post-growth planning's radical departure from established professional principles and practices. Drawing on a variety of encounters with planners, Lamker and Schulze-Dieckhoff conclude that planners are willing to consider alternatives to the mainstream logic, but find it hard to deliver on these alternatives while working as usual. These difficulties arise not just from demanding external conditions, but also from planners' inner struggles, which have to do with the fact that their profession is approaching a major crossroads.

In Chapter 14, Sandercock argues that the planner's transformative agency does not rely exclusively on different ways of knowing and doing in planning. Rather, the precondition for changing planning practice is a different way of being in the world. Accordingly, she calls for 'being skills' rooted in an ethic of relationality that is maintained with the ecosystem and the Other. This ethic, she expands, must rest on peoples' capacities for patience, listening, presence, courage, and humility. Reflecting on her work as a planner, teacher, activist, and community member with indigenous communities in what is known as British Columbia, she concludes that planning must foster an alternative growth paradigm that is qualitatively different from the currently dominant economy-centric growth approach. The time is ripe for planners to engage in work focused on repairing and healing.

## 4. Envisioning post-growth planning action and its vocabulary

Existing post-growth literature in urban studies offers examples of real-life alternatives to the dominant pro-growth logic of urbanisation. Some of these examples celebrate intentional communities that live together, sharing common resources and pursuing low-impact living in synergy with the natural environment. Although these concrete examples are very inspiring, they are unlikely to appeal to everyone or apply everywhere, at any time. It is probably best, then, for planners to avoid advocating standardised post-growth blueprints for urban development. Planning history has shown that a blueprint approach is not the way forward – indeed, it is a trap that leads decision-making processes to all sorts of dead ends (Faludi, 2000). Instead, we challenge planners to creatively engage with local people and their contexts so as to gradually materialise appealing yet feasible post-growth modes of collective organisation and living. We also challenge policymakers, leaders, members of private and public organisations, and people from all backgrounds to engage in this process. This path may be unexplored, but it has remarkable potential.

Building on the chapters in this volume, as well as on collective insights that we gathered during a symposium with all of the authors involved in it, we have compiled a manifesto for post-growth planning action. This manifesto (Chapter 15) captures some of the key messages that coalesced and developed during the book's production. In line with what we have already said, we hope that readers do not see this manifesto as an attempt to create a dogma for post-growth planning. Its primary goal is rather to prompt reactions, generate debate, promote controversy, and – hopefully – trigger concrete action.

This manifesto comes accompanied by a glossary for post-growth planning practices (Chapter 16), which covers this book's key contributions and concepts. Of course, there are other terms beyond those listed and new terms might yet emerge; nevertheless, the glossary should help readers better navigate this book. Still, the glossary's primary goal is more ambitious than that: we hope to equip planners and others with a vocabulary that transcends the obsession with growth, especially when thinking about the future of the places in which they live and work, socialise, and move about.

## References

Alexander S (2012) Planned economic contraction: the emerging case for degrowth. *Environmental Politics* 21(3): 349–368.
Alexander S and Gleeson B (2018) *Degrowth in the Suburbs*. Cham: Palgrave Macmillan.
Baabou W, Grunewald N, Ouellet-Plamondon C, Gressot M and Galli A (2017) The ecological footprint of Mediterranean cities: awareness creation and policy implications. *Environmental Science & Policy* 69: 94–104.
Brokow-Loga A and Eckardt F (eds) (2020) *Postwachstumsstadt. Konturen Einer Solidarischen Stadtpolitik*. Munich: oekom verlag.
Cattaneo C and Gavaldà M (2010) The experience of rurban squats in Collserola, Barcelona: what kind of degrowth? *Journal of Cleaner Production* 18(6): 581–589.

Chatterton P (2016) Building transitions to post-capitalist urban commons. *Transactions of the Institute of British Geographers* 41(4): 403–415.
Cosme I, Santos R and O'Neill D (2017) Assessing the degrowth discourse: a review and analysis of academic degrowth policy proposals. *Journal of Cleaner Production* 149: 321–334.
D'Alisa G, Demaria F and Kallis G (2015) *Degrowth: A Vocabulary for a New Era*. Abingdon: Routledge.
D'Alisa G and Kallis G (2020) Degrowth and the State. *Ecological Economics*, 169, 106486.
Daly H (1999) Uneconomic growth and the built environment: in theory and in fact. In: Kibert C (ed) *Reshaping the Built Environment: Ecology, Ethics, and Economics*. Washington D.C.: Island Press, pp. 73–86.
Daly H (2005) Economics in a full world. *Scientific American* 293: 100–107.
Drews S and Antal M (2016) Degrowth: a 'missile word' that backfires? *Ecological Economics* 126: 182–187.
Faludi A (2000) The performance of spatial planning. *Planning Practice & Research* 15(4): 299–318.
Ferreira A, Beukers E and Te Brömmelstroet M (2012) Accessibility is gold, mobility is not: a proposal for the improvement of transport-related Dutch cost-benefit analysis. *Environment and Planning B: Planning and Design* 39(4): 683–697.
Ferreira A and von Schönfeld KC (2020) Interlacing planning and degrowth scholarship: a manifesto for an interdisciplinary alliance. *disP – The Planning Review* 56(1): 53–64.
Fraser N (2014) Can society be commodities all the way down? Post-Polanyian reflections on capitalist crisis. *Economy and Society* 43(4): 541–558.
Gerber J-D and Gerber J-F (2017) Decommodification as a foundation for ecological economics. *Ecological Economics* 131: 551–556.
Gerber J-F (2020) Degrowth and critical agrarian studies. *The Journal of Peasant Studies* 47(2): 235–264.
Glaeser E (2011) *Triumph of the City: How Our Greatest Invention Makes Us Richer, Smarter, Greener, Healthier and Happier*. New York: Penguin Press.
Gorz A (1991) *Capitalism, Socialism, Ecology*. London: Verso.
Grant JL (2017) Growth management theory: from the garden city to smart growth. In: Gunder M, Madanipour A and Watson V (eds) *The Routledge Handbook of Planning Theory*. Abingdon: Routledge, pp. 41–52.
Jackson T (2017) *Prosperity without Growth: Foundations for the Economy of Tomorrow*. Abingdon: Routledge.
Kaika M, Heynen N and Swyngedouw E (2006) *In the Nature of Cities: Urban Political Ecology and the Politics of Urban Metabolism*. Abingdon: Routledge.
Kallis G (2011) In defence of degrowth. *Ecological Economics* 70: 873–880.
Kallis G (2018) *Degrowth*. Newcastle upon Tyne: Agenda.
Kallis G, Kerschner C and Martinez-Alier J (2012) The economics of degrowth. *Ecological Economics* 84: 172–180.
Kallis G, Paulson S, D'Alisa G and Demaria F (2020) *The Case for Degrowth*. Cambridge: Polity Press.
Kasraian D, Maat K, Stead D and van Wee B (2016) Long-term impacts of transport infrastructure networks on land-use change: an international review of empirical studies. *Transport Reviews* 36(6): 772–792.
Khreis H, Warsow K, Verlinghieri E et al. (2016) The health impacts of traffic-related exposures in urban areas: understanding real effects, underlying driving forces and co-producing future directions. *Journal of Transport & Health* 3(3): 249–267.

Kothari A, Demaria F and Acosta A (2014) Buen Vivir, degrowth and ecological Swaraj: alternatives to sustainable development and the green economy. *Development* 57(3): 362–375.
Latouche S (2009) *Farewell to Growth*. Cambridge: Polity Press.
Latouche S (2012) Can the Left escape economism? *Capitalism, Nature, Socialism* 23(1): 74–78.
Latouche S (2014) *Sortir de la société de consommation: Voix et voies de la décroissance*. Paris: Les Liens qui Libèrent.
Meadows D and Meadows D (1972) *The Limits to Growth*. New York: New American Library.
Molotch H (1976) The city as a growth machine: toward a political economy of place. *American Journal of Sociology* 82(2): 309–332.
Nelson A and Schneider F (2018) *Housing for Degrowth: Principles, Models, Challenges and Opportunities*. Abingdon: Routledge.
Okkels N, Kristiansen CB and Munk-Jørgensen P (2017) *Mental Health and Illness in the City*. Cham: Springer.
Peck J (2016) Transatlantic city, part 2: late entrepreneurialism. *Urban Studies* 54(2): 327–363.
Pickerill DJ (2016) *Eco-Homes: People, Place and Politics*. London: Zed Books.
Purcell M (2009) Resisting neoliberalization: communicative planning or counter-hegemonic movements? *Planning Theory* 8(2): 140–165.
Raco M and Savini F (eds) (2019) *Planning and Knowledge: How New Forms of Technocracy are Shaping Contemporary Cities*. Bristol: Policy Press.
Raworth K (2017) *Doughnut Economics: Seven Ways to Think Like a 21st-Century Economist*. London: Random House Business Books.
Rydin Y (2013) *The Future of Planning*. Bristol: Policy Press.
Sandercock L (2004) Towards a planning imagination for the 21st century. *Journal of the American Planning Association* 70(2): 133–141.
Savini F (2019) Responsibility, polity, value: the (un)changing norms of planning practices. *Planning Theory* 18(1): 58–81.
Savini F (2021) Towards an urban degrowth: habitability, finity and polycentric autonomism. *Environment and Planning A: Economy and Space* 53(5): 1076–1095.
Scott AJ (2019) City-regions reconsidered. *Environment and Planning A: Economy and Space* 51(3): 554–580.
Scott JC (1998) *Seeing Like a State: How Certain Schemes to Improve the Human Condition Have Failed*. New Haven and London: Yale University Press.
Tzaninis Y, Mandler T, Kaika M and Keil R (2020) Moving urban political ecology beyond the 'urbanization of nature'. *Progress in Human Geography* 45(2): 229–252.
UNEP (2020) *Preventing the Next Pandemic: Zoonotic Diseases and How to Break the Chain of Transmission*. Report by the Science Division of the United Nations Environment Programme (UNEP), Nairobi, Kenya.
Urry J (2004) The 'system' of automobility. *Theory, Culture & Society* 21(4–5): 25–39.
Urry J (2008) Climate change, travel and complex futures. *British Journal of Sociology* 59(2): 261–279.
von Schönfeld KC and Ferreira A (2021) Urban planning and European innovation policy: achieving sustainability, social inclusion, and economic growth? *Sustainability* 13(3): 1137.
Xue J (2015) Sustainable housing development: decoupling or degrowth? A comparative study of Copenhagen and Hangzhou. *Environment and Planning C: Government and Policy* 33(3): 620–639.

Xue J (2018) Space, planning and distribution. In: Nelson A and Schneider F (eds), *Housing for Degrowth*. Abingdon: Routledge, pp. 185–195.

Xue J (2021) Urban planning and degrowth: a missing dialogue. *Local Environment*: 1–19. Epub ahead of print, 4 January. DOI: 10.1080/13549839.2020.1867840.

Zukin S (1993) *Landscapes of Power: From Detroit to Disney World*. Berkeley: University of California Press.

# 2
# WHEN GREENING IS NOT DEGROWTH

## Cost-Shifting Insights

*Marta Conde, Giacomo D'Alisa and Filka Sekulova*

## 1. Introduction

The liberal, and largely colonial, idea that human beings have a legitimate right to extract, control, use, consume, waste, and dispose of all the resources deemed necessary in the pursuit of personal desire sets the imaginative horizon for growth in Westernised societies. This cultural bedrock, driven by individualism, patriarchal values (Mies, 1998), and colonial imaginaries (Nirmal and Rocheleau, 2019), has been the foundation of an expansion of capitalist socio-economic forces as the dominant vehicle for individual self-realisation (D'Alisa, 2019). Degrowth scholarship provides a grounded critique of this socio-ecological configuration, and documents the tight imbrications between constant economic expansion, surging global environmental damage, and social, cultural, and gender inequalities (Parrique et al., 2019; D'Alisa et al., 2015).

The ideas, movements, and proposals currently emerging in the field of degrowth are in a state of continuous evolution and aim to achieve a leaner societal metabolism (that is, one which requires less energy and material) (Georgescu-Roegen, 1971), while providing equitable conditions for supporting lives that are worth living. Degrowth presupposes a radical political and economic re-organisation of our capital-centric and unjust society in support of, and inspired by, global struggles for environmental and social justice (Anguelovski and Martinez Alier, 2014), as well as offering critiques of development (Escobar, 1999). The societal metamorphosis presupposed by degrowth is underpinned by principles of deep democracy (Zografos, 2019), feminism (Pérez Orozco, 2014), and decoloniality (Nirmal and Rocheleau, 2019). As such, degrowth draws inspiration from its sister movements across the globe, such as the multiple versions of Buen vivir, Ubuntu, and Ecosawaraj among many others, which have grown as a response to the monolithic imperative

DOI: 10.4324/9781003160984-3

of progress imposed on the global South by colonial and developmentalist regimes (Kothari et al., 2019).

The principles, visions, and claims of degrowth become even more pertinent in a context of rolling economic and environmental crises, such as the climate crisis and sharpening social inequalities, currently exacerbated by the COVID-19 pandemic (Wallace, 2016). Yet mainstream responses to the myriad socio-environmental pitfalls of our current system are predominantly spearheaded by calls for 'green' growth. Greening is a slogan beloved of mainstream political institutions and companies (Kenis and Lievens, 2016), who frame investments in clean energy, clean transport technology, and 'correct' market pricing as a global fix for our contemporary climate and socio-economic crises. This trend is clearly manifest in a plethora of Green New Deals in European and US political agendas as well as diverse social movements, and can be seen to branch out into the urban through the promotion of 'Nature-Based Solutions'. In this chapter, we critically engage with both concepts through the lens of degrowth.

The Green New Deal (GND) has become an umbrella term for different political visions and potentialities (Mastini et al., 2021), which aims to secure funds for a green transition. Under this banner we see initiatives such as the European Green Deal, a 'new growth strategy' (European Commission, 2019) that leaves capitalist neoliberal economics intact: the 'greening' project offers companies and investment funds new opportunities for business. We also, however, find a range of more progressive GND proposals: the initial US GND as presented by Alexandria Ocasio-Cortez in early 2019; the GND proposed by the Labour Party in the UK; those presented by civil society such as The Green New Deal for Europe (n.d.); and those pushed by activists from the South such as the Ecosocial Pact or the feminist GND (see Conde and Andreucci, 2020). The Green New Deal is thus a contested idea, where the imperative of the climate crisis can be invoked either to transition to a more social and just economy – as proposed by more progressive GNDs – or to harness another wave of capital accumulation – as established by growth-driven GNDs.

Nature-Based Solutions (NBS) is a new buzzword in environmental policy circles, frequently promoted as a way to implement green growth agendas. NBS represents a wide range of interventions that seek to harness natural functions and green aesthetics to meet challenges in urban sustainability. They are pursued as a win-win policy pack capable of simultaneously triggering economic growth, contributing to social cohesion and justice, and improving overall environmental performance (European Commission, 2015). Indeed, the pursuit of green aesthetics alters the perceived value of the landscapes in which we live (Gobster et al., 2007). Aesthetic features, however, do not necessarily match or represent healthy ecosystems, nor stand as a landmark for social justice (Anguelovski et al., 2018a). Although there is much about urban settlements' environmental conditions that could be improved, the current focus on aesthetic, technologically biased, and often elitist or exclusive approaches to nature in many world cities only conceals the root causes of urban socio-environmental degradation: harmful urban social metabolisms and deep social segregation.

The major argument that we set forth here is that greening the economy in pursuit of growth requires a constant and consistent shifting of costs away from privileged spaces and subjects, and towards more vulnerable ones (Kapp, 1963). Degrowth planning, as well as any progressive greening associated with NBS or GND projects, should thus aim to minimise the impacts of cost-shifting on other human and non-human beings and worlds.

The chapter is organised as follows: we begin by introducing the cost-shifting framework that underpins the unequal exchanges associated with various typologies of greening politics and projects. Then, for an example of this cost-shifting in the context of GND operational principles, we discuss two examples of NBS, and two from the energy complex nexus, a key component of the GND transition. These four examples have been chosen to illustrate cost-shifting at different scales, in different geographies, and across different modes of planning and participation. We conclude by reflecting on the kind of principles that planning and policy-making could take on board in order to pursue a degrowth agenda, to create more just and sustainable societies.

## 2. Cost-Shifting and Greening

According to William Kapp, the ability to socialise costs is perceived as a measure of a business's success. Most profit-driven private enterprises operate by shifting costs onto others; the more costs they shift and the better they become at doing it, the more prosperous their business (Kapp, 1963). In the pursuit of personal wants and desires, individuals also shift costs onto others. For example, for every person driving a Ferrari as a means of self-realisation, there is a concomitant socialisation of the cost of the $CO_2$ that that Ferrari emits.

Large-scale agribusiness uses huge quantities of pesticides to save on costs and maximise sales, even if this means polluting the land and harmfully impacting workers, as well as nearby residents. Relocating such operations to countries without restrictions on the extensive use of harmful pesticides is one way to maximise cost-shifting (Weir and Schapiro, 1981). Waste dumping is another successful strategy for cost-shifting, again driven by business, that allows highly urbanised and industrialised territories to socialise the costs of their waste generation onto both proximal rural areas and far-off marginalised regions (Demaria and D'Alisa, 2013). These strategies are completely in line with the mainstream economic approach. In most cases, mainstream economists theorise the costs of pollution as possible and occasional market failures – also known as externalities. Kapp (1963), on the other hand, demonstrated that the socialisation of costs is not external, but internal, or immanent to economic activities and standard business operations.

Cost-shifting has adverse consequences on human health and settlements, polluting and depleting ecosystems. Rob Nixon points to the slow violence of cost-shifting practices, and the consequences of contaminating activities (Nixon, 2011). These can manifest at different spatial scales and time frames (Gerber, 2016). At a local scale, this may be the slow contamination caused for example by a factory or industrial project, whilst at a wider scale the impacts of climate change could be described as a cost shifted onto socially vulnerable populations and future generations.

Cost-shifting occurs whenever (economic) agents generate social costs (financial or otherwise) that affect, whether directly or indirectly, third persons or the environment. Unless forced, economic agents that generate such costs generally do nothing to avoid or minimise them. Social costs are extra-economic in the sense that they are not the immediate result of a market transaction (Berger, 2008; Neves, 2018). Attempts have been made to find ways of minimising the socialisation of costs (or externalities): Pigou (1920) suggested taxes and subsidies, whereas Coase (1960) promoted a genuine reallocation of property rights. According to Kapp, however, scholars and policy makers should not address social costs simply or only in economic or monetary terms. Indeed, it is difficult to operationalise a quantitative approach to measuring – and thereby reducing – cost-shifting. One potential solution is a social multi-criteria evaluation method, which takes into account monetary as well as environmental and social criteria (Neves, 2016). Neves (2016) has suggested that the pervasiveness of systemic cost-shifting could be severely restricted through institutional reforms and the implementation of social norms. Following these interventions, we propose to use cost-shifting as an analytical framework to unveil the potential adverse implications of greening programmes.

Indeed, well-intentioned green policies can have unwanted cost-shifting consequences. Scholars and activists have begun to warn about the potential threats that the European Green Deal might pose for countries worldwide, as its implementation costs are socialised (Fuchs et al., 2020; European Environmental Bureau, 2020). For examples, we now turn to an analysis of renewable energy projects and Nature-Based Solutions, situating these within long-, medium-, and short-distance typologies of cost-shifting. Although we have chosen to focus on the spatial dimension, it is important to note that costs can also be shifted across different time frames, as well as across human and non-human beings.

## 3. Regional Cost-Shifting of NBS: The Eco-City of Tianjin, China

Funded through joint contributions from the governments of China and Singapore, the newly developed Tianjin eco-city is a large-scale flagship project. It is formally part of the state's movement towards building an ecological civilisation in China, where humans and nature, sustainability and growth are to coexist harmoniously.

The eco-city is located 40 kilometres from Tianjin city centre, within a region which lies between Beijing, Tianjin, and the Hebei Province, and which has been identified as 'the next growth engine' (Government of Singapore, 2019). The eco-city is projected to span over 30 square kilometres, and accommodate up to 350,000 inhabitants, though so far it has reached only one-fifth of this target (Katona, 2018).

It is planned as a compact area, with a mix of land uses and a variety of spaces for employment, residence, commerce, and recreation, all within walking distance from access points for public transport.

The deployment of Nature-Based Solutions is one of the underlying paradigms of the eco-city, visible in the revitalisation of polluted land, the presence of vegetation in central parts of the city, green belts (four kilometres of which have already been built), and various interlinked waterbodies. The previously polluted wastewater pond has been converted into a lake with a water purification system. The ecological features of the project are monitored across a large number of key performance indicators which cover air and water quality, as well as wetland and ecological shoreline protection rates. Other quality indicators include the accessibility of parks, recreational amenities, and social housing (20% of the homes are publicly subsidised). All buildings need to meet green standards along with a list of 'healthy living lifestyle' indicators. A minimum 50% of the residents are targeted for local employment, and at least 150,000 of these will be in the field of research and development, or technological innovation in general.

Although the project is the result of an impressive effort in terms of scale and finance, some of its key ecological and social premises merit further scrutiny. First and foremost, the eco-city has been discursively grounded upon vague notions of sustainability (Caprotti and Gong, 2017), rooted in practices of urban boosterism and green entrepreneurialism. Its philosophy closely resembles that of the mainstream versions of the Green New Deal, where economic growth is stimulated through real estate development (Wang and Mell, 2019) and the provision of grants and tax breaks for large companies willing to move their operations to a given location. Accordingly, the eco-city has been built on land with low acquisition value, the reclaiming of which can be seen as a form of 'green-grabbing' or the appropriation of land and resources for 'greening' objectives (Fairhead et al., 2012), a process which is accompanied by inherent and varied types of cost-shifting.

Second, whereas the eco-city is promoted as a space for green lifestyles and technological advancement, it remains silent on questions of social justice (Caprotti and Gong, 2017). The development of the Tianjin eco-city went ahead without a proper study of (or support for) the extant local culture. The original villages were demolished and their inhabitants displaced, leading to a loss of situated knowledge, such as maritime and cultural heritage, ocean folk customs, and the salt culture (Wang and Mell, 2019). This type of cultural cost-shifting has been largely ignored in the city's planning. The reclamation of the land was not planned with and for the previous inhabitants of the area, but despite them and in favour of an incipient techno-entrepreneurial Chinese class. The project development thus seems to have contributed to the widening of the gap between those undocumented migrant and precarious workers whose labour made the eco-city possible, and those privileged residents who can afford to live on the site.

Third, the 'eco' aspect of the project is primarily understood in terms of protecting the city's (financially well-off) occupants from environmental harm, rather than benefiting the global environment (Caprotti et al., 2015). The eco-city invites and promotes the expansion of lifestyles that are car-based and energy/resource-intensive, the costs of which are not borne locally (Wang and Mell, 2019). Flats in the Tianjin eco-city represent 'containers of a sanitized, or artificially "green" form of living', where air is filtered and garbage disappears directly from the apartments, sparing residents any views of garbage trucks (Caprotti et al., 2015). The energy and material costs of these green lifestyles and their associated smart infrastructure are, then, effectively shifted far away, onto incineration sites and extraction frontiers (Yang and Ho, 2018; Bondes and Johnson, 2017).

## 4. Short-Distance Cost-Shifting of NBS: The Glòries Park in Barcelona, Spain

Another example of a green redevelopment project is the Parc de les Glòries in Barcelona, Spain. This long-awaited urban transformation replaces, redirects, and buries underground a densely interwoven traffic hub, close to one of the city's main entrances. Its redevelopment involved demolishing an elevated ring road and underground traffic lanes, so as to enhance the liveability and pedestrian accessibility of the residential area. The location of the park is framed by two iconic buildings: Torre Agbar and the Barcelona Museum of Design, located right on its edge.

Glòries is an ambitious project in the making. It opens up new venues for connectivity and biodiversity, through so-called biodiversity nodes (used as nature refuges), wilderness areas, and lawns, as well as spaces for social interaction. Furthermore, the project has enhanced the natural interchange between sky and subsoil, improving permeability while expanding the existing tree canopy (IRBIS, 2014). Yet, while it does attend to local aesthetics, the project faces a number of wider sustainability challenges. Whereas its northern side is already complete and widely used as a green sports and recreation space, the development of the southern part has been paused, and is the object of numerous discussions due to the high financial, material, and energy costs that building the underground tunnel would entail. Furthermore, the park's central green lawn is hardly appropriate for the dry Mediterranean climate, favouring the diffusion of plagues (onto the plants) and requiring a huge amount of water. For this reason, the 'gran clariana', a large lawn designed to reproduce the experience of walking through a green field or an enjoyable space for relaxing, is continuously barred from use, a little more than a year after its completion. Water shortage costs are effectively shifted to the local community.

Another example of cost-shifting can be seen in the plight of parents whose children attend nearby schools, currently demanding the removal of large asbestos rooftops just next to the park – without much luck so far. The risks of breathing this toxic substance are being shifted onto the children and their families who use the park, meaning that while those who live in or use the area may enjoy an attractive open space, they cannot do this without running the gauntlet of its toxic perimeter.

It is a reasonable assumption that the Parc de les Glòries will have a gentrifying impact, given that green infrastructure frequently goes hand in hand with demographic changes (Anguelovski et al., 2018b). The park's influence on house prices in the area is yet to be seen; currently construction work around the park abounds, with ample luxury housing on sale. In the nearby neighbourhood of Poblenou, where the Parque del Centro was renovated, Anguelovski et al. (2018a) found that gentrification indicators (the percentage of residents with a high level of education, and therefore higher income) increased by nearly 28 percentage points on average for the areas around the park after its inauguration. Gentrification implies social, financial, and environmental cost-shifting onto families who can no longer cope with rising housing prices, and who are eventually forced to move away.

## 5. Contesting Cost-Shifting in Renewable Energy Planning in Catalonia, Spain

The green transition and accompanying investment in renewable energies are causing environmental conflicts in rural areas, where land is being occupied for large-scale renewable energy facilities. Zografos and Robbins (2020) have defined those areas onto which the costs of a supposedly just green transition are shifted as 'green sacrifice zones'. In Catalonia, Spain, the production of energy has long been a story of medium-distance cost-shifting 'successes' between peripheries and the centre. This can be seen, for example, between the city of Barcelona and its metropolitan conurbation, and rural areas. The centres operate through a constant accumulation of net energy, and displace entropy to the peripheries (Franquesa, 2018). Franquesa (2018) shows that three of the least populated counties in southern Catalonia host high-tension lines and pipelines, a nuclear energy station, natural gas power plants, and hydroelectric dams. The expansion of energy generation infrastructure in rural areas tends to be justified by presenting these regions and their inhabitants as unproductive or underdeveloped, with lingering agriculture and declining industry. In this way, governments and energy companies present renewable energy as an opportunity to 'develop' these areas. Yet, as seen in other parts of Catalonia, this only accelerates the processes of depopulation, agricultural and economic decline, and environmental degradation (Franquesa, 2018). A robust local opposition in southern Catalonia has thus far impeded the advancement of further energy facilities including two dams, three nuclear power plants, and two large storage facilities for natural gas and nuclear waste.

It is precisely this paradigm of greening the economy which means that renewable energy can be presented as an opportunity to 'develop' such areas, and which is key to the scores of renewable energy plants currently being proposed. This is the case not only elsewhere in Spain (Martinez Alonso et al., 2016) but throughout Europe more generally (Frolova et al., 2019).

The Farmer's Union in Catalonia, for example, has recently denounced projects to install large wind and solar plants which encroach onto the valuable arable lands of the farmers they represent. Most farmers only own small plots of land, and need to rent more terrain from landowners who are often located in urban areas, and who demand increasing returns. Farmers cannot compete with the land-rental prices offered by energy companies. The union, therefore, is organising to contest this move by proposing a different narrative. Although in favour of a green transition and a non-carbon future, they argue that such processes should be done radically differently, reducing the vulnerability of the energy system and promoting the right to energy as a common good. The farmers' union stresses transparency and participation in the planning process, particularly for those whose lives and territories are being affected. They demand the protection of agrarian lands and landscapes, suggesting instead that renewable energy projects focus on degraded, urban, or industrial plots, as a way to minimise costs and share them more fairly. Crucially, the farmers demand that the continuous cost-shifting of energy production be reversed, and they propose the implementation of what they call a 'distributed electricity generation' as a way to achieve this. Within this framework, energy would be produced as close as possible to where it is needed, thus limiting the cost-shifting of energy-intensive urban settlements onto rural areas. The union has organised a round table discussion forum, where promoters of renewable energy and representatives of municipal associations, along with other interest groups, can discuss paths forward and propose specific criteria for the development of potential future regulations.

## 6. The Increasing Demand for Lithium in Green Transitions, and its Long-Range Cost-Shifting

Lithium, used for batteries in electric cars and electricity storage, has become a key mineral for both the green economy and sustainable energy transitions. The increasing pressures of lithium extraction, however, suggest that it might end up exerting significant negative impacts within long-term transition projects (Greim et al., 2020). Chile, as the largest producer of lithium after Australia, is at the forefront of this extractivist pressure. The European Commission has been pushing for a Free Trade Agreement to guarantee supplies, and has already brought forward a clause stipulating the liberalisation of (and a zero-tariff on) lithium products (Ankersmit and Partiti, 2020). The manufacturing of green energy products and infrastructure is shifting the costs of extraction and production onto the people and territories where lithium is extracted – an example of long-distance cost-shifting. Indeed, the extraction of lithium entails a high level of degradation to the local environment, including vegetation decline and increased drought conditions (Liu et al., 2019). This is of high concern for the indigenous Atacama people who live on the arid salt flats between the borders of Chile, Bolivia, and Argentina, where one of the biggest lithium deposits worldwide is located. At the signing of a deal between six aboriginal communities and a mining company for the construction of a new mine, the leader of one of these communities stated, 'We know the lithium companies are taking millions of dollars from our lands, and we know they ought to give something back. But they're not' (Frankel and Whoriskey, 2016).

Since unequal power relations in decision making are prevalent in mining projects (Conde, 2017), some local groups trust neither the economic benefits nor the promises that 'sustainable development' will compensate for the environmental and social costs involved in the extraction. Indeed, the head of the Atacama Indigenous group has declared that the constituency he represents will 'not accept money in exchange for the subsistence of our people' (Sherwood, 2021). But is it possible for local groups to be compensated for the social and environmental costs of lithium extraction? How can they ensure that the environment is preserved? The idea of 'community mining', pushed by one of the main indigenous federations in Bolivia, has been put forward as a counter-proposal, demanding that minerals be owned and managed jointly by the state's agencies and community organisations, with an agreement on the distribution of benefits and burdens (Conde and Andreucci, 2020). Although such a move would not reduce the pressures of extractivism, it does represent a step towards community sovereignty in managing local resources, and their having the power to make decisions about their future.

## 7. Conclusion

The global turns to decarbonisation and green politics do not come without a cost. While progressive GNDs and Nature-Based Solutions construct a discourse of 'global sustainability', commitments to rapidly deploy major renewable energy infrastructure and implement large-scale urban projects shift the social and environmental costs onto marginalised territories and populations (Roy et al., 2020; Zografos and Robbins, 2020). Put differently, green narratives and 'greening' agendas are not inherently different to, and can often perpetuate, the cost-shifting practices of neoliberalism. Efforts to reduce or minimise short-, medium-, and long-distance cost-shifting practices should thus be at the forefront of degrowth planning. In the early sections of this chapter we placed various cost-shifting practices in the spotlight. Are there ways to distribute such (assumably unavoidable) costs more fairly?

First, we propose that any planning for a green transition should take into account the financial, environmental, social, and cultural costs associated with the extraction and use of materials and energy. The same should also go for considering the location of new so-called green infrastructures, and their implications for equity and justice. The importance of minimising cost-shifting must first be acknowledged, to then become a key ingredient of both public and private planning and operations. Although the socialisation of costs can be reduced, it cannot be completely avoided, as it is an immanent part of human activity and the social metabolism of our societies. Society must therefore decide which sectors and industries have unacceptably high levels of cost-shifting, with a view to responsibly and sensitively phasing them out. This has already been taking place over recent decades for some polluting industries, with asbestos a prime example. These are only a few suggestions, however, and more needs to be done; in the current transition, cost-shifting is increasing in many sectors and territories, and is justified by an uncritical green narrative.

Second, we have observed how top-down forms of renewable energy planning and urban NBS investments shift the cost of green energy and greening onto local inhabitants, as well as populations whose livelihoods depend on the territories in question. If cost-shifting practices in the name of a green transition were to increase they would most likely *deepen* existing inequalities. Affected groups respond to green or extractivist projects demanding a right to a veto, and a strong voice in the decision-making processes that concern their future. To this end, authentic and non-tokenistic participation practices (Arnstein, 1969) must be put in place in order to ensure that the benefits and costs of greening or green transitions are fairly distributed. These may include the right to say 'no' to a new project, multi-criteria iterative processes, as well as inclusive planning or decision-making initiatives. Following the 'Post-normal science' paradigm, controversial, urgent, and high-stakes issues such as the green transition should not be left only to 'professionals', but addressed via a plurality of legitimate perspectives, dialogue, and mutual respect (Funtowicz and Ravetz, 1993). Even if cost-shifting cannot be totally eliminated, a just settlement can be reached.

## Acknowledgements

Giacomo D'Alisa acknowledges under the contract SFRH/BPD/116505/2016 the support of the Portuguese Foundation for Science and Technology (FCT), through the 'Programa Operacional do Capital Humano' (POCH) co-funded by the European Social Fund.

## References

Anguelovski I, Brand A and Connolly J (2018a) From landscapes of utopia to the margins of the green urban life. *City* 22(3): 417–436.

Anguelovski I, Connolly J, Masip L and Pearsall H (2018b) Assessing green gentrification in historically disenfranchised neighborhoods: a longitudinal and spatial analysis of Barcelona. *Urban Geography* 39(3): 458–491.

Anguelovski I and Martínez Alier J (2014) The 'environmentalism of the poor' revisited: territory and place in disconnected glocal struggles. *Ecological Economics* 102: 167–176.

Ankersmit L and Partiti E (2020) *Alternatives for the 'Raw Materials and Energy Chapters' in EU Trade Agreements: An Inclusive Approach.* Berlin: PowerShift.

Arnstein SR (1969) A ladder of citizen participation. *Journal of the American Planning Association* 35(4): 216–224.

Berger, S (2008) K. William Kapp's theory of social costs and environmental policy: towards political ecological economics. *Ecological Economics* 67(2): 244–252.

Bondes M and Johnson T (2017) Beyond localized environmental contention: horizontal and vertical diffusion in a Chinese anti-incinerator campaign. *Journal of Contemporary China* 26(106): 504–520.

Caprotti F and Gong Z (2017) Social sustainability and residents' experiences in a new Chinese eco-city. *Habitat International* 61: 45–54.

Caprotti, F, Springer, C and Harmer, N (2015) 'Eco' for whom? Envisioning eco-urbanism in the Sino-Singapore Tianjin Eco-city, China. *International Journal of Urban and Regional Research* 39(3): 495–517.

Coase RH (1960) The problem of social cost. *Journal of Law and Economics* 3(1): 1–44.

Conde M (2017) Resistance to mining. A review. *Ecological Economics* 132: 80–90.

Conde M and Andreucci D (2020) Challenging extractivism. Available at: https://undisciplinedenvironments.org/2020/12/23/challenging-extractivism/ (accessed March 2021).

D'Alisa G (2019) Degrowth. In: *Dicionário Alice*. Available at: https://estudogeral.sib.uc.pt/bitstream/10316/87061/1/Degrowth_Dicionario%20Alice.pdf (accessed March 2021).

D'Alisa G, Demaria F and Kallis G (2015) *Degrowth: A Vocabulary for a New Era*. Abingdon: Routledge.

Demaria F and D'Alisa G (2013) Le nuove frontiere dell'accumulazione capitalistica. Rifiuti lotte ambientali in India. *Storie in Movimento* 30: 30–51.

Escobar A (1999) The invention of development. *Current History* 98(631): 382–386.

European Commission (2015) Towards an EU research and innovation policy agenda for nature-based solutions & re-naturing cities. *European Commission*, 3 July. Available at: https://ec.europa.eu/programmes/horizon2020/en/news/towards-eu-research-and-innovation-policy-agenda-nature-based-solutions-re-naturing-cities (accessed December 2021).

European Commission (2019) European Green Deal: what role can taxation play? *European Commission*, 11 December. Available at: https://ec.europa.eu/taxation_customs/commission-priorities-2019-24-and-taxation/european-green-deal-what-role-can-taxation-play_en (accessed December 2021).

European Environmental Bureau (2020) Civil society concerns on EU critical raw materials plans. Available at: https://eeb.org/library/civil-society-concerns-on-eu-critical-raw-materials-plans/ (accessed March 2021).

Fairhead J, Leach M and Scoones I (2012) Green grabbing: a new appropriation of nature? *Journal of Peasant Studies* 39(2): 237–261.

Frankel TC and Whoriskey P (2016) Tossed aside in the 'white gold' rush. *The Washington Post*, 19 December. Available at: www.washingtonpost.com/graphics/business/batteries/tossed-aside-in-the-lithium-rush/ (accessed March 2021).

Franquesa J (2018) *Power Struggles: Dignity, Value, and the Renewable Energy Frontier in Spain*. Bloomington: Indiana University Press.

Frolova M, Centeri C, Benediktsson K, Hunziker M, Kabai R, Scognamiglio A, Martinopoulos G, Sismani G, Brito P, Muñoz-Cerón E, Słupiński M, Ghislanzoni M, Braunschweiger D, Herrero-Luque D and Roth M (2019) Effects of renewable energy on landscape in Europe: comparison of hydro, wind, solar, bio-, geothermal and infrastructure energy landscapes. *Hungarian Geographical Bulletin* 68(4): 317–333.

Fuchs R, Brown C and Rounsevell M (2020) Europe's Green Deal offshores environmental damage to other nations. *Nature* 586: 671–673.

Funtowicz S and Ravetz J (1993) Science for the post-normal age. *Futures* 25(7): 739–755.

Georgescu-Roegen N (1971). *The Entropy Law and the Economic Process*. Cambridge, MA: Harvard University Press.

Gerber JF (2016) The legacy of K. William Kapp. *Development and Change* 47(7): 902–917.

Gobster PH, Nassauer JI, Daniel TC and Fry G (2007) The shared landscape: what does aesthetics have to do with ecology? *Landscape Ecology* 22(7): 959–972.

Government of Singapore (2019) The Sino-Singapore Tianjin Eco-city. Available at: www.mnd.gov.sg/tianjinecocity/who-we-are (accessed February 2021).

Greim P, Solomon AA and Breyer C (2020) Assessment of lithium criticality in the global energy transition and addressing policy gaps in transportation. *Nature Communications* 11: 4570.

IRBIS (2014) Canòpia Urbana, Proyecto ganador del concurso para el Proyecto Urbano para el espacio libre de la Plaça de les Glòries (Barcelona). Available at: www.irbis.cat/es/project/canopia-urbana-plaza-de-las-glories/ (accessed February 2021).

Kapp KW (1963) *Social Costs of Business Enterprise*. Bombay/London: Asia Publishing House.

Katona A (2018) Tianjin Snapshot report. Available at: https://naturvation.eu/location/asia/cn/tianjin (accessed February 2021).

Kenis A and Lievens M (2016) Greening the economy or economizing the green project? When environmental concerns are turned into a means to save the market. *Review of Radical Political Economics* 48(2): 217–234.

Kothari A, Salleh A, Escobar A, Demaria F and Acostam A (2019) *Pluriverse. A Post-Development Dictionary*. New Delhi: Tulika Books.

Liu W, Agusdinata DB and Myint SW (2019) Spatiotemporal patterns of lithium mining and environmental degradation in the Atacama Salt Flat, Chile. *International Journal of Applied Earth Observation and Geoinformation* 80: 145–156.

Martinez Alonso P, Hewitt R, Pacheco JD, Bermejo LR, Jiménez VH, Guillén JV, Bressers H and de Boer C (2016) Losing the roadmap: renewable energy paralysis in Spain and its implications for the EU low carbon economy. *Renewable Energy* 89: 680–694.

Mastini R, Kallis G and Hickel J (2021) A Green New Deal without growth? *Ecological Economics* 179: 106832.

Mies M (1998) *Patriarchy and Accumulation on a World Scale: Women in the International Division of Labour*. London: Zed Books.

Neves V (2016) What happened to Kapp's theory of social costs? A case of metatheoretical dispute and dissent in economics. *Review of Political Economy* 28(4): 488–503.

Neves V (2018) The theory of social costs of K. William Kapp: some notes on Sebastian Berger's *The Social Costs of Neoliberalism*. *Forum for Social Economics* 49(301): 1–13.

Nirmal P and Rocheleau D (2019) Decolonizing degrowth in the post-development convergence: questions, experiences, and proposals from two Indigenous territories. *ENE: Nature and Space* 2(3): 465–492.

Nixon R (2011) *Slow Violence and the Environmentalism of the Poor*. Cambridge, MA: Harvard University Press.

Parrique T, Barth J, Briens F, Kerschner C, Kraus-Polk A, Kuokkanen A and Spangenberg JH (2019) Decoupling debunked: evidence and arguments against green growth as a sole strategy for sustainability. Report, European Environmental Bureau, July. Available at: https://eeb.org/library/decoupling-debunked/ (accessed February 2022).

Pérez Orozco A (2014) *Subversión feminista de la economía. Aportes para un debate sobre el conflicto capital-vida*. Madrid: Traficantes de Sueños.

Pigou AC (1920) *The Economics of Welfare*. London: Macmillan.

Roy B, Hanaček K, Kallis G and Avila S (2020) Ecological economics and degrowth: proposing a future research agenda from the margins. *Ecological Economics* 169: 106495.

Sherwood D (2021) Inside lithium giant SQM's struggle to win over indigenous communities in Chile's Atacama. *Reuters*, 15 January. Available at: www.reuters.com/article/us-chile-lithium-sqm-focus-idUSKBN29K1DB (accessed March 2021).

The Green New Deal for Europe (n.d.) Available at: www.gndforeurope.com/ (accessed March 2021).

Wallace R (2016) *Big Farms Make Big Flue*. New York: Monthly Review Press.

Wang X and Mell I (2019) Evaluating the challenges of eco-city development in China: a comparison of Tianjin and Dongtan eco-cities. *International Development Planning Review* 41(2): 215–242.

Weir D and Schapiro M (1981) *Circle of Poison: Pesticides and People in a Hungry World*. San Francisco, CA: Institute for Food and Development Policy.

Yang X and Ho P (2018) Conflict over mining in rural China: a comprehensive survey of intentions and strategies for environmental activism. *Sustainability* 10(5): 1669.

Zografos C (2019) Direct democracy. In: Kothari A, Salleh A, Escobar A and Demaria F (eds) *Pluriverse: A Post-Development Dictionary*. Chennai: Tulika Books.

Zografos C and Robbins P (2020) Green sacrifice zones, or why a Green New Deal cannot ignore the cost shifts of just transitions. *One Earth* 3(5): 543–546.

# PART 2
# Dwelling

# 3
# HOUSING COMMONS AS A DEGROWTH PLANNING PRACTICE

Learning from Amsterdam's de Nieuwe Meent

*Federico Savini and Daan Bossuyt*

## 1. Degrowth, autonomy and commoning

The commoning of housing is the strongest available way of prefiguring a degrowth imaginary of planning. Housing is one of the most valuable goods in our economic system and residential real-estate development fuels GDP growth. Both housing and land constitute immovable, limited and easily excludable goods. As such, they have become cornerstones of capitalism. The commodification of housing, through which it becomes a growth-boosting market, depends on the endurance of a legal and ideological infrastructure that sees private ownership as a way of securing well-being and individual success. In surpassing public and private property schemes, the commoning of housing cuts against these premises, becoming a horizon for degrowth.

From a degrowth perspective, housing is not a commodity but an essential social good. Commoning turns housing into a degrowth practice, creating living spaces that are free from market logics in their physical, social and ecological aspects (Alexander 2018; Chatterton 2016; Lietaert 2010). These spaces entail commoning in that they denote collective ownership, democratic control, conviviality and solidarity. Housing commons are based on intentional communities that operate in terms of sharing and togetherness (Jarvis 2017). They become nests of political emancipation through the everyday practice of organising inclusive and collective living, which plants the seeds of politics (Nelson and Schneider 2018).

If the commoning of housing is a practice, autonomy is its condition. The degrowth critique of contemporary society is historically premised on the study (and pursuit) of autonomy because it directly relates to theories of direct democracy (for a review see Asara, Profumi, and Kallis 2013). From a degrowth perspective, autonomy means society's emancipation from the hegemony of the imperatives of growth and their ideology of competition and productivity (Fotopoulos 2007). As

DOI: 10.4324/9781003160984-5

Deriu puts it, 'it is hard to imagine any real form of autonomy and self-government without questioning the central imperative of economic growth' (Deriu 2015: 57).

By unpacking the notion of autonomy, it is possible to articulate the philosophical premises of degrowth housing, as well as its political, institutional and ecological meanings (Bonaiuti 2012). In this context, autonomy calls for housing collectives to be governed autonomously, managing their members' fundamental right to shelter through direct and participative forms of democratic decision-making. Yet, it also calls for institutions able to protect and crystallise networks of solidarity and cooperation, so as to ensure the long-term provision of autonomous housing. Autonomy is also ecological in that it stresses the importance of collective housing being low-impact and self-sufficient in catering for essential needs such as food, heating, water and energy and caring for different age groups. Finally, autonomy pursues human well-being, seeking to provide secure long-term living and collective care through commoning.

Despite the close relations and codependency among commoning, autonomy and degrowth, it is not a given that housing commons enable degrowth, understood as a socio-economic practice that explicitly fulfils the imperative to live ecologically. Housing commons assume a variety of forms, varying from independent housing squats to legally sanctioned housing cooperatives (Bossuyt 2021; Lang, Carriou, and Czischke 2020; Salet et al. 2020). Within this diversity not all models are associated with autonomy, degrowth or decommodification. Autonomy can be achieved through different collective appropriation strategies. Housing commons can be identified as degrowth housing initiatives by the way in which they maintain this autonomy and organise their political and architectural dimensions.

In this chapter we look at how the commoning of housing enables autonomy and degrowth. We do so recognising that State hierarchies and market competition pose a constant threat to autonomy. Housing commons face the risk of marketisation, marginalisation and co-optation. Marketisation implies that housing commons are parcelled into individually tradable properties, leading to effective commodification (Bruun 2018; Starecheski 2019). Inward-looking groups become marginal in seeking to preserve themselves in the face of internal and external conflict (Sørvoll and Bengtsson 2018). To a degree, social housing has addressed some of these problems through centralised public management, which has come at the expense of autonomy. This points to the looming threat of co-optation through the imposition of hierarchical and professionalised management upon democratic association (Beekers 2012; Bossuyt, Salet, and Majoor 2018). Accounts of housing cooperatives in Europe have highlighted how these processes play out to the detriment of housing affordability and accessibility (Bruun 2018; Chiodelli 2015).

Housing commons and an institutional environment that is shaped by economic growth are constantly in tension. Under these conditions, the maintenance of autonomous housing presents a central challenge for a degrowth planning practice. In what follows, we address this challenge by exploring the institutional architecture of a housing cooperative built around degrowth ideals. In so doing, we devise a compass that identifies the conditions under which autonomy in urban housing markets can be maintained. This compass comprises four rights that serve to articulate collective, self-managed and democratic living: commissioning, management, inclusion and income rights. Even though these rights can be applied in any housing tenure or form, we contend that it is only when they are 'collectivised' – that is, when the property regime is dispersed and disputable – that they institute autonomous housing.

We illustrate how these rights are articulated in practice by looking at a concrete experiment of a housing initiative in Amsterdam: de Nieuwe Meent, a housing cooperative completely built around degrowth principles. Two years ago, the cooperative started designing and building an estate of about 33 housing units. We examine these two years of work to explain how the commoning of housing, and its striving towards a degrowth living, require building a nested internal structure. This allows the collection to maintain two conditions: the disputability and dispersal of rights. These insights, we conclude, are far from being universally applicable prescriptions. Still, depending on the specific institutional context, they can inform a planning practice that explicitly and deliberately seeks to promote autonomous forms of housing from a degrowth perspective.

## 2. The institutional architecture of housing commons from a degrowth perspective

In economic terms, housing appears as the quintessential private good. Housing supply is limited, especially in dense urban areas, and housing's material qualities facilitate the exclusion of other users, rendering it a rivalrous and excludable good. However, these qualifications are primarily based on the owner-occupied single-family home, which is hardly the only type of housing across the world. Much of the world's urban population lives in housing developments that combine elements of private and common property, such as condominiums, homeowner associations and cooperatives (Ostrom 2000: 351). These provide goods such as shared spaces, gardens or joint facilities to a limited group of people. Although walls or fences render such housing easily excludable, it is not rivalrous. Institutionalist economists argue that such residential communities provide club goods (Manzi and Bill 2005). These are collectively accessible, yet only to members of an exclusive group. Setting clear, exclusionary boundaries, these economists argue, safeguards spaces. However, these accounts of collective housing conceive it purely in terms of efficient resource allocation. They overlook the social value of commoning, which does not exclusively lie in self-management but in the production of a socio-political autonomy too.

As a social practice, the commoning of housing does not rely on the materiality of the good in itself. Rather, it involves the social interaction that is necessary to sustain and reproduce that good, including both the everyday work of caretaking, management and improvement as well as the political decision-making that coordinates those activities (Linebaugh 2008). The practice of commoning rests on social norms and codified rules that are inherently political because they are subject to the commoning process (De Angelis 2017: 123). Commoning necessarily involves a dynamic relationship between subjects and a normative framework coproduced through daily interactions.

The challenges of housing commons are not solely those of consolidating self-management structures; there is also the question of how to ensure that those structures are subject to political dispute. Autonomy depends on commoners collectively establishing an institutional architecture, which might assume various configurations (Bossuyt, Salet, and Majoor 2018). To grasp this variety, we draw on the property regime approach, as developed by Schlager and Ostrom (1992), who identify a set of essential norms for regulating a good's production, maintenance and consumption. A property regime includes a bundle of rights, each of which regulates what certain actors can do with respect to a resource (Ostrom 2000; Schlager and Ostrom 1992; Von Benda-Beckmann 1995). It also defines how responsibilities and duties are articulated; in so doing, the regime questions the power relations that comprise the rights in question (Blandy, Dixon, and Dupuis 2006). Four rights constitute the essential institutional parameters for housing commons: commissioning, management, inclusion and income.

- *Commissioning rights* concern who decides on a building's spatial characteristics, housing units and any joint facilities. This includes decisions on whether to create convivial architectures able to balance collectivism and individualism by prescribing which facilities may be shared. Architecture shapes social interactions in a place, promoting interaction, conviviality and intergenerational care. From a degrowth perspective, commissioning rights ensure residents' autonomous control over their own living space and allow the development of architectural forms that are oriented to reducing the consumption of materials and land.
- *Management rights* identify how a building is used and organise self-governance. Involving more than operational problem-solving, management concerns the everyday use and maintenance of spaces as much as the constitutional foundations by which the community is governed. Management rights in degrowth housing concern decision-making with respect to different elements of the development. These decisions might concern, for example, how shared spaces are used or the improvement of the estate. We understand management as political because it defines how these spaces are used, who can enjoy them at different times, and how the social labour needed to produce them is organised.
- *Inclusion rights* identify the capacity to be a member of a housing commons. As a good, housing generally requires a degree of exclusiveness. Households expect a place to themselves and demand security of tenure, guaranteeing them the right to use the development over the long run. A decommodified and collectivised conception of housing, however, must establish access conditions for non-residents. Inclusion concerns the right not to be excluded from housing; it is a necessary condition for housing commons to avoid enclaving. Commodified housing property relies on legally codified and culturally legitimated rights of exclusion – an owner's right to deny access to a property.

Inclusion rights instead stress the possibility of non-owners accessing the good and demanding it as an essential need. Inclusion rights require a crafted practice of allowing non-residents to get involved in enjoying a housing estate and its spaces.
- *Income rights* concern the transfer of one's use, commissioning and management rights to others in exchange for money. Privately held income rights are the ideological pillar of commodified homeownership. They are deeply rooted in the expectation that housing's exchange value increases over time. Redefining income rights is vital for the long-term decommodification of housing. It demands, on the one hand, that the right to earn money from housing is subject to collective control and, on the other, that this collectivisation is maintained, avoiding a collective decision to privatise housing. As we explain later, the dispersion of these rights across different institutional subjects is crucial to this end.

Institutional economists taxonomise rights to understand how commonly held resources are managed (Colding et al. 2013; Pokharel 2014). Yet, in so doing they assume that it is possible to find a right balance between this bundle of rights, maintaining long-term commoning in the face of internal conflicts, free-riding or external authorities. Understanding commoning purely as an arrangement, however, obscures the politically charged process that generates the bundle of rights previously enumerated. In supposing that there exists a 'right' configuration of rights to maintain autonomy, this politically neutral perspective leaves the normative conditions that determine 'rightness' unspecified. It thus relies on the residents' subjective perceptions of fairness and tends to assume that there is a stable model of self-management that can satisfy everybody. Autonomy essentially implies that commoners define the 'right' balance of rights and that this value judgement is always potentially politically disputable.

The constitution of these rights involves conflict, negotiation and cooperation. These interactions are part of the necessary labour that goes into commoning processes, which produce autonomy. Yet, it is the possibility of contesting and negotiating the bundle of rights that ensures that autonomy is maintained. Conversely, the possibility of autonomy lies in residents' ability to redefine how the bundle of rights are articulated. Housing commoning can be considered a degrowth practice insofar as it decommodifies property, making it an essential good subject to political dispute, not a commodity on which more investments can be leveraged. Yet, we argue that housing commons' capacity to maintain autonomy – and thus embrace a degrowth imaginary – depends on the degree to which the bundle of rights is dispersed and disputable.

By dispersion, here, we mean how rights are distributed among different subjects. It implies avoiding concentrations of rights in a single individual or collective subject. Although concentration can expedite decision-making, it might frustrate autonomy, as illustrated by the legacy of state-owned public housing. Whereas social housing has guaranteed affordability, concentrations of rights in single actors have rendered it vulnerable to neoliberal reforms. The dispersion of rights balances powers and opens up a political space in which interests can be articulated and consensus created. Dispersion also functions as a safeguard against internal enclaving or marketisation. It reduces the risk that individuals or groups can change rules regarding tenure conversion, apartment sale or open membership policies. Dispersion also allows non-residents and other parties to participate in internal organisation. A dispersed, tiered and layered structure makes housing developments less vulnerable to internal strife or political pressures from state and market players, and guarantees the maintenance of autonomy.

Disputability is the degree to which the content of the commissioning, membership, management and income rights can be challenged and redefined by processes of democratic engagement involving commoners. It demands and ensures moments of dialogue and contestation regarding a housing estate's management. Yet, there is a limit to disputability, which should not be used to foreclose further dispute in the future. Disputability ensures that commoning remains a political activity, a process of substantiating rights. Yet it must come with the condition that prevents commoners from disputing the possibility that others can engage in disputation. Dispersion, as we shall show, might realise this limit.

Disputability rests on a process of direct, democratic decision-making. As such, it has serious limits. First of all, participants' differential ability to take part in deliberations, whether in terms of the time or knowledge needed to do so. Even though commoners might all consider themselves equal, political deliberation may still be affected by unequal power relations, which emerge through interpersonal differences. For example, an epistocracy may arise when certain commoners, by virtue of their talents or expertise, subjugate others (Vrousalis 2021). In this case, formal direct democracy disguises unequal relations behind a veil of legitimacy. Problems with formal equality might also be compounded by interpersonal differences based on gender or ethnicity. For any community of commoners, explicitly acknowledging interpersonal differences represents a first step towards recognising one another as equals. In concrete organisational terms, consensual decision-making remains subject to a dispersed system of rights, with different groups having different responsibilities. Internal democracy does not mean that everybody takes all decisions. Rather, it stresses the deliberative character of the decisions taken.

At their inception, commoning processes are imbued with social vigour. To successfully develop a housing project, its participants must cement this energy in a legal-organisational framework. As Thompson (2020: 181) shows, however, there might be a trade-off between radical political energy and the perseverance and technical expertise required to sustain housing developments over time. The legacy of cooperative housing associations in northwestern European countries testifies to how this trade-off can easily tip towards professionalisation and managerialism, leading to a situation in which the bundle of rights is hardly disputable (Harloe 1995). In our view, disputability refers to housing commoners' ability to challenge this managerial mutation of commoning. It must be possible to challenge the articulation of rights in such a way as to allow a housing commons to match the changing composition of its community.

The degree of a housing development's dispersion and disputability depends on its legal, social and architectural properties, as well as the commoners' profile. The terms dispersion and disputability are not prescriptive. Rather, they are intended to enable commoners to maintain a degree of reflexive critique that decreases the risks of co-optation or professionalisation.

In what follows, we present an example of how disputability and concentration have played out in a case of housing commoning organised around degrowth principles. This case illustrates one particular way of autonomous housing self-management, which is specific to the legal and institutional context of Amsterdam and should not be understood as a blueprint for housing commoning elsewhere.

## 3. A degrowth housing collective: autonomy in de Nieuwe Meent

de Nieuwe Meent is a housing cooperative built around degrowth principles. Conceived in late 2018 by an initially small collective of activists, architects, engaged scholars and professionals, it has grown into a community of over 50 people, who work collectively to realise a vision of affordable living in Amsterdam. The project seeks to create a pocket of affordable housing set up in explicit contrast with Amsterdam's overstretched housing market. First, private homeownership in Amsterdam has become increasingly dominant yet unattainable, with average house prices coming to over 480,000 euros (as of 2020). This renders living in the city highly exclusive. Second, social housing providers have become increasingly managerial, growing in scale as a result of mergers and adopting risky entrepreneurial strategies to capitalise on their assets (Aalbers, Loon, and Fernandez 2017). Meanwhile, Amsterdam's social housing stock had rapidly shrunk over the previous years (declining from constituting 70% to 50% of the city's overall stock in one decade) as a result of neoliberal urban reform aimed at tenure diversification. Residents are objects of a hierarchical relationship that leaves them little room to exert control over their housing conditions (Bossuyt, Salet, and Majoor 2018).

de Nieuwe Meent explicitly rejects the ecomodernist ideal of housing efficiency, with its mainstream goals of energy neutrality and technical improvements. Instead, it proposes an ecological lifestyle anchored around principles of reduction through sharing, operating at three levels: *woongroepen*, shared facilities and caretaking. First, sharing translates into the creation of 'collective living groups' (*woongroepen*). People in these groups share essential facilities such as bathrooms, kitchens, living rooms and appliances while retaining a private unit. The project hosts five of these groups with each sharing one floor of about 200 sqm. It has 25 housing units in total, with group size varying from four to five residents. The project also hosts 15 independent social housing units. Second, all residents share facilities around the building's entrance, such as a dining space, library, day-care centre and courtyard. These are all accessible to both residents and non-residents from the neighbourhood. The garden is the socioecological core of the project. It is a shared space that nurtures community-supported agriculture and ecological education for children. Third, living collectively is understood as a caretaking process in which each resident contributes to maintaining the community through interpersonal care, solidarity and do-it-yourself architecture. All members give their time to building the estate and its community, performing maintenance and sharing essential tasks such as introducing new members to the collective. Given that these practices require time and care, the project seeks to reduce individual rent as much as possible, allowing residents to work less.

Overall, de Nieuwe Meent pursues a multidimensional understanding of autonomy. First, autonomy is political in that it works through consensus-based democratic decision-making. Autonomy is here a condition for allowing all residents and non-residents to participate in making the residential estate and its surrounding spaces. Second, autonomy is understood economically in terms of collective ownership as part of a cooperative. Third, it is understood ecologically as the creation of a community of care that ensures long-term inclusion and affordable living.

## 4. Distributing commissioning, management, inclusion and income rights

de Nieuwe Meent offers a mode of dwelling that radically differs from established housing in Amsterdam. The project distinguishes itself by translating autonomy into a legal architecture that guarantees self-management, while ensuring inclusion. de Nieuwe Meent directly confronts the risk that a housing development might be parcelled into alienable private units or transformed into an enclave for a few engaged individuals. The distribution and disputability of commissioning, management, inclusion and income rights are essential in facing these challenges.

Inclusion rights are organised by carefully integrating legal membership of the cooperative (signatories of the statute) with the practised membership of the community (individuals contributing to the project), which is organised around workgroups. Workgroups are open to the general public and provide new members with a point of entry into the cooperative. Groups are organised around the domains of community, media, finances, legal issues and design. As will be explained, each has de facto commissioning rights. The community workgroup aims to enlarge the community by organising inclusion events, informing new members, and monitoring the degree of heterogeneity within the group, primarily generationally. Participation in the workgroups grants one neither a place to live nor legal membership of the cooperative, which is reserved for those who will obtain a dwelling in the estate. Yet the workgroups foster close connections among the engaged community of commoners and residents. Engagement becomes a precondition for residence.

Admission and unit allocation occur through open applications. For the living groups, applications can be submitted only by groups of people that, as one subject, apply for an entire floor. When applying, groups are asked to share their view on the project, express their understanding of its core principles and explain how they would contribute to its functioning. A representative from the assembly and advisors evaluate the application. Once granted, residence entails a fee of 4000 euros, which will be restituted upon leaving (plus 2% inflation and 2% interest). Residents are not obliged to buy shares (as we will discuss).

Commissioning rights, which concern the right to define the building's operations and form, are performed through de Nieuwe Meent's physical and political architecture. The project won a tender issued by the Municipality of Amsterdam in late 2018 as part of its program to promote pilot housing cooperative projects in the city (Municipality of Amsterdam 2018a). The municipality tendered the right to build on a central plot in the city under the conditions that the building would be owned by a cooperative, respect a maximum residential density and offer both social and affordable rental units.

Commissioning rights in de Nieuwe Meent are not concentrated in the hands of a single developer that works within an existing cooperative. Instead, they are articulated by a general public of commoners. Until the tender deadline, the cooperative organised weekly Sunday meetings, which were open to anyone interested in engaging with degrowth living. Ideals and community grew alongside each other within the project. As an organisation, the cooperative was created only after the project's main profile had been defined. This step was necessary to attain the right to build on the plot. Still, the members of the cooperative were not yet initially identified (with the exception of a chair, treasurer and secretary); rather, this question was left open to be addressed through the inclusion process previously explained.

After the award of the tender, this inclusive form of commissioning developed further. It gave rise to a horizontal network of working groups, each responsible for specific aspects of the building process: legal, economic, architectural, sustainability, media and community (as mentioned previously). The groups develop specific plans for the building that are then discussed in a general assembly (*Algemene ledenvergadering*), which decides upon the plan through democratic consensus. Although the cooperative formally holds commissioning rights (it signs the contracts), commoners acquire and exert these rights through active participation in workgroups.

According to the principle of autonomy, management is as decentralised and inclusive as possible, while remaining coordinated across the different decision-making arenas. de Nieuwe Meent proposes a nested self-management structure, which couples a legal statute with open engagement on the part of both residents and non-residents (see Figure 3.1).

The cooperative's structure has three layers: the *meentraad* (commons council), which is formed by all building residents and endowed with decision-making power on all management issues; the *meentbestuur* (commons board), which fulfils the formal tasks of reporting the yearly budget; and the *comité voor de Meent* (committee of the commons), which operates in an advisory role, stepping in when consensus cannot be reached. Although the council remains the project's official

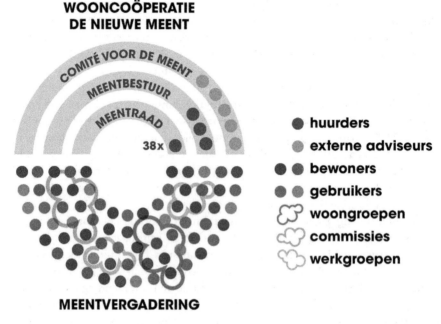

FIGURE 3.1 The management architecture of de Nieuwe Meent

Source: de Nieuwe Meent

decision-maker (through consensus), the actual inputs and agenda of issues to be decided upon are defined by the *meentvergadering*, the assembly of commoners. Unlike in a traditional cooperative, the assembly is open to both residents and non-residents alike, including neighbours, advisors and users. A horizontal political body, it defines the management agenda, which is organised according to the different workgroups.

de Nieuwe Meent's financial structure presupposes a distribution of income rights among different parties. The project has a total budget of about 6 million euros, with construction being the largest share of costs (about 4 million). Of the budget, 68% is covered by a bank loan, issued by a cooperative bank (GLS); 22% is covered by a range of public subsidies and funds, which have been granted specifically to improve the estate's social and ecological sustainability; 8% is crowdfunded, through the issuing of bonds to anybody who wishes to support and invest in the project (5- to 10-year interest rates); and 2% is covered by the membership fee. The loan and interest are repaid through the rent for both residential and non-residential spaces.

The cooperative holds the legal title for the building. Incremental increases in its value go towards the cooperative and may not be turned into individual revenue. For the first 30 years, part of the rent will be used to cover the loan. Most importantly, the land remains publicly owned. The land lease comes with the condition that the cooperative may not subdivide, sublease or sell the building. The municipality prohibits tenure conversion (Municipality of Amsterdam 2018b).

After the bank loan is repaid, the rent will be used to maintain the building and create a solidarity fund. Although this fund's function is as yet undefined, there is increasing agreement among the members that the fund should be used to support dwellers in economic hardship and sustain similar projects in the city (and elsewhere), possibly through a federation of cooperatives. Residents can but are not obliged to purchase shares. In this legal sense, de Nieuwe Meent differs from a full-equity cooperative and is similar to a limited-equity cooperative, with residents being exclusive members. de Nieuwe Meent is registered as a cooperative association under Dutch law. Residents do not capitalise on real-estate appreciation when they leave. In the expectations of the group at this stage, the return on their investment of time, energy and money will be covered through a highly affordable rent, long-term housing security, and the possibility of accessing care within the community.

## 5. Housing commons as a transitional practice towards degrowth?

The long history of neoliberal housing reforms was driven by an imaginary of individual freedom. This served to concentrate rights in the hands of one owner per property as a pathway towards efficient management and market exchanges. In the received ownership model of property, individual owners (who are clearly identifiable by titles) retain absolute rights to commission and manage their property as well as decide who uses it (Singer 2000). These individuals also claim full ownership of any rent and investment returns, which are understood as an index of the individualised risk in housing purchases (through debt). These rights are indisputable because they are concentrated. The legal infrastructure of property laws has been geared towards protecting the indisputability of those rights and limiting public claims on private property. Cooperative forms of housing provision partially disperse property rights. In collectivising commissioning, management and income rights, such housing aims both to preserve its long-term affordability and to improve the quality of cohabitation. However, dispersing rights does not necessarily ensure a project's disputability or long-term affordability.

In this chapter, we have argued that a degrowth imaginary of housing prefigures a form of autonomous housing provision that is practised through commoning. This is a way of life that is not limited to instituting collective self-management, decommodification and ecological living. It also strives for a collective form of internal democracy, in which inclusion and political disputability lay the foundations of autonomy. As a strategy for decommodifying real estate, housing commons embed the essential degrowth imperative to interrupt perpetual accumulation in housing markets and its ecological impact. de Nieuwe Meent offers an example of this form of housing, at least in its inception and early development. We have illustrated how the project builds on a bundle of rights that is both dispersed – across commoners, public governments and even financing institutions – but also disputable through internal democracy within the cooperative. These principles are formalised in a statute and articulated through a nested hierarchy of sub-collectives. This setup reflects the project's ideological premises, in which the socio-political values of commoning overlap with the estate's physical and institutional architecture.

This degree of disputability – the ability to question perpetually how the bundle of rights are distributed – can hardly be justified in terms of efficient and rational thinking. Instead, it is recognised as a value that is reproduced through the political practice of commoning. The community behind de Nieuwe Meent belongs to the fringe of heteronomous culture and radical environmentalism. As such, it forms a small niche of Amsterdam's population. In this context, the project is a radical experiment of living.

Given their experimental nature, projects such as de Nieuwe Meent persistently confront themselves with two risks: on the one hand, that of turning into enclaves for the happy few activists who are able to organise and sustain an internal practice of engaged democracy. On the other, they always run the risk of being co-opted by the market. In the former case, projects such as this may remain marginal, hardly issuing any institutional change into housing markets or simply being marketed as the first steps towards gentrification. In the latter case, they may simply turn into new prototypes of real-estate development, which are directed by a group of professional commoners able to replicate these projects, yet without their internal democratic profile. These are real risks, which will always be present for as long as urban commons take place under the hegemony of economic growth and its ideology.

In our view, though, a degrowth transition will likely take place through these practices. A multitude of different prefigurative degrowth practices, in their synergy, will challenge existing institutional structures. This is a much more likely pathway to degrowth than a direct and authoritative programme of reform towards a degrowth politics, imposed 'from above'. In this vein, de Nieuwe Meent's early development already sketches the contours of a compelling alternative housing model. It stresses, first, the need to make housing political through commoning. The project prefigures degrowth living as a practice of cohabitation enacted through sharing and caring. It sees housing not just in terms of dwelling but also as a nest of politics. Second, de Nieuwe Meent understands autonomy as the institutional condition for housing commoning. Autonomy is maintained for as long as it remains possible for the collective to define its own goals through democracy and inclusion; this in turn is ensured through the dispersion and disputability of rights. Third, de Nieuwe Meent reveals the resources necessary to re-enact autonomy over time. Affordability – achieved through low rents and collective ownership – is an economic premise for democracy and participation in housing provision. The work of care necessary for the commoning process is made possible by the community that provides this care. The architecture of sharing, collectivisation of investment risks, reduction of individual indebtedness, long-term low rents, and provision of internal/external solidarity funds are some of the elements that tend in this direction.

# References

Aalbers MB, Loon JV and Fernandez R (2017) The Financialization of a Social Housing Provider. *International Journal of Urban and Regional Research* 41(4): 572–87.

Alexander S (2018) *Degrowth in the Suburbs*. Singapore: Springer.

Asara V, Profumi E and Kallis G (2013) Degrowth, Democracy and Autonomy. *Environmental Values* 22(2): 217–39.

Beekers WP (2012) Het Bewoonbare Land. PhD Thesis, Vrije Universiteit Amsterdam.

Blandy S, Dixon J and Dupuis A (2006) Theorising Power Relationships in Multi-Owned Residential Developments: Unpacking the Bundle of Rights. *Urban Studies* 43(13): 2365–83.

Bonaiuti M (2012) Growth and Democracy: Trade-Offs and Paradoxes. *Futures* 44(6): 524–34.

Bossuyt D (2021) Who Owns Collaborative Housing? A Conceptual Typology of Property Regimes. *Housing, Theory and Society*. Epub ahead of print, 21 February. DOI: 10.1080/14036096.2021.1888788.

Bossuyt D, Salet W and Majoor S (2018) Commissioning as Cornerstone of Self-Build Housing. Assessing the Constraints and Opportunities of Self-Build in The Netherlands. *Land Use Policy* 77: 524–33.

Bruun MH (2018) The Financialization of Danish Cooperatives and the Debasement of a Collective Housing Good. *Critique of Anthropology* 38(2): 140–55.

Chatterton P (2016) Building Transitions to Post-Capitalist Urban Commons. *Transactions of the Institute of British Geographers* 41(4): 403–15.

Chiodelli F (2015) What is Really Different between Cohousing and Gated Communities? *European Planning Studies* 23(12): 2566–81.

Colding J, Barthel S, Bendt P et al. (2013) Urban Green Commons: Insights on Urban Common Property Systems. *Global Environmental Change* 23(5): 1039–51.

De Angelis DM (2017) *Omnia Sunt Communia: On the Commons and the Transformation to Postcapitalism*. London: Zed Books.

Deriu M (2015) Autonomy. In: D'Alisa G, Demaria F and Kallis G (eds) *Degrowth: A Vocabulary for a New Era*, 55–8. Abingdon: Routledge.

Fotopoulos T (2007) Is Degrowth Compatible with a Market Economy? *Journal of Inclusive Democracy* 5(1): 1–16.

Harloe M (1995) *The People's Home? Social Rented Housing in Europe and America*. Oxford: Blackwell.

Jarvis H (2017) Sharing, Togetherness and Intentional Degrowth. *Progress in Human Geography* 43(2): 256–75.

Lang R, Carriou C and Czischke D (2020) Collaborative Housing Research (1990–2017): A Systematic Review and Thematic Analysis of the Field. *Housing, Theory and Society* 37(1): 10–39.

Lietaert M (2010) Cohousing's Relevance to Degrowth Theories. *Journal of Cleaner Production* 18(6): 576–80.

Linebaugh P (2008) *The Magna Carta Manifesto: Liberty and Commons for All*. Berkeley: University of California Press.

Manzi T and Bill S-B (2005) Gated Communities as Club Goods: Segregation or Social Cohesion? *Housing Studies* 20(2): 345–59.

Municipality of Amsterdam (2018a) *Actieplan Wooncoöperaties*. Report, Municipality of Amsterdam.

Municipality of Amsterdam (2018b) *Selectiebrochure Archimedeplatsoen*. Report, Municipality of Amsterdam.

Nelson A and Schneider F (2018) *Housing for Degrowth: Principles, Models, Challenges and Opportunities*. Abingdon: Routledge.

Ostrom E (2000) Private and Common Property Rights. *Encyclopedia of Law and Economics* 2000: 332–79.

Pokharel A (2014) A Theory of Sustained Cooperation with Evidence from Irrigation Institutions in Nepal. PhD Thesis, Massachusetts Institute of Technology.

Salet W, D'Ottaviano C, Majoor S and Bossuyt D (2020) *The Self-Build Experience: Institutionalisation, Place-Making and City Building*. Bristol: Policy Press.

Schlager E and Ostrom E (1992) Property-Rights Regimes and Natural Resources: A Conceptual Analysis. *Land Economics* 68(3): 249–62.

Singer J (2000) *Entitlement: The Paradoxes of Property*. New Haven, CT: Yale University Press.

Sørvoll J and Bengtsson B (2018) The Pyrrhic Victory of Civil Society Housing? Co-Operative Housing in Sweden and Norway. *International Journal of Housing Policy* 18(1): 124–42.

Starecheski A (2019) Squatters Make History in New York: Property, History, and Collective Claims on the City. *American Ethnologist* 46(1): 61–74.

Thompson M (2020) *Reconstructing Public Housing: Liverpool's Hidden History of Collective Alternatives*. Liverpool: Liverpool University Press.

Von Benda-Beckmann F (1995) Anthropological Approaches to Property Law and Economics. *European Journal of Law and Economics* 2(4): 309–36.

Vrousalis N (2021). Public Ownership, Worker Control, and the Labour Epistocracy Problem. *Review of Social Economy* 79(3): 439–53.

# 4
# DWELLING BEYOND GROWTH

Negotiating the state, mutualism and commons

*Anitra Nelson and Paul Chatterton*

## 1. Dwelling beyond growth

How might we dwell — live and house ourselves — in a post-growth world? Certain 'eco-collaborative housing' models offer glimpses of such futures, as prefigurative hybrids pointing to a post-growth world. Eco-collaborative housing communities follow environmentally sustainable household practices, and build and retrofit their housing with low-carbon and environmentally sustainable facilities. Their members cogovern and share spaces, amenities and facilities as an intentional community. They often engage in self-provisioning such as food gardening and maker workshops, including re-use, repair, sharing and caring practices. Such multi-household communities are ideally placed to install and operate efficient and cost-saving collective neighbourhood systems for energy provision, water supply, grey water and black water management, Internet access, and shared use of cars and other appliances. Typically, certain spaces and facilities are shared with their wider neighbourhood. The cases of housing cooperatives discussed in this chapter offer two distinctive models within a suite of eco-collaborative housing types (see Chapter 16).

In best-practice eco-collaborative housing, residents develop skills in co-governance and establish ways of collectivising economic burdens, through participatory processes, nonmonetary economies, and cooperative structures of joint housing loans and mutual finance. These forms of housing and living strive to embed themselves in their natural, built and social environments in mutually beneficial ways. This creates a sense of solidarity between the self, community and their wider locality in various forms of what the degrowth movement terms 'open re-localisation', outward-looking semi-autonomous communities celebrating diversity in all its forms (Liegey and Nelson, 2018). They maximise opportunities for collectively regenerating local areas environmentally, and socially through joint caring, learning

DOI: 10.4324/9781003160984-6

and working. Examples might include promoting local food growing, the uptake of micro renewables or local car-sharing clubs.

Typically struggling against planning, legal and financial regulations developed by and for growth-oriented market-based economies supported by capitalist states, it is no surprise that even the most successful eco-collaborative communities are often complex hybrids rather than fully worked out examples of post-growth living and dwelling. In this chapter we critically analyse the transformative efforts and experiences of two leading types of practising eco-collaborative communities through three distinct characteristics that inform discourse and practice on broader socio-political and economic transformation to post-growth futures.

## 1.1 The state, mutualism and commoning

The first characteristic relates to state legislation, power and politics. All social change projects need to navigate state apparatus even if in radical opposition to the state or working interstitially, at a distance (Cumbers, 2015). Eco-collaborative projects engage with the state, especially regarding planning and building regulations. The second characteristic is mutualism, the deep bonds of association that support new ways of being and relating that underpin the wider degrowth movement. Eco-collaborative communities incorporate deep forms of democratic practice, such as consensus decision-making, nonviolent communication and sociocracy — learning skills for a degrowth society (Nelson, 2018: 214–245).

The third characteristic is the commons. A fundamental aspect that underpins human flourishing is common ownership and control of land and of the housing built upon land. Key to unlocking the potential of housing beyond growth is access to physical, material, commons as well as a broader knowledge commons based on open and shareable information. For instance, DemoDev, drawing on the approach of WikiHouse, is an open-source project to reinvent ways homes are made and works with the UK Land Registry and national mapping agency Ordinance Survey in collaboration with Birmingham City Council to unlock underused land and turn it into open-designed, sustainable, adaptable homes.

These key characteristics involve enabling and disabling roles of state agencies and regulations, internal strategies of mutualism and solidarity, and visions and practices of cogoverning associated land as commons. Taking a lead from the late Erik Olin Wright (2010), we acknowledge that social change projects such as eco-collaborative communities reflect complex and often contradictory relationships to the state, market economy and civil society within which they operate. As such we identify disabling barriers and enabling factors to establishing and scaling up eco-collaborative housing types.

## 1.2 Enabling and disabling mechanisms

Enabling policies and practices prioritise social justice, ecological sustainability, close mutual social relations and subsidiarity. Cogoverning communities enhance the democratic skills and knowledge of members, as such pointing towards post-growth polities; they enhance collective sufficiency in food provisioning and, by pursuing caring practices, form bases for post-growth caring economies; and, through regenerating local ecologies, they support broader ecological sustainability. Devolving powers to dwellers to collectively self-govern for sustainability offers feedback loops, buy-in and learning that can maximise environmental sustainability by creating internal circular and sharing economies. If expanded in number and variety, such decentralised settlements would strengthen both socially and environmentally sustainable practices within post-growth cities, acting as transitionary vehicles to a post-growth world.

It is clear that housing alternatives that value and respect basic human needs for shelter are fundamental to creating post-growth housing and households. Moreover, post-growth visions and goals demand housing forms that not only minimise material and energy use in constructing, maintaining and operating dwellings but also enhance householder equity and democracy. In particular, our examples explore post-growth practices in establishing housing that responds to both climate breakdown and the deep social injustice and dysfunction built into contemporary global housing markets. Eco-collaborative housing represents a particularly productive laboratory through which post-growth housing models can emerge and develop new ways of living that integrate shelter, work, finance, food and energy in grassroots-led change.

## 1.3 Case studies and methods

This chapter identifies disabling and enabling structures that have made possible two pioneering examples, each of which takes a different route to housing beyond growth. Lilac (low impact living affordable community) is an eco-cohousing settlement based around a mutual ownership model with 20 households in West Leeds in the United Kingdom (UK). Kraftwerk1 and Kalkbreite are examples of Zürich's twenty-first-century radical 'young housing cooperatives' based on a rental-type model in Switzerland.

Significantly, we identify as activist-scholars in this space (Routledge and Derickson, 2015). We have been inspired by a diversity of housing struggles around the world: Barcelona's Platform For Mortgage Victims (*Plataforma de Afectados por la Hipoteca*, 'PAH'); London Renters Union, which was set up in 2017 in the face of the chronic shortage of affordable homes in the UK; the broader Right To The City Alliance, a response to gentrification and calls to halt displacement of low-income groups, people of colour and marginalised communities; and majority world struggles to defend and reclaim housing, such as the South African Shack Dwellers Movement (*Abahlali baseMjondolo*) and the Brazilian Homeless Workers Movement (*Movimento Dos Trabalhadores Sem Teto*).

Paul Chatterton is a founding and current resident member of Lilac, which he analyses using autoethnography and critical theory (Chatterton, 2013, 2015, 2016). Anitra Nelson spent more than a decade living in two Australian eco-collaborative housing models. Both authors have stayed in and visited various intentional communities in the UK, United States and Europe. Anitra is an experienced action researcher applying ethnographic and critical skills to her research. Both authors have published on post-growth futures, planning and eco-collaborative housing models (Chatterton, 2013, 2015, 2016; Nelson, 2018; Nelson and Schneider, 2018).

## 2. The Lilac cooperative: creating a degrowth, mutual housing commons

Lilac is a cooperative cohousing project in Leeds, in the North of England. It comprises 20 homes based around the central common house, constructed from straw and timber. Lilac is a member-led cooperative where residents co-manage their living and land spaces. Through their Mutual Home Ownership financial model, residents buy a mutual stake in their property, the value of which is capped to ensure permanent affordability. Moreover, the settlement has many ecologically sustainable features supporting post-growth practices (Baborska-Narozny et al., 2014; Stevenson et al., 2016).

Lilac is part of a cohousing movement that emerged over the last few decades to build gregarious intentional communities that maximise interaction and mutual association between neighbours (Field, 2004). There are hundreds of cohousing projects in Denmark, commonly understood as the birthplace of the cohousing movement in the 1960s; around 300 projects in The Netherlands; and over 100 in North America. According to the UK Cohousing Network, in 2020, there were 21 cohousing communities in the UK, with 32 in development and 20 forming.

### 2.1 The role of the state

The idea for Lilac was citizen- and activist-led, rather than state-led. Both the national and local state context in the UK reflects low levels of eco-collaborative housing types, and a lack of central support for and institutional interest in these types. Much of this reflects the highly privatised and deregulated housing market and dominance of large volume-building corporate housing providers, who control land supply and values (Hodkinson, 2015). Momentum for the Lilac project emerged in 2006 through a group of community activists who spent five years developing the idea. A number of key priorities were identified, including using natural materials and low car use to tackle the climate emergency, responding to the dysfunction of the speculative housing market, and overcoming social isolation. These became key guides to create what became the 'Lilac' model, a 'low impact living, affordable, community'. The main motivator and broader public interest in the Lilac model emerged from the use of a cooperative structure and mutual finance to tackle housing exclusion and develop permanent affordability.

Lilac founders took the model to the local municipality to broker support in terms of land and finance. Lilac was a classic early disruptive innovation within the traditional model of municipal housing provision and support. The city council in Leeds was cautious and unfamiliar with eco-collaborative housing types such as cohousing and cooperatives. Some limited staff time, rather than land or resources, was offered to support the testing of the model. The Lilac group bought an affordable plot of land from the local state at open market value for inner-city Leeds — low enough to permit the affordability of the model. After its completion in 2013, the Lilac project has gone on to provide support to other community-led equal collaborative housing groups.

Although the local state now recognises it as a pioneering model of how citizen-led housing can emerge, Lilac remains a small-scale prototype, without formal state backing. Due to its complexity especially in terms of community self-governance, it presents many challenges in terms of replicability and scalability for large-scale local authorities. Moreover, incorporating what is essentially a community-led process into large-scale municipal processes and structures would undermine much of the innovation underpinning this form of eco-collaborative housing. The key challenge going forward for creating favourable conditions for housing beyond growth is to understand how these disruptive small-scale innovations can integrate and influence large-scale processes and practices of the local and national state.

## 2.2 Creating degrowth through mutualism

Legally, Lilac is a cooperative society, which exists for the benefit of its members. This kind of legal form embeds the idea of mutual association between members. Mutualism has a rich historical tradition enmeshed in and emerging from the idea that association and interdependence can be beneficial and increase well-being. Mutualism enables people to conduct relationships based on free and equal contracts of reciprocal exchange (Woodin et al., 2010; Field, 2011). It is based on a passionate desire for people to govern themselves and not have authority imposed upon them. From the nineteenth century onwards, through a strong cooperative movement, mutualism provided a strong bulwark against the rampant individualism of the fast-expanding free-market capitalist economy.

For Lilac, this legal cooperative framework creates fertile ground for creating practices and social relations key to post-growth economies. One particularly notable strand is the use of deliberative democracy to ensure that all members have a voice and decisions are made equally and without coercion. Consensually made 'community agreements' are used for community life in Lilac, such as for using shared spaces, food and pets. Members contribute to the self-management of Lilac through various task teams, ranging from landscape to food maintenance. A governing board made up of voluntary participating members oversees the legal and financial aspects. Central to the daily practices of housing beyond growth are institutional arrangements where people are not individuals or consumers of housing, but members of a broader community-based collective.

Following this, post-growth practices can also be observed in the Lilac housing model through the kinds of interpersonal relations that it promotes. A significant focus of Lilac is on building a strong sense of community and interpersonal ties. In Lilac, residents have a different housing tenure from the mainstream housing market. Rather than being owner-occupiers of private property, residents are members of a cooperative society and lease their homes after paying a member charge, set at one-third of their net monthly income. Through this regular payment, members accrue equity in their housing. But the value of this equity is linked to average wages in the UK rather than average house prices (Chatterton, 2015). Therefore, housing in Lilac is not a speculative commodity that can be bought and sold according to the vagaries of market conditions. Instead, a home in Lilac is a product that is decoupled from typical housing growth and, since its value is linked to what you earn, it remains affordable in perpetuity for future generations. This is a significant shift, as it gives texture to what degrowth practices mean, especially in terms of increasing stability in local housing markets and reducing tendencies towards volatile local economies. Although money certainly circulates within Lilac, and the project depends on much debt financing, it has attempted to embed less marketised forms of financial and social interactions.

## 2.3 Housing commons and degrowth

The third aspect of degrowth practices in Lilac relates to how the physical layout, or spatiality, of daily practices points towards Lilac as a housing 'common'. The common has become an important tool for exploring forms of social reproduction and collective property ownership and social organisation which challenge individualised notions of property and ownership, and celebrates the co-ownership, co-production and co-management of social goods and spaces (Caffentzis and Federici, 2014; De Angelis, 2017; Bollier, 2002). The common is not only a series of goods and spaces that require defending from capitalist enclosures and commodification, but also a means to create subjectivities and forms of value beyond growth that are produced and held in common.

Lilac represents a complex interplay between private, public and common spaces. One of the key principles of cohousing is to combine private self-contained homes with shared spaces held in common. Residents have to continually negotiate the boundaries between private and more shared, communal spaces. This negotiation relates to openness and availability in public spaces. The site has been designed to increase natural surveillance and neighbourly encounters. Therefore, residents set their own boundaries and tactics for moderating levels of interaction with residents, and others who might visit the project.

Moreover, the boundary of the site represents the gateway to the broader public realm and requires mediation. Although the grounds of Lilac are private, other people are not discouraged from entering, which blurs a traditional boundary between public and private, setting Lilac apart from the rapid growth of privatised housing estates. Lilac has not fully resolved this issue but there is a great desire to allow Lilac to be open to the public, to reduce concerns about being perceived as a gated community. This raises key questions as to how eco-collaborative housing models create spaces outside the market, and what the spatiality of degrowth actually feels and looks like (Chatterton and Pusey, 2019).

## 3. The radical twenty-first-century housing cooperative movement in Zürich

Two similar housing cooperatives, Kraftwerk1 and Kalkbreite, exemplify Zürich's radical 'young housing cooperatives' movement that essentially emerged in the twenty-first century. They developed within a strong enabling structure of city support for housing cooperatives that started more than a century ago to become a key feature of the city's housing typology. Housing cooperative stock is prominent in Zürich, while young housing cooperatives show ways in which post-growth alternatives can point beyond the market and state. As such they represent prefigurative hybrid forms suggesting pathways to post-growth futures. Significantly, they arose in an essentially unaffordable housing market, a common characteristic of contemporary cities.

Beyond relevant literature, this section is informed by in-depth interviews conducted in mid-July 2019 with two activist-residents of Zürich's young housing cooperatives: writer Hans Widmer (P.M.) and Fred Frohofer, a prominent member of the Kalkbreite *Leicht Leben (Simple Living)* group working at shrinking residents' eco-footprints. Participant observation was enabled by a two-night stay in Hardturmstrasse (Kraftwerk1) in 2018 and, in 2019, a week-long stay in the Kalkbreite guest house, touring both establishments and attending a three-hour public meeting of the NeNa1 Collective pursuing post-growth visions and strategies detailed at the o500 and New Alliance sites (o500, undated; New Alliance, undated).

### 3.1 The state and city as bulwark

In Switzerland, housing cooperative stock accounts for scarcely 1 in 20 dwellings, yet around 7 in every 20 dwellings in Zürich belong to housing cooperatives. Whereas around two-thirds of the Swiss cooperatives each own fewer than 100 dwellings, Zürich's largest housing cooperative owns 5,000 dwellings (COOP, 2020). Municipal authorities insist that any city-subsidised construction is subject to architectural competitions so cooperative housing is quality housing (Claus, 2017: 20). A municipal government representative sits on every cooperative board of management. In short — in sharp contrast to Lilac's relationship with the Leeds city council — Zürich's housing cooperatives partner with their quasi city-state.

The city's support of housing self-provision is impressive. In 2007 citizens celebrated a *century* of housing cooperatives that Zürich's authorities had made feasible through building rights, planning provisions and facilitating finance. Cooperatives initially started as unions sought to provide adequate, secure and affordable housing for members. Since 1924, housing cooperatives have only been required to pledge a minimum 6 percent of the project cost (equity) to get approval from the city's mayor to guarantee diverse mortgages managed by the state bank (Claus, 2017: 18). Cooperatives' member-tenants self-manage repayment of around 50-year-long loans. As co-owners with shares in the cooperative, they pay affordable rents typically around 20 percent lower than private rents (COOP, 2020).

Dire housing conditions in the city in the late nineteenth century drove municipal authorities' intervention with 'new guiding urban-planning principles and the city's municipal housing subsidy policies' (Claus, 2017: 19). Supporting self-help in preference to direct provisioning of social housing, municipal land was sold for housing cooperative use, low-interest loans arranged and cooperative shares purchased. By the latter half of the 1920s, the City of Zürich's housing cooperative program already offered 'an urban-planning blueprint with a dual focus on methodical civic development and social improvement' (Kurz, 2017: 32). The city still purchases dwellings in such constructions and owns some of its own stock, both managed as low-income social housing benefiting eligible households. In this way, a community-led housing alternative to market or state housing provision has burgeoned for generations. Well-established cooperatives are so financially stable and viable that they often save the requisite capital to spawn more construction. The cooperatives are regenerative and often scale up.

Such safe, secure, affordable and quality housing tends to set a standard for privately owned housing and a ceiling for private rental rates in Zürich. Dense urban cooperative housing is so popular that the city had to legislate a maximum income eligibility. A late-1990s referendum made the provision of 10,000 affordable apartments within a decade a target. Then, not content with one in four city apartments belonging to housing cooperatives or the city, a 2011 referendum committed the municipality to a new target of one housing cooperative apartment in every three.

The specifically 'young housing cooperatives' in Zürich are a special subset of all housing cooperatives whose memberships have been variously criticised over the years as apathetic, passive, managed and gentrified. Clearly, membership, motivations, processes and governance of housing cooperatives matter. The key difference between radical and other housing cooperatives is their semi-autonomous self-management addressing both environmental challenges and social justice — they are 'more than housing' (Hugentobler et al., 2016). This approach is characterised by practices that align with principles of mutual aid and solidarity.

## 3.2 Mutualism and solidarity

The cooperative model has a long history, spreading internationally as an alternative to profit-making enterprises during the nineteenth century, with prominent advocates such as Pierre-Joseph Proudhon in France and Robert Owen in the UK. The cooperative form was hailed as superior to capitalist enterprises and the cooperative movement has been intentionally based on solidarity and mutual aid, or mutualism. Yet detractors have criticised the tendency of cooperatives to compromise on principles of self-management (as in taking a bureaucratic approach to functions that might be hived off to paid project managers and administrators); to fall victim to market-oriented pressures, especially if they produce for trade; and to exclusively contain their solidarity to their membership.

Aware of such pitfalls, the political founding members of Zürich's young housing cooperatives — who had previously fought for collective rights to their city — viewed the cooperative as a vehicle for transformation to a post-growth future. In Zürich its ubiquity gives the housing cooperative relative power within the city council and among the construction industry and allied professionals. Housing cooperatives are outward-looking enablers of city housing policies, taking participatory democracy steps in the direction of citizenry self-provisioning.

Well-oiled collaborations between architects, construction firms, bankers, lawyers, planners, councillors and city building bureaucrats support cogoverned housing cooperatives to function and deliver in socially and environmentally sustainable ways (Boudet, 2017). Similarly, legal and financial models are well-established (COOP, 2020). New projects attract architectural competitions assessed by all stakeholders. Cooperative members participate in the design and realisation of urban housing and planning while maintaining their cooperative neighbourhood in physical, material, social and political ways. Emerging in a comparatively progressive context of Swiss democratic processes, those political skills developed in actively co-managing residential activities and the construction and maintenance of their housing exemplify the direct democracy necessary to collectively limit production and consumption and enhance a post-growth quality of life in urban futures. Thus, the Hans Widmer political model of 'taking the people with you' (Widmer, 2018).

In the last quarter of the twentieth century, a novel cohort of cooperative drivers included ex-squatter-activists with strong social and environmental values, and an association of housing and planning professionals, INURA (1991–). Both saw the existing housing cooperative model as a means to realise eco-sustainable urban housing, dwellings that were affordable, adaptable and inclusive, supporting self-managing neighbourhoods, incorporating sustainable practices and minimising ecological footprints (Hugentobler et al., 2016). For instance, compared with the Zürich average of 45 m$^2$ residential space per capita, each Kalkbreite resident takes up just 32 m$^2$ housing space. Their standard practice is to provide each household with a dwelling of one room per resident plus one room per household. As such they practise solidarity in absorbing contractions necessary to respect Earth's limits.

If housing cooperatives are often criticised as 'for the middle-class', Widmer (2018) points out that two in every three Zürich citizens *are* middle class. Moreover, *any* citizen has a right to apply to join a cooperative even if they often have to wait for a vacant dwelling. For instance, in mid-2020, just 700 of Kraftwerk1's 1664 members were tenants. All housing cooperatives abide by the city's policy of social mix so Kraftwerk1 aims for a housing demographic mirroring Zürich's profile. Given that more than one in four Zürich residents are non-Swiss, at least one in four residents need to be non-Swiss. Then, given that, at some point, each resident gains Swiss citizenship, the constant intake of non-Swiss tends to amplify cultural diversity in Kraftwerk1. Similarly, 15 percent of places are reserved for those 50 years and older. The housing cooperative's social values mean that dwellings are adapted for residents with disabilities or other special needs so the cooperative community is inclusive, following European community-led housing models (LaFond and Tsvetkova, 2017).

In short, mutualism and solidarity are displayed through the democratically self-managed form of the cooperative and its inclusive operation for all members equally. The cooperative maintains open, responsible and outward-looking relations with Zürich citizens, municipal authorities and the housing industry more generally. Moreover, enforcing principles of environmental sustainability protects and ensures solidarity with and for future generations.

## 3.3 Commons and co-governance

Post-growth visions incorporate commons, the concept and practice of sharing land and other resources such as housing on the basis of use rights and co-governance. In contrast to private property with owner occupiers, investor landlords and private tenants with various levels of precarity, Zürich's cooperative members have permanent, full and equitable rights in co-managed housing on co-owned land (via members' cooperative shares). In short, both Kraftwerk1 and Kalkbreite represent a model of secure and socialised rental tenancy with limited equity through shareholding. Yet, even as the borrowing costs of their buildings diminish over time, the cooperative invests in maintenance, renewal and expansion. This model conceptually points to, and practically works towards, post-growth futures based on commons and commoning. Such cooperative housing integrates dwelling with production and consumption, social inclusion and efforts to live within Earth's limits.

Hans Widmer, strongly instrumental in the movement visioning and realising such progressive futures for Zürich's cooperative housing, lives in Kraftwerk1's first construction, Hardturmstrasse (2001–). Established in a brownfield area of Zürich, apartments occupy 9,251 m$^2$ of the space along with 175 m$^2$ of common space across 4 co-located buildings. There are 57 variations in apartment layouts and 2,440 m$^2$ was reserved for offices, workshops and retail or hospitality spaces.

Kraftwerk1 went on to acquire more marginally sited buildings to retrofit. Kraftwerk1's Heizenholz (2011–) pioneered the 'cluster' or 'satellite' apartments that also feature in Kalkbreite (2014–). Here collectives of individuals who chose to live more communally are provided with several studios (with bedsit spaces, ensuites and kitchenettes) clustered around a large communal living room, kitchens and bathrooms. Elsewhere, if any apartment household shrinks or grows, they move into a more appropriately sized apartment as it becomes free. More recently, Kraftwerk1 became a partner in the massive Zwicky-Süd (2016–) complex of 280 apartments, with retail and other commercial activities, and living-work spaces with special account for the needs of those with disabilities, youth and seniors. Clearly, members of each cooperative can avail themselves of various housing options over time.

Established in a niche space atop and alongside a tram depot and overlooking the railway line to Zürich's international airport, 40 percent of Kalkbreite (2014–) is commercial, including a cinema, florist, cafes and restaurant. Sited in central Zürich, it has only two carparks but ample bike storage for around 250 residents in 88 dwellings, and some 200 workers. The seven-storey complex curls around a first-floor public courtyard with dwellings overlooking it or having external views of the city. There are ten types of apartment layouts and sizes from two-room apartments to multi-room clusters. Although space is limited for food gardening there is a commercial guest house, common library, laundromat, hobby and workshop spaces, and flexible 'joker' rooms for temporary purposes.

Moreover, Kalkbreite is responsible for the Zollhaus project, sited alongside a Zürich railway line on land bought from Swiss Federal Railways. Here, 400 m$^2$ of communal spaces service some 56 apartments, with a few restaurants, a guesthouse, shops, offices, a nursery and a kindergarten. Commercial spaces make the cooperative more financially viable. Neighbouring wasteland is a mixed-use Zollgarten.

The young housing cooperatives present their driving visions at their site, concluding that:

> We can reduce energy consumption massively and still improve our quality of life by living together and using resources collectively instead of owning them individually. This strategy is more efficient than technological innovation. What more could we want?
>
> *(o500, undated)*

They aim to develop cultures and dwelling spaces within Earth's limits, meaning that the planet can support 10 billion people at a similar level of basic needs. Drawing on work such as the 2,000-watt society model pioneered by the Swiss Federal Institute of Technology (ETH Zürich), their calculations ultimately aim for around 20 m$^2$ private space and a few more square metres of communal space per person. Similarly, they refer to a range of consumption options, including for transport, food and internet, within a Swiss one planet lifestyle 'menu' (New Alliance, 2019). Their grand vision includes food self-provisioning through a peri-urban agricultural/gardening cooperative *ortoloco* within which residents work and from which they benefit.

As such, the radical 'more than housing' cooperatives that have sprung up this century in Zürich offer planners in other cities, cultures and nations food for thought in promoting post-growth housing (Hugentobler et al., 2016). We ask planners:

> How might the city and state authorities whom you work with, or for, cultivate similar types of housing cooperatives that exist in Zürich, adapted to your cultural and social contexts?

What are the enabling and disabling factors at work in your cultures and under your planning laws?

Young housing cooperatives demonstrate that the built and social forms of the housing that they provide and cogovern are peculiarly consistent with environmental, social and political values for post-growth futures. Both projects highlighted here have been realised by grassroots collectives on an independent non-profit model, rejecting speculation but committed to social inclusion and deep environmental sustainability. They are typical of an upsurge in politicised, citizen-led, ecologically oriented communal forms of living in Vienna, Berlin and many more European cities. They occupy the city's future under glocal principles of planetary limits and local governance. They have developed internal processes and built structures that accommodate transitions beyond market economies and polities. In his interview, Hans Widmer (2018) asserted that they even have the potential to function as commons without the state, market and money (Nelson and Timmerman, 2011; Nelson, 2016).

## 4. Conclusion

This chapter uses eco-collaborative housing — specifically, a cohousing project in the UK and two representatives of a housing cooperative sub-group in Zürich — as examples of prefigurative, messy and hybrid forms for achieving housing beyond growth. We focused on three characteristics to explain our case studies: relationships to the state, the potential and practices of mutualism, and the idea of the 'commons' as a way to own and govern land and assets. Our cases place an emphasis on shared use-rights of land and housing, community-based relationships of collective self-provisioning and care (rather than alienating and commodified relationships), and neighbourhood-oriented co-governance using horizontal techniques of communicating and decision-making.

Their limits and complexities reveal ways around market and state barriers in order to create a more general shift to a post-growth society. In particular, both cases display the realpolitik of local and national states, in terms of securing finance and land using conventional ways of transacting and securing tenure rights for residents. Participants in these projects engage in myriad social relationships, some more mutualistic and some still heavily commodified. They represent islands of building common ownership within broader structures of power and privatisation. Nevertheless, both are disruptive examples of open re-localised economies and socio-political cultures that incorporate relationships of solidarity and care for nature and for people. Their values abstract from the dominating capitalist exchange value of monetised markets. In short, they point purposively in a post-growth direction.

It is worth noting that the implications of the COVID-19 pandemic have brought many of these issues into stark relief, and generated a number of new tensions and solutions for eco-collaborative housing. First, shared spaces and communal facilities have presented challenges for social distancing and, in intimate community settings, protocols were developed, including rotas for the safe use of shared spaces. Particular attention was required to meet the needs of children to use outside and indoor spaces safely without creating concern for vulnerable or shielding adults. However, looking to the future, eco-collaborative housing models display many elements of post-COVID resilience, including access to plentiful green space during lockdowns, the use of natural surveillance of vulnerable and senior residents, greater possibilities for safe and socially distanced interactions between residents, and shared shopping rotas to minimise unnecessary journeys. Some COVID-19-imposed state limits on citizen interaction and movement could be dealt with in collaborative and caring ways. There were more options for satisfying individual and household needs compared to 'nuclear households'.

In sum, we argue for these types of eco-collaborative housing that have the potential to respond to our urgent triple — social, nature and climatic — emergencies and to attend to deep-seated social and geographical injustices. The challenge is to continue building links between civic housing innovations and broader regimes of power and governance to scale up these realistic utopias.

## References

Baborska-Narozny B, Stevenson F and Chatterton P (2014) A social learning tool — Barriers and opportunities for collective occupant learning in low carbon housing. *Energy Procedia* 62: 492–501.

Bollier D (2002) Reclaiming the commons. *Boston Review* 27(3–4).

Boudet D (ed) (2017) *New Housing in Zürich: Typologies for a Changing Society*. Zürich: Park Books.

Caffentzis G and Federici S (2014) Commons against and beyond capitalism. *Community Development Journal* 49(S1): i92–i105.

Chatterton P (2013) Towards an agenda for post-carbon cities: Lessons from Lilac, the UK's first ecological, affordable cohousing community. *International Journal of Urban and Regional Research* 37(5): 1654–74.

Chatterton P (2015) *Low Impact Living: A Field Guide to Ecological Affordable Community Building*. London: Routledge.

Chatterton P (2016) Building transitions to post-capitalist urban commons. *Transactions of the Institute of British Geographers* 41(4): 403–415. DOI: 10.1111/tran.12139.

Chatterton P and Pusey A (2019) Beyond capitalist enclosure, commodification and alienation: Postcapitalist praxis as commons, social production and useful doing. *Progress in Human Geography* 44: 27–48. DOI: 10.1177/0309132518821173.

Claus S (2017) The impressive development of housing cooperatives in Zurich. In Boudet D (ed) *New Housing in Zürich: Typologies for a Changing Society*. Zürich: Park Books.

COOP (2020) About Switzerland. Cooperative Housing International. Available at: www.housinginternational.coop/co-ops/switzerland/ (accessed 13 February 2021).

Cumbers A (2015) Constructing a global commons in, against and beyond the state. *Space and Polity* 19(1): 62–75. DOI: 10.1080/13562576.2014.995465.

De Angelis DM (2017) *Omnia Sunt Communia: On the Commons and the Transformation to Postcapitalism*. London: Zed Books.

Field M (2004) *Thinking about Cohousing: The Creation of Intentional Neighbourhoods*. London: Diggers and Dreamers Publications.

Field M (2011) *Housing Co-operatives and Other 'Mutual' Housing Bodies*. Warwick: Consult.

Hodkinson S (2015) All that is solid: The Great Housing Disaster. *International Journal of Urban and Regional Research* 39(3): 641–3.

Hugentobler M, Hofer A and Simmendinger P (eds) (2016) *More than Housing: Cooperative Planning — A Case Study in Zürich*. Basel: Switzerland.

Kurz D (2017) City and cooperatives, a housing-policy symbiosis. In Boudet D (ed) *New Housing in Zürich: Typologies for a Changing Society*. Zürich: Park Books.

LaFond M and Tsvetkova L (2017) *CoHousing Inclusive: Self-Organized, Community-Led Housing for All*. Berlin: Jovis.

Liegey V and Nelson A (2018) *Exploring Degrowth: A Critical Guide*. London: Pluto Press.

Nelson A (2016) 'Your money or your life': Money and socialist transformation. *Capitalism Nature Socialism* 27(4): 40–60. DOI: 10.1080/10455752.2016.1204619.

Nelson A (2018) *Small is Necessary: Shared Living on a Shared Planet*. London: Pluto Press.

Nelson A and Schneider F (eds) (2018) *Housing for Degrowth: Principles, Practices, Challenges and Opportunities*. London: Routledge.

Nelson A and Timmerman F (eds) (2011) *Life without Money: Building Fair and Sustainable Economies*. London: Pluto Press.

New Alliance (2019) A Proposal. New Alliance. Available at: https://newalliance.earth/a_proposal.pdf (accessed 23 February 2021).

New Alliance (undated) New Alliance. Available at: https://newalliance.earth (accessed 13 February 2021).

o500 (undated) 500 now! Pechakucha. o500. Available at: http://o500.org/pechakucha.html (accessed 13 February 2021).

Routledge P and Derickson KD (2015) Situated solidarities and the practice of scholar-activism. *Environment and Planning D: Society and Space* 33(3): 391–407.

Stevenson F, Baborska-Narozny M and Chatterton P (2016) Resilience, redundancy and low-carbon living: Co-producing individual and community learning. *Building Research & Information* 44(7): 789–903. DOI: 10.1080/09613218.2016.1207371.

Widmer H (2018) I primarily write science fiction novels and not by-laws for cooperatives: A talk with Hans Widmer aka P.M. In Hamelijnck R and Terpsma N (eds) *International Edition Zürich: What Life Could Be, and the Ambivalence of Success*. Zürich: Contemporary Art Publishers.

Woodin T, Crook D and Carpentier V (2010) *Community and Mutual Ownership: A Historical Review*. York: Joseph Rowntree Foundation.

Wright EO (2010) *Envisioning Real Utopias*. London: Verso.

**PART 3**
# Moving

# 5
# INDIVIDUAL WELL-BEING BEYOND MOBILITY GROWTH?

*Luca Bertolini and Anna Nikolaeva*

## 1. Background and vision

Mobility growth confronts us with an obstinate dilemma (Bertolini, 2012): we (households, organizations, cities, countries) depend on mobility for our welfare and well-being, but our mobility practices are not sustainable. The current sustainable mobility paradigm (Banister, 2008) seeks a way out of the dilemma by trying to balance between the two sides: on one hand trying to make lifestyles and business models marginally less dependent on mobility, and on the other trying to make mobility practices marginally more sustainable. However, the sustainable mobility paradigm is not delivering. There is as yet no convincing evidence that modern lifestyles and business models are on the way to becoming sufficiently independent of mobility, nor that our mobility practices are on the way to becoming sufficiently sustainable (Holden et al., 2019).

Trends documented by the European Environmental Agency (EEA, 2019a; 2019b; 2019c) sum up the conundrum. First, although there have been recurrent calls and attempts to decouple mobility growth and economic growth, the two keep showing a strong correlation. When the economy grows mobility grows, and it is only when the economy declines that mobility declines. The trends in transport demand and gross domestic product in the EU documented by the EEA (2019b; 2019c) are a poignant indication of this. Both passenger kilometres and ton kilometres have been substantially growing in the past two decades. Reversals of this trend are limited and temporary and are correlated with the 2008 financial crisis and ensuing economic recession, rather than with a substantial and consistent decrease in the mobility intensity of the economy. Second, and similarly, although there have been recurrent calls and attempts to decouple mobility growth and carbon emission growth (a key measure of lack of sustainability), the two keep showing a strong correlation. As shown by the EEA (2019a), carbon emissions from

DOI: 10.4324/9781003160984-8

transport in the EU keep growing, and the only reversals are correlated with the decreases in passenger kilometres and ton kilometres shown in EEA (2019b; 2019c) and correlated in their turn with periods of economic decline.

In this accumulating evidence we see an urgent call to go beyond the balancing approach of the sustainable mobility paradigm and instead question at its roots the link between mobility growth and human welfare and well-being. In the context of this broader questioning, which should for instance also extend to a critique of business models and organizational practices, we need to better understand to which degree, and in which sense, individual well-being depends on mobility growth, or might even be impaired by it. And we need to understand what individual well-being independent of mobility growth could look like, and what could be enablers and barriers to achieving them. We acknowledge that there are important, unsolved debates around definitions and measurements of individual well-being, as well as its relationships with collective welfare. In this chapter, however, we use the term to loosely refer to the combination of material and immaterial processes and resources that make a human life 'good' (Rosa & Henning, 2018) in the understanding of those living that life.

The current pandemic has triggered a unique natural experiment in this respect, as individuals in a great variety of contexts are confronted with unprecedented restrictions of their mobility and challenged to find ways of pursuing their well-being independently of mobility growth, and rather in a context of mobility decline. Which risks and opportunities do these experiences document? With reference to the Multi-Level-Perspective (MLP) on socio-technical transitions (Geels, 2011), we see the pandemic as a landscape shock, providing a sudden 'window of opportunity' for emergent 'low mobility' niches to challenge the 'high mobility' regime. In this view, the pandemic shapes a context in which to explore 'for real' a range of material and symbolic dynamics both between and within the mobility niches, regime, and landscape (Sheller, 2012). In a similar vein, we see the pandemic as a disruption of the dominant mobility routines and arrangements, forcing adaptations in individual practices that might reveal latent, and previously hidden, possibilities for alternative mobility routines and arrangements (Marsden & Docherty, 2013; Marsden et al., 2020).

To structure the analysis, we will make use of the distinction between a 'local' and a 'stagnant' society introduced by Ferreira et al. (2017). In both a local and a stagnant society low-mobility practices are dominant, as presently forced by the pandemic. However, in a local society low mobility is preferred and the dominant social norm, whereas in a stagnant society high mobility is preferred and the dominant social norm.[1] In this perspective, instances of a local society could point at enablers of a transformation towards a society where individual well-being is independent of mobility growth. Instances of a stagnant society could instead point at barriers to a transformation towards such a society. Ferreira et al. (2017) further articulate the distinction between a local and a stagnant society with the help of the dimensions of 'mobility as capital' identified by Kaufmann et al. (2004), and the dimensions of 'social practices' identified by Shove et al. (2012). Combining the two, they identify the four analytical elements of *access, competence, appropriation and meaning*, and *materials*. *Access* is about the resources that are within reach of individuals, and about the ways they have of acquiring them. *Competence* is about the skills required for everyday life, and about the ways of developing such skills. *Appropriation and meaning* are about the measures by which and the ways in which individuals take control of and shape their everyday practices and environment. Finally, *materials* are the physical artefacts that are mobilized in all the other processes (for a more extensive discussion, see Ferreira et al., 2017). The resulting characterization of a local and a stagnant society is summarized in Table 5.1.

With the help of this analytical framework, we will seek answers to the questions of: in which way and degree are mobility practices and values in the pandemic evocative of a local or a stagnant society? And what might be the implications for

**TABLE 5.1** Characterization of localism and stagnancy

| *Analytical element* | *Type of society* | |
| --- | --- | --- |
| | LOCAL: *Proximity as available capital* | STAGNANT: *Mobility as unavailable capital* |
| **Access** | Individuals have in their proximity enough valued people and resources to meet their needs and aspirations up to high levels of satisfaction | Individuals operate within imposed and confined geographical areas without proper access to critical resources, social contacts, and institutions |
| **Competence** | Individuals master the best skills to thrive in the environment where they are, and it is easy to develop new skills there | The skills which individuals have are not useful in the environment where they operate; learning new skills is difficult |
| **Appropriation and meaning** | Individuals feel rooted to their area and geographical landscape; they are deeply connected to local people, social practices, and institutions | Individuals feel that they belong 'elsewhere' and that this place is not reachable. Local practices and symbols are perceived negatively or convey no meaning |
| **Materials** | Use and disposal of materials is primarily based on local supplies and arrangements; bikes, cargo-bikes, and pedestrian pathways are highly valued, as is public space. Local environment and resources are well managed | Needed materials become scarce because they are not available locally and the necessary transport means are unavailable |

Source: Ferreira et al. (2017)

a transformation towards a society where individual well-being is independent of mobility growth?

## 2. The COVID-19 pandemic as the trigger of a global experiment in a post-mobility growth society?

The outbreak of COVID-19 in 2020 has led to severe physical mobility restrictions around the world: various governments issued decrees limiting movements of their citizens on multiple scales from international and intercity travel to daily walks. Although policies have varied, some degree of mobility restriction became part of the daily lives of hundreds of millions of people around the world. As such, the COVID-19 pandemic has become the trigger of a unique global experiment in mobility reduction and multiple scholars have attempted to measure the effects of this.[2] In this chapter we will do something different: we will discuss the reduction of mobility under COVID-19 in the context of our theoretical framework outlined earlier to understand the potential for what kind of society this experiment has unlocked or at least has shown. Has COVID-19 pushed the world towards a LOCAL or a STAGNANT type of society? How is this articulated in terms of access, competence, appropriation and meaning, and materials? And which questions does this all raise for a transformation towards a post mobility growth society?

Our entry point for this discussion is an analysis of the qualitative data collected in the summer of 2020 by a team of researchers, led by Anna Nikolaeva, as a follow-up of a survey on experiences with working from home with more than 1000 respondents globally (see Rubin et al., 2020). The team sent written interview requests to 300 survey respondents who had expressed interest in participating in the follow-up study. Of the contacted respondents 50 people from 12 countries participated and filled in the written interview forms. The written interview consisted of one leading question that was meant to invoke a story of individual experiences with reduced mobility in the context of the pandemic: 'How has COVID-19 changed your daily mobility, and how do you feel about these changes?' This question was followed by an elaboration and some optional prompt questions. The aim of such an open approach was to allow for the exploration of meanings of mobility and of reduction thereof without a predetermined framework. The responses offer a glimpse into what it means to live a life less mobile – not by choice, not for a long period (or, at least, so it was believed), and yet, precisely because of the abrupt nature of that change the observations and reflections of our interviewees offer a striking count of losses, discoveries, and questions that might accompany a transformation to reduced mobility.

We have applied the framework described in Table 5.1 for coding the data with the reservation that we focus on people's *perceptions* of the changes in their daily lives, and thus the type of data at hand lends itself best to discussing the analytical elements of *competence* and *appropriation and meaning*. Another important reservation is that our interviewees are mainly knowledge/white collar workers based in Europe, the US, and Australia who are in full-time or part-time employment and who in their stories, with a couple of exceptions, have not reported economic hardship, deep distress, and uncertainty about their future. It is also likely that a self-selection bias was at play as people who participated had an interest in the subject and had the time and energy to write down their stories. Our analysis is exploratory in nature and we pose some questions in the discussion that address the limitations of the dataset.

Before we dig into the data, we need to make two important disclaimers. First, we by no means want to suggest that the current pandemic is *prefigurative* of a post mobility growth world, be it local or stagnant. There are too many additional and even contradictory factors at play. One evident one is the restrictions on social interactions in physical space, both public and private, which would be key ingredients of a local, proximity-focused world (see Table 5.1). Also, the pandemic takes place in a world which is still dominated by economic, social, and cultural institutions assuming mobility growth, which have only marginally, if at all, adapted to the reality of a world with great constraints on physical mobility. Second, we do not want to suggest that the perceptions of our respondents can be used as evidence of any loss or gain in well-being. Subjective assessments are notoriously questionable and, in any event, insufficient means of reaching any such conclusion, which should also, if not most importantly, rely on objective assessments of well-being (O'Neill, 2018). In addition, the subjective assessments of our respondents might also be muddled by the awareness (right or wrong) that the mobility reduction is temporary and reversible. What we instead claim is that this crisis offers a unique chance to explore in the field what *could be* risks and opportunities of a transformation towards a post mobility growth society, from the point of view of the lived experiences of individuals affected by drastic reductions in their everyday mobility. We aim to generate questions, rather than to give answers.

## 2.1 Access

In terms of access the stories of our interviewees for the most part report situations that lie between the LOCAL and the STAGNANT society characteristics. Most respondents had to stop going to their workplace completely at some point during the period between March and July 2020 and experienced other limitations on personal mobility beyond their commute. Many interviewees report missing going to work for various reasons, while also underscoring some benefits of working from home in general or not having to commute in particular. Missing social contacts was a very important theme in almost all interviews. For some people socializing at work is a key part of their social life, whereas others see those interactions as pleasant and important for the quality of work:

> Though we were able to carry out the work, we all felt that we are missing the face-to-face interaction. We had to make an extra effort to maintain the quality of work. [...] The current situation feels like an overdose of remote interactions. I feel that the face-to-face interaction with my students and

colleagues is essential. I can see that the quality of interaction (depth) is significantly inferior.

*(F, 58, Israel)*

The lives of our interviewees were largely not designed for staying in one place; their social connections, sometimes including close family, are often beyond their reach under the conditions of a lockdown:

I didn't move about nearly as much, which I like a lot, except that I have missed international travel the most, friends and family in faraway places.

*(F, 51, Austria)*

Many interviewees had to spend most of their time at home and in its surroundings, which for some has exposed that they had relied on mobility for satisfying multiple needs and now cannot find replacements for activities, experiences, and contacts they crave. Others report rediscovering their local environment and enjoying that. A university professor from a small English village discusses the sense of constraint:

Colleagues who live further from the university (but in cities or larger towns) look forward to not having to travel in. They are happy with the prospect of mostly working from home. I feel distant from this anticipation – we don't have places we can walk and see people, parks where at least we could hear others' voices and have social encounters, pavement cafes where one could sit when distanced. These are things that require me to travel deliberately into town. For me, the prospect of continued instruction to work from home fills me with fear. My mobility is entirely the source of my social interaction.

*(M, 56, the UK)*

Another university professor does not seem to feel confined to the same degree in her village in Israel:

My home is located in a small village in the middle of a rural area. That helped to prevent feelings of confinement and enabled me to carry out the physical activity I am used to (jogging). During this period, I had much more interactions with my neighbors from the village (mainly chatting while walking or jogging in the fields) than in normal times.

*(F, 58, Israel)*

Many interviewees reported enjoying long walks and learning more about architecture and nature in places where they live:

Because I try to go on a daily walk through my neighbourhood (about 45 mins) I spend a lot more time in my direct environment than before. I have noticed things that I didn't really notice before – breeding birds, for example…

(F, 30, The Netherlands)

While discussing their local environments many interviewees raised issues around walkability and bikeability. A student who moved from Davis to Phoenix in the US to stay with his parents during the pandemic comments:

If I wanted to travel anywhere including the park, I had to drive a car. […] Spending so much time inside made me realize how inaccessible a lot of the same destinations that I travel in Davis are in my neighborhood in Phoenix. […] It wasn't necessarily a new realization but it was definitely apparent that destinations are more accessible by bike in Davis, which is a small college town with extensive bike infrastructure, than in Phoenix.

(M, 23, the US)

His fellow countryman, who recently became a father, discusses the dangers of walking and related constraints in Houston, Texas:

One thing that inhibits me from taking the baby and wife with me (aside from the weather – Texas summers are extremely hot!) is that I live in a neighborhood that, unfortunately, does not have sidewalks, and people tend to drive pretty fast even on the residential roads. This hasn't stopped me from walking, but I am a lot more protective of the kid, and frankly I don't trust drivers here to slow down just because they see someone walking with a baby in a stroller.

(M, 33, the US)

Some interviewees (especially people who use public transportation) also mentioned concerns regarding using public transportation because of fear of contracting COVID-19 and thus potential reduction in access to places.

To sum up, no one reported losing access to critical resources or facilities, but we must emphasize that we have a non-representative sample and our interviewees could be considered as a comparatively privileged group of people. The main impacts that they have experienced in terms of access have to do with (very) limited social contacts and the lack of variety and change in their daily life. Some, however, were also able to find new opportunities for social interaction and spare-time activities close to home.

## 2.2 Competence

Most of our interviewees discussed the adjustment to new routines in ambiguous terms. Many of them mastered or began mastering new skills necessary in the situation and enjoyed that, whereas others experienced stress, anxiety, and boredom.

Examples of skills and competencies that people began mastering include learning more about the neighbourhood and socializing with neighbours (see some examples in the previous section), adopting new self-care practices, developing a different working rhythm and distribution of chores with their partner, and doing their shopping and planning vacations differently. Sometimes adopting new skills and routines is discussed as a direct result of struggles with separation between private life and work, loneliness, lack of physical movement, new digital tools, etc. For example, a marketing consultant from Germany comments on the already changing meeting culture and the future transformations of personal meetings triggered by the pandemic:

> I think we have all learned that meetings do not need to be in person all the time. I am certain that we will have a larger number of virtual meetings in lieu of personal meetings. And we will cherish personal meetings a lot more. Meeting culture will change, as well. We have all learned that the level of being 'private' can be much higher on occasion and you still get work done.
> *(43, M, Germany)*

A university lecturer from The Netherlands explains how he adapted to the sense of social isolation during lockdown by becoming a more active member of the local community:

> I also miss the simple daily informal meeting opportunities like going for lunch or a drink with colleagues. On the other hand, because I recently chose to become more active in a local organization (I applied for a voluntary position in the board of that organization, and was chosen for that position), I am building up new social networks in my city. This might have happened without the pandemic too, but maybe the pandemic and having to be at home much more was an incentive to make this choice.
> *(47, M, The Netherlands)*

An Italian researcher describes how the initial relief of not having to commute vanished and gave way to a sense of containment, inability to concentrate, sadness, and loneliness. Eventually she developed new routines and self-care practices to lift her spirits:

> [...] during the first period I didn't miss anything of my travels from Modena to Bologna and back. Especially, I didn't miss the anxiety of getting to the train at the right time, in order to be able to arrive to work or home in time for all the already planned things. I didn't miss the frequent and regular delays of the trains. I didn't miss the crowd on the train [...]. I dint' miss the loss of time (2.30 hours per day) to commute. [...]
>
> After the first two/three weeks at home, however, I started to feel depressed, like a tiger in the cage [...]. During the first two weeks of lockdown I found

it really difficult to force myself to follow a routine. I couldn't focus and I couldn't follow any schedule. Partially because I was worried, the situation was completely new and I never expected – as many other people – that I would experience a similar global situation. Partially because being at home all the time, waking up alone, living alone, eating alone, working in the same room every day and never changing environment was not giving me the motivation to have regular days, regular meals, regular working hours. [...] So, at some point I decided I needed to react and I forced myself to wake up at certain time, working from x to x, eating healthy, doing some gym. After this, days started to flow again a bit faster, even if the mood was not great in any case.

*(F, 33, Italy)*

The ease of mastering new skills and competencies varied across the stories of our respondents, with some painfully pointing out that their circumstances, such as the built and social environment around them, were too constraining when they tried to adapt (see section 2.1 on *access*). Thus, again we see a mixture of characteristics of a LOCAL and a STAGNANT society. Most interviewees discuss a variety of successful adaptation strategies – from building their own gym facilities to developing well-thought-out routes for daily walks – but the successes of such adaptations as well as difficulties reported by others are linked in complex ways to their personalities and unique circumstances.

## 2.3 Appropriation and meaning

Perhaps as a reflection of the growing competencies discussed in the previous section, as well as possibly related to the nature of our dataset (relatively well-off respondents, living in environments they largely seem to like), we see a lot of appreciation of living locally and living 'slower'. A Scottish lawyer thus summarizes her experience:

My Life [sic] is much less frantic which is most pleasant. [...] Most of those I speak to – generally busy people are all saying we enjoy this slower pace of life…

*(F, 64, the UK)*

Many respondents explained why they appreciate the new rhythm of life, how they managed to make it their own and find joy, peace, and meaning in life under lockdown:

With no commute I get to sleep in an hour longer and instead of being in the car I walk for half an hour in my neighborhood and still start on time. I truly enjoy my new morning routine. I get to have lunch with my husband, check on my flowers in the garden, take an hour off when I am waiting on materials from others, and can fill that time with something useful at home. I can be flexible with promising my time since I am not under pressure to take a train or be on the road to avoid traffic.

*(F, 55, the US)*

Many interviewees reported feeling more connected locally, learning more about places where they lived, and enjoying that new sense of place:

We are lucky to live in an area with shops, restaurants, a vibrant high street (well, during normal times) within walking distance and with very good transport connections (tram and train) also within walking distance. As we have walked more (than riding to specific destinations), we have learned a bit more about our neighborhood and have enjoyed being here more.

*(M, 53, Australia)*

And yet there is also a sense of the meaninglessness and emptiness of this 'local' life:

In lockdown, immobile, nothing is unexpected, there are no memories.

*(M, 56, the UK)*

Some people also gave meaning to the situation by connecting it to the issue of environmental degradation and the disastrous consequences that were revealed by the pandemic:

The corona lockdown for me is a confirmation how brutally privileged we are that we can do nothing for three months and still get strawberries and kiwis at the supermarket for a reasonable price and so how brutal we are towards others in the world and our offspring that we keep raping our planet because of shareholders value… We know that it can be different.

*(M, 57, Dutch living in Germany)*

I hope more generally the travelling behavior will change and will tackle problems like congestion and excessive plane use.

*(M, 41, The Netherlands)*

Similarly to the discussion of competences, we see in our data an effort to find meaning in the current circumstances, to make sense of the situation, to enjoy it even. Some interviewees report growing connection to places and communities, adopting and enjoying a new pace of life. Yet, given the perceived temporary nature of these changes and the possible effect of novelty of all those pleasant experiences, one can hardly conclude that a LOCAL society has materialized. Rather, our respondents got acquainted with some glimpses of it and tried to make it their own.

## 2.4 Materials

The interviews not surprisingly document a radical step-up in the presence and reach of digital technologies in all aspects of daily life. But the pandemic has also forced people to reconsider the role of the home as a place to not just live, but also work and physically exercise, and the direct surroundings of the home as a place for shopping, socializing, and recreation. These shifts have been met by ambivalent appreciation, as illustrated by the quotes which follow.

For example, some welcomed the replacement of face-to-face meetings, whereas others suffered:

> Many of our clients all of a sudden are allowing us to do things remotely and electronically which we asked for in the past. It is more efficient and better for the environment.
>
> *(F, 55, the US)*

> Going to the office normally allows me to have some distance, now everything is absorbed into am amorphous blob and a small house does not allow for separation between intimate domestic space and the domain of my employer. I hate the communications technologies available. The way that they level all communication to a single undistinguished plane of distorted visual and compressed audio signal.
>
> *(M, 56, the UK)*

Quite a few interviewees comment on the relative advantages of digital communication technologies while at the same time highlighting that for some purposes they are a poor fit:

> At work I find it largely ok how much you can exchange and decide, now that everyone is comfortable using online tools. Now we can have meetings on one day that would have otherwise taken place in the Hague, Utrecht and Zaandam. That part of travelling I don't miss at all, sitting in the train half of the day, searching for an unfamiliar location at […] But [I do miss] a bit networking after such meetings. Now everyone waves to the screen and the meeting is over in 5 seconds.
>
> *(F, 48, The Netherlands)*

Many people discussed lacking a dedicated working space, as this Scottish transport policy officer comments:

> The biggest change with COVID-19 is the lack of change in my daily routine. I now work, exercise, eat, home-school, and relax in the same room of my apartment.
>
> *(M, 32, the UK)*

Yet, some highlight how they realized that office space is not as necessary as it seemed. What is necessary is the social contact:

> The only part it's made me realize is how little of my work is really necessary to be in the office for. I could do 90% of it from home, however the social aspect of seeing colleagues is VERY important for mental health and productivity.
>
> *(M, 26, The Hague, The Netherlands)*

As discussed earlier for the category *access*, the local built environment becomes key for quality of life and for mobility options that people consider when they do decide to go out. Many interviewees report lack of access to walkable and bikeable environments which, combined with the reported fear of using public transportation due to the perceived danger of contracting COVID-19, points in the direction of a STAGNANT society. Quite a few interviewees changed their views on their neighbourhoods because of the new balance of modes and new routines:

> My view of the neighbourhood has changed too. I walked around a lot more than I did before, so I noticed new spots that are nice to go to. However, I also noticed I live in a really busy street. There is a lot of noise from cars / motor bikes and this annoys me while working. Also, it's hard to walk on the side walk and keep 1,5 m distance, especially in the afternoon and weekends.
>
> *(M, 26, Utrecht, The Netherlands)*

Others acknowledge that they are 'lucky' to live in areas where they can walk or cycle safely anywhere they need to:

> I've also gotten to know my local area very well, I'm lucky to live in a very walkable neighbourhood, with a shopping strip that supports most of daily needs, so I often combine a walk around the neighbourhood with a trip to the shops.
>
> *(F, 28, Australia)*

## 3. Conclusions and discussion: what do we need to know and do?

Taken together our interviews point at four broader, underlying themes, each also highlighting directions in which further enquiries into the contours and conditions of a society where individual well-being is independent of mobility growth could go. They point at:

- An *ambivalent picture:* both a stagnant and a local society are evoked. Following Rosa (2018), on one hand people seem to suffer from the sudden impossibility of pursuing the modern ideal that *ever more* resources and opportunities should be 'available, accessible, and attainable'; on the other hand, they seem to appreciate the value of an alternative ideal of 'resonance' with people and places that are *already* within their reach. And this raises the question: is this ambivalence caused by the fundamentally and intrinsically ambivalent impact of the reduction of mobility on individual well-being? Or is it instead caused by the path dependency of routines, habits, and networks developed in a high-mobility world?

- Great *heterogeneity*: positive or negative perceptions are very diverse and are much affected by personal characteristics (e.g. household composition) leading to reinforcing existing and creating new inequalities; a more diverse sample of respondents (e.g. including people who could not work from home, or could only do so with much difficulty; the unemployed, the elderly, the young, people with serious health concerns) would most likely show even bigger variation and inequality. What are the implications of all these personal and contextual differences for the pursuit of a society where individual well-being is independent from mobility growth?
- *Trade-offs*: on one hand respondents miss more faraway (and possibly more diverse) social interactions and place experiences, on the other they enjoy more close by (and possibly more intense) social interactions and place experiences. This raises the question of whether these different types of experience are interchangeable, commensurable, and cumulable, or in other words: do we have to choose between being rooted in a local world and connected in a global world? If we don't, what could that look like? If we do, what are the implications for individual well-being?
- *Cues for a post-growth society*: although we believe that any such choice should be the outcome of political and inclusive deliberation (see also the next point), the narratives of our respondents do provide some cues of what enabling a transformation towards a post mobility growth world might entail:
  - reconfiguration of social contact networks in a way that does not rely exclusively on travel;
  - working more locally or working both remotely and locally, working less, volunteering locally;
  - developing enjoyable, diverse, and accessible public spaces in close proximity to where people live;
  - enabling easy, safe, inclusive low-carbon mobility locally;
  - providing access to basic services within walking or cycling distance, or remotely.
- *Discovery and opening*: in spite of all the differences, the crisis is for everybody a moment of discovery and opening – not necessarily pleasant, but nevertheless forcing the reconsideration of old habits and routines and the exploration of new ones; as such, it seems a unique opportunity to redirect the course and shape the future (Marsden & Docherty, 2013; Marsden et al., 2020). However, a collective appreciation of this opportunity seems necessary, as physical and

situational conditions determined by collective decisions heavily affect the scope of possibilities and the type of impacts at the individual level, as poignantly shown in the interviews by the impacts of the built and social environment on lived experiences. There is no built-in irreversibility in the mobility practices emerging during the crisis, including those experienced as positive, and any continuation of them would require a conscious, collective choice to enable their survival proactively (and arguably, also selectively). In other words: it would require moving beyond identifying emerging individual practices towards questioning collective institutions as well. How, then, can individual discoveries add up to collective articulations of meaning? Can we common (Nikolaeva et al., 2019) the new meanings of mobility arising in a world less mobile?

## Notes

1 Ferreira et al. (2017) not only distinguish a local and a stagnant society, but also a 'global' and a 'liquid' society. In both a global society and a liquid society high-mobility practices are dominant. However, in the former they are preferred and in the latter they are not. Both these options are precluded during the pandemic and are thus not relevant for our analysis.
2 For a review of the research, including references to other reviews, see https://airtable.com/tblWYkmqFZ3riUsA8/viwxIuFgPcFDhb0Ob?blocks=hide.

## References

Banister, D. (2008). The sustainable mobility paradigm. *Transport policy*, *15*(2), 73–80.
Bertolini, L. (2012). Integrating mobility and urban development agendas: A manifesto. *disP – The planning review*, *48*(1), 16–26.
European Environment Agency (EEA) (2019a). *Greenhouse gas emissions from transport*. Copenhagen: EEA. Available at: www.eea.europa.eu/data-and-maps/daviz/transport-emissions-of-ghgs-6#tab-chart_1.
EEA (2019b). *Inland freight transport volumes and GDP*. Copenhagen: EEA. Available at: www.eea.europa.eu/data-and-maps/daviz/freight-transport-volumes-and-gdp-7#tab-chart_4.
EEA (2019c). *Trends in passenger transport demand and gross domestic product*. Copenhagen: EEA. Available at: www.eea.europa.eu/data-and-maps/daviz/trends-in-passenger-transport-demand-7#tab-chart_1.
Ferreira, A., Bertolini, L., & Næss, P. (2017). Immotility as resilience? A key consideration for transport policy and research. *Applied Mobilities*, *2*(1), 16–31.
Geels, F. W. (2011). The multi-level perspective on sustainability transitions: Responses to seven criticisms. *Environmental innovation and societal transitions*, *1*(1), 24–40.
Holden, E., Gilpin, G., & Banister, D. (2019). Sustainable mobility at thirty. *Sustainability*, *11*(7), 1965.
Kaufmann, V., Bergman, M. M., & Joye, D. (2004). Motility: Mobility as capital. *International journal of urban and regional research*, *28*(4), 745–756.
Marsden, G., Anable, J., Chatterton, T., Docherty, I., Faulconbridge, J., Murray, L., ... & Shires, J. (2020). Studying disruptive events: Innovations in behaviour, opportunities for lower carbon transport policy? *Transport policy*, *94*, 89–101.

Marsden, G., & Docherty, I. (2013). Insights on disruptions as opportunities for transport policy change. *Transportation research part A: Policy and practice*, *51*, 46–55.

Nikolaeva, A., Adey, P., Cresswell, T., Lee, J. Y., Nóvoa, A., & Temenos, C. (2019). Commoning mobility: Towards a new politics of mobility transitions. *Transactions of the Institute of British Geographers*, *44*(2), 346–360.

O'Neill, J. (2018). How not to argue against growth: Happiness, austerity and inequality. In H. Rosa & C. Henning (eds), *The good life beyond growth. New perspectives* (pp. 141–152). New York, NY: Routledge.

Rosa, H. (2018). Available, accessible, attainable: The mindset of growth and the resonance conception of the good life. In H. Rosa & C. Henning (eds), *The good life beyond growth. New perspectives* (pp. 39–54). New York, NY: Routledge.

Rosa, H. & Henning, C. (eds) (2018). *The good life beyond growth. New perspectives*. New York, NY: Routledge.

Rubin, O., Nikolaeva, A., Nello-Deakin S., & te Brömmelstroet, M. (2020). *What can we learn from the COVID-19 pandemic about how people experience working from home and commuting?* Amsterdam: Centre for Urban Studies, Universiteit van Amsterdam.

Sheller, M. (2012). The emergence of new cultures of mobility: Stability, openings and prospects. In F. Geels, R. Kemp, G. Dudley, & G. Lyons (eds), *Automobility in transition? A socio-technical analysis of sustainable transport* (pp. 180–202). New York, NY: Routledge.

Shove, E., Pantzar, M., & Watson, M. (2012). *The dynamics of social practice: Everyday life and how it changes*. Los Angeles, CA: SAGE.

# 6
# BEYOND THE RULE OF GROWTH IN THE TRANSPORT SECTOR

Towards "clumsy mobility solutions"?

*António Ferreira and Kim Carlotta von Schönfeld*

## 1. Introduction

The dominant transport planning narrative of our times is characterised by values such as economic growth and capital accumulation, efficiency and predictability, time value and travel time savings, innovation and techno-centrism. This has remained the case even as the sustainability agenda has been increasingly accommodated. Without arguing that these values are necessarily problematic in all circumstances and contexts, we propose that allowing a key activity sector to be subjugated to them is necessarily problematic. We will briefly review today's dominant transport planning narrative and its major alternatives, all of which, we will argue, have major shortcomings. To address the lack of suitable strategies that the transport sector presently experiences, it is necessary to promote a greater diversity of perspectives in the conduct of transport-related decision-making processes. This requires creatively integrating contributions from a range of worldviews that are not only radically dissimilar from the one that dominates today, but which also potentially conflict with one another. Such an integrative approach (Ferreira, 2018; 2020) will lead to what we call *clumsy mobility solutions*, ultimately following the line of thinking initiated by Douglas (1970; 1978; 1989) on cultural biases. According to Schmitt and Hartmann (2016), there are inspiring similarities and remarkable synergies between Douglas' work and that of Jane Jacobs (1972), who famously explored imperfection as a positive value for urban planning and the good city. We will transpose this argument from urban planning and cities to transport planning and mobility, refining and expanding it as we do so. But first, we need to critically analyse the dominant transport planning narrative of our times: that of innovation-led, sustainable mobility for economic growth.

DOI: 10.4324/9781003160984-9

## 2. The dominant pro-growth mobility narrative (and its drawbacks)

The central premise of the dominant mobility narrative is that both economic and mobility growth should be promoted. Not only is each considered desirable on its own terms, but their mutual reinforcement is also considered positive (European Commission, 2011; Department for Transport, 2011). The logic underlying so-called "sustainable transport growth" closely follows this premise. This purportedly new approach still assumes that the key benefit of promoting transport growth is economic growth (and its supposed derivatives, e.g. jobs, well-being, happiness), but brings in the novelty that the environmental degradation that grows proportionally with it must be resolved through continuous innovation. Such faith in the power of innovation is displayed in a large variety of policy documents (and academic literature). A summary of the argument is provided by Tsakalidis et al. (2020: 1):

> Transport makes a significant contribution to economic growth and higher quality of life by facilitating the movement of people and goods. On the flipside, it causes externalities that have detrimental effects on the environment and public health. These externalities are the main impetus to support innovation that makes transport greener, safer and more efficient.

Perhaps due to its inherent optimism and forward-looking qualities, the pro-growth mobility narrative has strong political and research appeal. However, even though it has delivered some constructive outcomes across history, it is reaching a point of rupture. This happens primarily for six reasons.

First, because it is questionable to what extent, beyond a certain threshold, economic growth produces benefits that justify its costs. As noted by Daly (1999), when that threshold is surpassed, *uneconomic growth* emerges. This means that economic growth ceases to promote the public good. Instead, it becomes a source of social, environmental, and – paradoxically – also economic drawbacks and vulnerabilities (Kallis, 2018; Jackson, 2017).

Second, because the relationships between economic growth and mobility growth are not straightforward (Banister, 2012). Consider this: transport improvements typically lead to additional mobility, which in turn can lead to congestion in some links of the transport network. Congestion can then suppress mobility within those links (Hills, 1996), which represents accessibility problems for those using them. This process leads to a variety of reconfigurations of social and economic activities throughout time and space due to accessibility gains and losses, which, in turn, lead to a new pattern of induced versus supressed traffic (Janelle, 1969; Wegener and Fürst, 1999). Some geographical areas and social groups are benefited whereas others are punished by this ongoing process (Knowles, 2006). Assuming that transport growth homogeneously and predictably leads to economic prosperity is, therefore, imprecise and a source of social injustice.

Third, because promoting innovation entails risks and costs. Innovation can lead to the proliferation of novelties that fail to solve any actual problems while creating new problems that result from their implementation. And then yet more innovations are developed to solve these problems (Morozov, 2014; Soete, 2013; von Schönfeld and Ferreira, 2021). An excessive focus on innovation can also induce maladaptive policymaking whereby innovation becomes a goal in itself at the expense of public goals proper such as sustainability, justice, and well-being (Ferreira et al., 2020).

Fourth, because the environmental impacts of the transport sector are likely to remain massive and proportional to mobility growth. Despite all the transport-related innovations witnessed in the last few decades, the transport sector has failed to reduce energy consumption at a rate compatible with sustainability (IEA, 2020). Furthermore, increasing transport efficiency can induce mobility growth which, in turn, neutralises the efficiency gains achieved – this is called Jevons' Paradox (Alcott, 2005; Sorrell, 2009).

Fifth, because continuously improving mobility does not consistently lead to positive outcomes. Research on mobility and accessibility (e.g. Bertolini et al., 2005; Handy, 2002) suggests that increasing mobility can have a net negative impact on individuals' access to key social contacts, services, goods, and opportunities. Individuals might have to engage in increasingly extensive, frequent, and costly travelling to continue accessing what they used to have in their close proximity. Amenities can be incrementally displaced to remote locations due to the middle- and long-term consequences of mobility growth. As a result, the costs of travelling can become unbearable for many, and mobility becomes a driver of social exclusion (Kenyon, 2003; Social Exclusion Unit, 2003). Furthermore, authors such as Urry (2004) and Bauman (2007) argue that many of the neurotic characteristics of contemporary societies derive from continuous mobility growth. Mobility is also becoming a burden and a driver of dispossession and precarity, and not just a source of freedom and endless possibilities, as the pro-growth mobility narrative argues.

Sixth, and finally, because – as was also observed during the Eyjafjallajökull ash cloud disruption (Guiver and Jain, 2011; Birtchnell and Büscher, 2011) – the COVID-19 crisis has shown that the impacts resulting from mobility disruptions are proportional to the extent to which a given society or individual is mobility dependent, and particularly the extent to which one is dependent on long-distance, high-speed, and frequent mobility. These impacts become stronger when individuals have caring responsibilities, as is the case for parents with young children (Rubin et al., 2020). Promoting mobility growth and mobility dependence induces non-negligible collective and individual vulnerabilities (Ferreira et al., 2017).

Clearly then, alternatives to the dominant pro-growth mobility narrative are deeply needed. However, the existing alternatives also have drawbacks.

## 3. The alternative mobility narratives (and their drawbacks)

There are two major alternatives to the dominant mobility narrative. These rely on *virtual mobility* and *accessibility-by-proximity* as their core concepts. Virtual mobility means accessing what one needs or wants via digital means. It has delivered positive results. For example, it enabled many to continue working and socially interacting during the COVID-19 pandemic. However, virtual mobility can aggravate obesity problems induced by lack of physical activity. Obesity already constitutes a global health issue (Nieuwenhuijsen and Khreis, 2019; Pucher and Buehler, 2010) and is likely to be further aggravated as the COVID-19 pandemic continues (Clemmensen et al., 2020). Furthermore, virtual mobility is a technologically mediated, long-distance form of interaction potentially leading to a gulf between reality and perception. It can promote impoverished and even perverse human interactions. The problem is not limited to the absence of physical mobility and face-to-face contact, nor to the expectable forms of perceptual distortion induced by any medium of communication, as noted by McLuhan (1995). A deeper perversion of human interaction derives from the fact that corporations such as Facebook, Amazon, and Google (i.e. "Big Tech") are transforming essentially *all* digital means of communication into devices for surveillance, commodification, and control of human behaviour (Zuboff, 2019). As a result, the value of the data economy of the EU27 and the UK was estimated at above 400 billion euros in 2019 (Cattaneo et al., 2020). Such value shows the extent to which virtual mobility was integrated into the economic growth agenda. To aggravate matters, the sustained investment in digital technologies will require a continuous demand for rare minerals. Accessing these materials might soon constitute not only serious environmental, but also geo-political problems (Stegen, 2015) – a threat about which there is a surprising lack of awareness (Hofmann et al., 2018).

Accessibility-by-proximity means performing changes in land use patterns and societal arrangements so that individuals can find what they need (e.g. jobs, health care, education, goods, social contacts) in their close vicinity. This allows individuals to travel less and to use non-motorised modes such as walking and cycling (Ferreira and Batey, 2007; Bertolini et al., 2005). However, accessibility-by-proximity requires a variety of desirable amenities in the vicinity of housing, which often leads to increases in residential property values (Koster and Rouwendal, 2012; Song and Knaap, 2004). In turn, high land values constitute a key driver of social exclusion and housing precarity. Even though this can be partially addressed by state-sponsored measures aimed at stabilising housing prices, the present trend is for governments to facilitate the conversion of real estate into financial assets, which are then speculated upon by both the state itself (through taxes) and global investors (through rents and mortgages) (Stein, 2019). The accessibility-by-proximity approach is being gradually converted from an idealistic vision of planners concerned with social justice and environmental sustainability into a mechanism to raise land values in the name of capital accumulation.

Despite good intentions, transport planning has a strong tendency to reinforce and assist, instead of counteract, the pro-growth economic rationale (Ferreira and von Schönfeld, 2020). This, in turn, makes current transport planning incapable of effectively addressing environmental sustainability and social justice challenges. The next section offers an explanation as to why this is the case.

## 4. Mobility, time, and value

A possible way to understand the bond between economic growth and transport planning starts at home. In the past, washing clothes or dishes were manual tasks that consumed substantial time and labour. Now, many households across the world have machines to perform such tasks. The free time saved for people in general, and women in particular, had a monetary cost (for purchase as well as maintenance). This cost was accepted because the benefit was spread out across the multiple time intervals people could now supposedly enjoy. These time intervals could also be used to perform additional work.

Since the dissemination of private washing devices, countless other devices have inundated our lives. Computers and the internet are perhaps the most impressive: they allow individuals to instantaneously have access to, send, and process unfathomable amounts of information. Although computers and the internet also have a relevant monetary cost, this is almost unanimously considered well-spent money due to the reduction of waiting times, the productivity gains achieved, and the opportunities for enjoyment offered.

All these machines are associated with both *hedonistic* principles, concerned with creating free time and facilitating a greater enjoyment of life through reduced labour; and with *austere* principles, concerned with reducing waiting times and increasing productivity. These two, apparently antagonistic, principles have followed converging trajectories that are progressively merging them. This paradoxical assemblage is characterised by configurations where duty and fun, guilt and triumph, private and public, stress and release permanently replace each other in rapid succession. Rosa (2003; 2015) relates these dynamics to *social acceleration*. Social acceleration is expressed in three different, but intertwined and synergistic, categories: acceleration of technologies (which become ever faster and more productive), acceleration of social change (as institutions experience ever faster transformations), and acceleration of the pace of life (as individuals experience an increasing sense of rush).

At the core of social acceleration lies the transport sector and its allegiance to economic growth and capital accumulation. It became well accepted in policy-making circles that new transport investments should be assessed through time gains and losses converted into economic value. In other words, the pro-growth narrative effectively integrated hedonistic and austere principles in a seamless way for the benefit of elites. Mobility was the mixer and the glue. The mechanism behind this elitist integration of opposites through mobility is simultaneously compelling, intuitive, and absurd. Consider the simplified example in Box 6.1:

---

**BOX 6.1: ECONOMIC APPRAISAL OF NEW TRANSPORT INFRASTRUCTURE**

Mary commutes every day. The return trip takes 1 hour and she earns £25 per hour at work. This means that, per day, she uses a £25-worth hour travelling.

> If a new transport infrastructure is built and reduces her travel time by 50%, the value of her time spent travelling will be reduced to £12.50 per day. At the regional level, 1,000,000 people experience a daily situation somewhat comparable to Mary's. This means that, every day, the regional economy is wasting about £25,000,000 in travel time. If built, the travel infrastructure in question will, therefore, have a positive economic effect of £12,500,000 per day in travel time savings. Assuming that these people commute 260 days per year, this transport infrastructure represents an economic benefit of £12,500,000 × 260 = £3,250,000,000 per year.
>
> But then remember that Mary needs to have fun and enjoy life besides work. With the construction of the new transport infrastructure, she can now reach a hitherto inaccessible sport facility within a one-hour return trip. This is excellent, as Mary can now have fun and socialise in this prime facility once a week instead of doing so near her residence, as she used to. Since the year has 52 weeks and there are about 50,000 people in the region comparable to Mary, for whom one hour is worth £25, the value of the infrastructure for the economy is £25 × 52 × 50,000 = £65,000,000 per year. Therefore, the overall annual value of the new infrastructure is at least £3,250,000,000 (from austere practices related to work) + £65,000,000 (from hedonistic practices related to social life, sports, and fun). These values are extremely conservative, as they do not include John's trips and the trips of those like him, nor any other activities, for example.

As the simplified (yet troublingly realistic) example in Box 6.1 shows, assuming that travel time has monetary value leads economic appraisal to present new or enhanced transport infrastructures as nothing less than gold mines (Ferreira et al., 2012). Remarkably, if enhanced transport infrastructure and induced mobility actually drive social contacts, services, and jobs away from people, this too can be made economically positive: it creates the opportunity to summon new gold mines in the form of additional transport enhancements that will induce even more mobility. This circular logic can be repeated as many times as desired, as long as the natural environment can sustain it and people are willing to endure the drawbacks of continuously travelling more. It should immediately be added, however, that these supposed gold mines are *fictitious*, as Polanyi might have put it (Polanyi, 2001 [1944]): the wealth creation assumed by transport-related econometric appraisal methods is, to a large extent, imaginary. Indeed, where are the *£3,250,000,000* + *£65,000,000* calculated above? This wealth does not necessarily exist; it is mostly an abstract figure in a transport appraisal spreadsheet. Still, the additional trips and their environmental impact, as well as the costs of building and maintaining the infrastructure, are very real.

Besides the negative environmental consequences, the socially unjust and unethical nature of this assessment logic must also be emphasised (Naess, 2006). If Mary and her peers earned just £5 per hour at work, the economic gain of performing the same transport enhancement would be much lower. Note the injustice of the reasoning: the more a given social group earns, the more economically relevant it becomes to plan new transport initiatives for them. The opposite is also true: providing mobility for the deprived becomes a waste of economic, environmental, and energy resources. As their purchasing power is low, it also leads to the displacement of desirable services and jobs away from their vicinity.

Another important detail must not be missed: as was referred to in the example, transport-related economic appraisal does not subtract new travel times from the time savings resulting from the delivery of enhanced transport conditions. Instead, it *adds* them to each other as it assesses *both* time savings and additional time travelling as proof of the satisfaction of individual needs and desires. It does the same with time spent travelling for austere as well as hedonistic practices: everything is summed up. We will return to the profound meaning of this paradoxical aggregation process in what follows.

Note that both virtual mobility and accessibility-by-proximity are harmonious with, and actually further reinforce, the overall logic of valuing travel time in a socially unjust way. Virtual mobility reduces travel time to essentially zero, facilitating both hedonistic and austere practices to be performed without waiting times – provided that individuals have the means to afford a high-speed digital connection coupled to an up-to-date digital device. Accessibility-by-proximity facilitates extremely convenient access to desired places, people, and activities – but only for the privileged few who can live and work in the exclusive geographical areas where that is made possible.

## 5. A typology of transport-related worldviews

As we have critically analysed, the three most noteworthy narratives framing transport planning theory and practice today all display serious shortcomings. This happens, we propose, because they are in harmony with a set of fundamentally unjust and unsustainable underlying premises. First, that time (and therefore also travel time) has economic value. Second, that the value of travel time is determined by the level of economic wealth of the traveller. Third, that the economic gains resulting from mobility efficiencies are proportional to the economic value of the traveller's time.

In order to fundamentally challenge the dominance of economic growth and efficiency in transport planning, it will be necessary to integrate very different concepts and values, and perhaps even different ways of perceiving the world, into its foundations. In what follows, the term *worldview* will be employed to mean the lenses adopted by individuals to make sense of their own socially constructed reality. A given transport planner or policymaker's worldview would shape how they respond to the following classical planning questions (to which we will return later):

- Which *values* should guide transport planning practice?
- Which forms of *knowledge* should be endorsed?
- Who are the relevant *stakeholders* to be included in planning processes?
- How should planning *processes* be conducted? And finally,
- Which *substantive measures* should be implemented?

In order to understand why empowering alternative worldviews is key to advancing post-growth transport planning, it is important to understand how current answers to these questions, and with them our perceived mobility needs, are deeply influenced by the dominant worldview. Indeed, both travel time savings and new trips, as well as mobility for both austere and hedonistic purposes, are all supposed to be converted into pro-growth capital accumulation mechanisms. In fact, and as we have argued, all three of the mobility narratives described are being co-opted, or were originally developed, so that they could reinforce the dominant pro-growth logic. As a result, what we have witnessed for decades is individuals across the world being prevented from making slow and contemplative trips, as well as physically active, fun, and exploratory trips – unless they pay for them as special commodities to be performed at the edges of the mainstream, highly efficient and pro-growth, transport flows. Likewise, land use patterns and all sorts of societal arrangements are being developed or actively rearranged so that they too can promote commodification, growth, and capital accumulation.

In other words, the *accelerating* worldview has dominated transport planning for decades (and urban planning as well): that worldview which prioritises economic growth and capital accumulation, efficiency and predictability, innovation and techno-centric econometric decision-making. The result is longstanding shortcomings such as the incapacity to reduce carbon emissions and environmental impacts, or to promote social inclusion. To be clear, the problem is not that the accelerating worldview is *present* but that it *completely dominates*. Alternative logics have been systematically and purposefully reworked to reinforce the accelerating worldview, or else excluded altogether. The reason that transport planning struggles to deliver serious improvements is that it has insistently aimed to solve problems using the same worldview that has created them – and, in many cases, in an increasingly intensified and autistic manner.

This takes us to the cornerstone of our reasoning. Contemporary transport planning is dominated by an unsustainable and unjust fixation on growth and capital accumulation, efficiency and predictability for the benefit of the few. In this moment of history, it is crucial that without altogether quashing values of growth and efficiency, we nonetheless explicitly integrate the opposite values and principles into transport planning. Encouraging a comfort with disorder and experimentation is an important but, on its own, insufficient component. We must also actively push an agenda of degrowth and commoning for the benefit of the many. Suitable solutions for the future of transport will be those that strike a suitable balance between a variety of opposites. Doing this follows, to a significant extent, the theoretical mechanisms initially employed by Dame Mary Douglas in her classical writings (Douglas, 1970; 1978; 1989), which eventually led to the development of the term *clumsy solutions* (for some uses of the term, see Verweij et al., 2006; Schmitt and Hartmann, 2016; Hendriks, 1999). These can be defined as solutions that can be accepted by radically different worldviews on the grounds that they synthetise the key aspirations held by each of them. They are called "clumsy" because they naturally lack the inner consistency and streamlined properties of solutions developed by a single worldview. This lack of inner consistency is in fact their greatest strength, and their source of flexibility, adaptive capacity, and resourcefulness.

The proposed typology of worldviews (also called cultural biases) is represented in Figure 6.1. We will describe them next, using the key questions of planning already outlined. We invite the reader to ponder which worldview best describes his or her current understanding of reality.

First, we will address the *accelerators*: those whose worldview currently dominates the transport planning discipline. Individuals adopting this worldview consider economic growth and efficiency key values to be delivered through the development and employment of econometric and innovative technical knowledge. In line with this, they prioritise the engagement of engineers and economists in the design of transport systems, which should follow a techno-centric econometric process. To deliver results, accelerators preferably make use of innovative transport technologies and approaches. As we have seen, as a result of their worldview, these individuals find it intuitive to add travel time savings to new trips induced by transport enhancements. They also find it intuitive to add trips made for both austere and hedonistic purposes; and convert all these items into econometric sums in ways that favour elites, which they belong to or aspire to be part of.

Second, we have the *rebels*: they are diametrically opposed to the accelerators in their understanding of the world. They radically oppose the idea that economic growth is a legitimate goal for transport policy, and are moreover repulsed by efficiency and predictability (and elites). They support values such as improvisation,

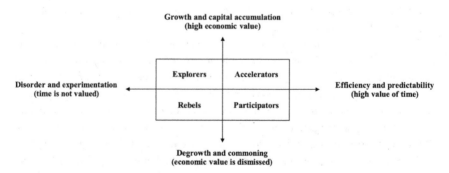

**FIGURE 6.1** A typology of worldviews for transport planning

Source: authors

spontaneity, and self-organisation. The very notion of *planning* is problematic for them because it has an imperialistic connotation. Decisions should be based on what people subjectively know and feel. On the same basis, processes of deliberation should be conducted by lay citizens and focused on local issues identified by local residents. The substantive measures preferred by rebels are as variable as they are context specific. Their substantive preferences might include the private car, the bike, skateboards, or whichever means of transport best facilitate autonomy.

*Explorers* share with rebels their allegiance to experimentation and improvisation at the local level, as well as to citizen participation. But the explorers see local transport experiments as means to achieve economic growth and capital accumulation for their own benefit. They mix an interest in bottom-up approaches with econometric assessments of prosperity and well-being that integrate the local, the national, and the global. They thus combine bottom-up and top-down approaches, and have some tolerance for experts on econometrics and engineering at both ends of the process. They are likely to appreciate and promote cycling and walking in their neighbourhoods, provided these improve the value of their properties, but they also expect high levels of accessibility to high-speed trains and airports.

Finally, we have the *participators*: those who want the transport sector to be ruled by an efficient and predictable logic, but who oppose the dominance of growth and capital accumulation. Instead, they want to see the common folk developing high-quality, self-organised initiatives, which involve bottom-up forms of governance that are beyond the market logic. Their focus on efficiency and predictability is directed at other goals besides economic growth. These goals are likely to be well-being, environmental sustainability, social inclusion, and biodiversity. This means that participators would welcome ecologists and landscape architects, and particularly nature-friendly technological innovators, while promptly excluding neoliberal economists and civil engineers wanting to build heavy transport infrastructures (especially roads). They would probably support local and self-managed public transport initiatives.

## 6. Towards clumsy mobility solutions for post-growth transport planning

The theoretically driven typology presented makes it possible to describe the fundamental tenets of our vision for post-growth transport planning. This would be a form of planning that creates space for all of the worldviews previously described, and with them the multifarious conceptual frames, expectations, and solutions they offer for the problems facing the transport sector. Underlying this logic is the assumption that all worldviews have specific merits and drawbacks when made agents of change in transport planning. Readers may have identified with one, multiple, or none of the preceding worldviews. In any case, this process of self-reflection provides a starting point for identifying and compromising between different aspirations and requirements. We invite all readers to consider how a given transport-related decision could be enhanced by integrating aspirations and requirements associated with worldviews other than those they may have identified with, and to think about how joint decision-making among conflicting worldviews could be orchestrated.

Achieving this form of planning would necessarily be a complex task because the presented worldviews are extremely different and, in fact, antagonistic by definition. However, if a given transport solution could represent a suitable compromise for all of them, it could have the merit of not only being willingly supported and adopted by an unprecedentedly large number of individuals and organisations. It could also have the capacity to promote transport sector configurations characterised by humanity, complexity, and diversity. In this way, we might repurpose Jacobs' (1972) thinking about imperfect cities (see also Schmitt and Hartmann, 2016) for the transport sector.

In practice, clumsy mobility solutions could be achieved in two distinct ways (that could be combined in various creative manners). The first way is *integrative*: each mobility solution in itself achieves a compromise between the aspirations and requirements of all the worldviews described here (and, possibly, also the aspirations and requirements of other worldviews). The second way is *combinative*: even though no mobility solution in itself addresses the aspirations and requirements of all worldviews involved, a range of solutions are promoted in parallel so that – in aggregate terms – a suitable compromise is achieved for all worldviews.

## 7. Concluding remarks

The vision we propose for post-growth transport planning is not specifically concerned with (de)commodification, the commons or capital accumulation, the expansion or reduction of GDP, the minimising of carbon emissions, or any other idea or goal of a similar nature. Instead, we are concerned with the dynamic integration of worldviews that would simultaneously radically support and radically oppose any dominant concept, both in fundamental terms and in their application to the transport sector. What we propose is the advancement of clumsy mobility solutions as a foundational transport planning concept: these are ways of addressing the problems affecting the sector that achieve a suitable compromise regarding the aspirations and requirements of all worldviews involved.

At present, transport planning is dominated by an accelerating worldview that prioritises concepts such as economic growth and capital accumulation, efficiency and predictability. We propose that alongside this worldview, transport planning needs to integrate alternative worldviews that are fundamentally opposed to such concepts. Now, it is important to note that once we challenge the dominant status of these concepts, others may simply arise to take their place. There is a human tendency to champion superordinate categories that give a sense of order to reality by systemically excluding true alternatives – a topic discussed in relation to planning professional practice by Ferreira (2018; 2020) and Verma (1998). This means that the process of including opposing worldviews should be dynamic and iterative, always alert to the major criticisms and negative reactions resulting from the latest developments. Clumsy mobility solutions therefore provide an understanding of mobility that remains open to continuous agonistic debate (Mouffe, 2013), or at least to a continuous, situated reinterpretation of priority setting (Lennon, 2017). This includes the possibility that in a post-growth future, economic growth, efficiency, and capital accumulation will continue playing a role in mobility choices. But their presence will be fully counterbalanced through the integration of worldviews that contest such values with the same force that they are defended.

## References

Alcott B. (2005) Jevons' paradox. *Ecological Economics* 54: 9–21.
Banister D. (2012) Transport and economic development: Reviewing the evidence. *Transport Reviews* 32: 1–2.
Bauman Z. (2007) *Liquid Life*. Cambridge: Polity Press.
Bertolini L., le Clercq F. and Kapoen L. (2005) Sustainable accessibility: A conceptual framework to integrate transport and land use plan-making. *Transport Policy* 12: 207–220.
Birtchnell T. and Büscher M. (2011) Stranded: An eruption of disruption. *Mobilities* 6: 1–9.
Cattaneo G., Micheletti G., Glennon M. et al. (2020) *The European Data Market Monitoring Tool: Key Facts & Figures, First Policy Conclusions, Data Landscape and Quantified Stories (2.9 Final Study Report)*. Brussels: European Commission.
Clemmensen C., Petersen M. and Sørensen T. (2020) Will the COVID-19 pandemic worsen the obesity epidemic? *Nature Reviews* 16: 469–470.
Daly H. (1999) Uneconomic growth and the built environment: In theory and in fact. In: Kibert C. (ed) *Reshaping the Built Environment: Ecology, Ethics, and Economics*. Washington D.C.: Island Press, pp. 73–86.
Department for Transport. (2011) *Creating Growth, Cutting Carbon: Making Sustainable Local Transport Happen*. London: Her Majesty's Stationery Office.
Douglas M. (1970) *Natural Symbols: Explorations in Cosmology* (1st edition). New York: Pantheon.
Douglas M. (1978) *Cultural Bias*. London: Royal Anthropological Institute.
Douglas M. (1989) A typology of cultures. In: Haller M., Hoffmann-Nowotny H., Zapf W. et al. (eds) *Kultur und Gesellschaft. Verhandlungen des 24. Deutschen Soziologentags*. Zürich: Campus Verlag, pp. 85–97.
European Commission. (2011) *White Paper: Roadmap to a Single European Transport Area – Towards a Competitive and Resource Efficient Transport System*. Brussels: European Commission.
Ferreira A. (2018) Towards an integrative perspective: Bringing Ken Wilber's philosophy to planning theory and practice. *Planning Theory and Practice* 19: 558–577.
Ferreira A. (2020) Dilemmas, conflicts, and worldview diversity: Exploring the relevance of Clare Grave's legacy for planning practice and education. *Journal of Planning Education and Research*. DOI: 10.1177/0739456X20940797.
Ferreira A. and Batey P. (2007) Re-thinking accessibility planning: A multi-layer conceptual framework and its policy implications. *Town Planning Review* 78: 429–458.
Ferreira A., Bertolini L. and Næss P. (2017) Immotility as resilience? A key consideration for transport policy and research. *Applied Mobilities* 2: 16–31.
Ferreira A., Beukers E. and Te Brömmelstroet M. (2012) Accessibility is gold, mobility is not: A proposal for the improvement of transport-related Dutch cost-benefit analysis. *Environment and Planning B: Planning and Design* 39: 683–697.
Ferreira A. and von Schönfeld K.C. (2020) Interlacing planning and degrowth scholarship: A manifesto for an interdisciplinary alliance. *DisP – The Planning Review* 56(1): 53–64.

Ferreira A., von Schönfeld K.C., Tan W. et al. (2020) Maladaptive planning and the pro-innovation bias: Considering the case of automated vehicles. *Urban Science* 4: 1–17.

Guiver J. and Jain J. (2011) Grounded: Impacts of and insights from the volcanic ash cloud disruption. *Mobilities* 6: 41–55.

Handy S. (2002) *Accessibility- vs. Mobility-Enhancing Strategies for Addressing Automobile Dependence in the U.S.* Davis, CA: Department of Environmental Science and Policy, Prepared for the European Conference of Ministers of Transport.

Hendriks F. (1999) The post-industrialising city: Political perspectives and cultural biases. *GeoJournal* 47: 425–432.

Hills P. (1996) What is induced traffic? *Transportation* 23: 5–16.

Hofmann M., Hofmann H., Hagelüken C. et al. (2018) Critical raw materials: A perspective from the materials science community. *Sustainable Materials and Technologies* 17: e00074.

IEA. (2020) *Tracking Transport 2020*. Paris: International Energy Agency.

Jackson T. (2017) *Prosperity without Growth: Foundations for the Economy of Tomorrow*. Abingdon: Routledge.

Jacobs J. (1972) *The Death and Life of Great American Cities: The Failure of Town Planning*. London: Pelican.

Janelle D.G. (1969) Spatial reorganization: A model and concept. *Annals of the Association of American Geographers* 59: 348–364.

Kallis G. (2018) *Degrowth*. Newcastle upon Tyne: Agenda Publishing Ltd.

Kenyon S. (2003) Understanding social exclusion and social inclusion. *Proceedings of the Institution of Civil Engineers* 156: 97–104.

Knowles R.D. (2006) Transport shaping space: Differential collapse in time-space. *Journal of Transport Geography* 14: 407–425.

Koster H. and Rouwendal J. (2012) The impact of mixed land use on residential property values. *Journal of Regional Science* 52: 733–761.

Lennon M. (2017) On 'the subject' of planning's public interest. *Planning Theory* 16: 150–168.

McLuhan M. (1995) *Understanding the Media: The Extensions of Man*. London: MIT Press.

Morozov E. (2014) *To Save Everything, Click Here: Technology, Solutionism, and the Urge to Fix Problems that Don't Exist*. London: Penguin Books.

Mouffe C. (2013) *Agonistics: Thinking the World Politically*. London: Verso.

Naess P. (2006) Cost-benefit analyses of transportation investments: Neither critical nor realistic. *Journal of Critical Realism* 5: 32–60.

Nieuwenhuijsen M. and Khreis H. (2019) *Integrating Human Health into Urban and Transport Planning: A Framework*. Cham: Springer.

Polanyi K. (2001 [1944]) *The Great Transformation: The Political and Economic Origins of Our Time*. Boston, MA: Beacon Press.

Pucher J. and Buehler R. (2010) Walking and cycling for healthy cities. *Built Environment* 36: 391–414.

Rosa H. (2003) Social acceleration: Ethical and political consequences of a desynchronised high-speed society. *Constellations* 10: 3–33.

Rosa H. (2015) *Social Acceleration: A New Theory of Modernity*. New York: Columbia University Press.

Rubin O., Nikolaeva A., Nello-Deakin S. et al. (2020) *What Can We Learn from the COVID-19 Pandemic about How People Experience Working from Home and Commuting?* Amsterdam: Centre for Urban Studies, University of Amsterdam.

Schmitt S-M. and Hartmann T. (2016) Clumsy city by design—A theory for Jane Jacobs' imperfect cities? *Urban Planning* 1: 42–50.

Social Exclusion Unit. (2003) *Making the Connections: Final Report on Transport and Social Exclusion*. London: Social Exclusion Unit, Office of the Deputy Prime Minister, UK.

Soete L. (2013) Is innovation always good? In: Fagerberg J., Martin B.R. and Andersen E.S. (eds) *Innovation Studies: Evolution and Future Challenges*. Oxford: Oxford University Press, pp. 134–144.

Song Y. and Knaap G-J. (2004) Measuring the effects of mixed land uses on housing values. *Regional Science and Urban Economics* 34: 663–680.

Sorrell S. (2009) Jevons' paradox revisited: The evidence for backfire from improved energy efficiency. *Energy Policy* 37: 1456–1469.

Stegen K. (2015) Heavy rare earths, permanent magnets, and renewable energies: An imminent crisis. *Energy Policy* 79: 1–8.

Stein S. (2019) *Capital City: Gentrification and the Real Estate State*. London: Verso Books.

Tsakalidis A., van Balen M., Gkoumas K. et al. (2020) Catalyzing sustainable transport innovation through policy support and monitoring: The case of TRIMIS and the European Green Deal. *Sustainability* 12: 1–18.

Urry J. (2004) The 'system' of automobility. *Theory, Culture & Society* 21: 25–39.

Verma N. (1998) *Similarities, Connections and Systems: The Search for a New Rationality for Planning and Management*. Boston, MA: Lexington Books.

Verweij M., Douglas M., Ellis R. et al. (2006) Clumsy solutions for a complex world: The case of climate change. *Public Administration* 84: 817–843.

von Schönfeld K.C. and Ferreira A. (2021) Urban planning and European innovation policy: Achieving sustainability, social inclusion, and economic growth? *Sustainability* 13: 1137.

Wegener M. and Fürst F. (1999) *Land-Use Transport Interaction: State of the Art*. Dortmund: Deliverable 2a of the project TRANSLAND (Integration of Transport and Land Use Planning) of the 4th RTD Framework Programme of the European Commission.

Zuboff S. (2019) *The Age of Surveillance Capitalism: The Fight for a Human Future at the New Frontier of Power*. London: Profile Books.

# PART 4
# Governing

# 7
# THE CITY AS A COMMONS

Diffused Governance for Social and Ecological Reproduction

*Massimo De Angelis*

## 1. (Re)production and Governance

Governance systems should be designed with one purpose in mind: to address the grave multiple crises concerning the reproduction of both a social and ecological nature, while at the same time promoting a good life for all. This of course implies deaccumulation of capitalist social relations, as well as the creation of new social processes of production, distribution, and exchange that are in line with ecological and social objectives. Where does one start? The answer to this is with (re)production itself, as it is a field of social cooperation within which multiple issues and subjectivities can be situated and recomposed. Additionally, if reclaimed along novel organisational and institutional lines, (re)production might allow us to rearticulate our multiple interdependencies, by redefining both the quantitative and the relational/qualitative aspects of social reproduction as a whole. The main hypothesis at the basis of my argument is the following: the more we can collectively subtract processes of accumulation from the spheres of (re)production, the more we will be able to:

- reduce our dependency on capitalist markets and become less vulnerable to its competitive, alienating, ecologically destructive, and exploitative logic;
- contrast the processes of capitalist subjectification with the creation of alternative subjectivities through commoning.

It is for this reason that in what follows I locate (re)production as the main purpose of a system of diffused governance within a city.

I want to propose that the notion of (re)production is related to and sits between the reproduction of labour power in the domestic sphere as discussed by classic Marxist feminist texts and more recent literature (Dalla Costa and James, 1975;

Federici, 2012; Fortunati, 1995; Bhattacharya, 2017; Barca, 2020), and the general question of social reproduction within a socio-economic system, including both waged and unwaged work, as a whole (Caffentzis, 2002). By (re)production, I mean the sphere of social cooperation that has a bodily, cognitive, affective, emotional, and relational preoccupation with the production of human beings by means of human beings (Hardt and Negri, 2009: 136–137).

The online Oxford etymology dictionary helps us to understand reproduction as "bringing forth" (producing) something "back to the original place; again, anew, once more" (the "re-" of "reproduction"). What does this mean when applied to us as human beings? Clearly, that human beings are both the means and the ends of production. Beyond the infinite scenarios of its concrete systemic manifestations, however, this radical circularity also implies that cooperative processes could be designed in such a way as to favour a coincidence of means and ends: their connections and articulations balanced in an endless dance of self-perpetuation. Thinking in terms of (re)production means, therefore, to think first and foremost about what those human beings who serve as a means have in common with those who serve as an end, in particular social relations and contexts (not only care, education, and health, but also culture and the arts, as well as manufacturing, mining, and so on). The problematic of (re)production in turn opens a space for collective reflection on the socially just forms that would be necessary for a model in which all human beings are seen to be both the means and ends of social endeavour.

Clearly, there can be no question of producing human beings by means of human beings without touching on that of life in general: we are part of an ecosystem from which we derive all forms of energy, and to which we return everything that we use as waste. Therefore, the sphere of (re)production must also include a bodily, cognitive, affective, emotional, and relational preoccupation with safeguarding the ecological preconditions for human existence, present and future. Our necessary and vital entanglement with all that is alive serves to remind us that the need to balance means and ends – their mutual adjustment processes – also involves our relation to the living. Capital, in its race to commodify everything, has turned all of nature (both within and without the human body) into a means, by treating it as a resource. My definition of (re)production does not ignore the living, and recognises that it is the responsibility of human beings to bring about this rebalancing and mutual adjustment of means and ends. This is the role of cognitive commoning, a particular form of cognitive labour embedded in commons systems which this chapter locates within a new system of governance.

Finally, (re)production is not seen as concentrated in a particular sector, but as a layered and transversal social phenomenon: layered, in that it occurs through a multiplicity of practices at different levels of social action, mobilising different kinds of social power and systems of governance; and transversal, because the preoccupations of (re)production apply to all areas of human social cooperation. There is a lot of emotional labour involved in the factory, the office, and the school. (Re)production thus cuts across both paid and non-paid activities, across services, agriculture, and industry, and across households, commons, corporations, and state offices. Given this transversality, (re)production is a potentially huge terrain, through which the social recomposition of imaginaries and struggles can be explored.

(Re)production, therefore, constitutes a realm of social cooperation made up of many systems, institutions, and modes of production that mix, collide, cooperate, or attempt to subordinate each other. Capital, the state, and the commons are here understood as systems of production, regimes of governance, and political principles for the further development of the forms and objectives of social cooperation.

## 2. Emergent Messy Governance

If the main purpose of the city as a commons is (re)production, then it is important to establish what form of governance will be adopted to pursue this. How is a city governed? I want here to propose two distinct definitions of governance. The first, in line with current literature, is "governance proper" (Jessop, 2016), a networked forum of different stakeholders in which specific issues are to be resolved. The second is "emergent messy governance", understood as the entirety of a city's actual governance, in all of its divergent and perhaps conflicting forms, exercised through different nodes of social cooperation. This distinction is introduced in order to problematise the current state of governance, faced as it is with the huge problems that exist within social reproduction.

"Emergent messy governance" is, therefore, the actual governance of a given entity (a neighbourhood, a city, a region, a nation, etc.) as it springs from a potentially messy variety of models and practices of governance, all of which pursue different and often contradictory objectives. This might entail, for example, simultaneous campaigns of capitalist accumulation on one side, and socially just and ecologically sound social reproduction on the other. Through its many strands, emergent messy governance is linked to circuits of social reproduction at different scales, which affect ecologies and distribute resources, thus impacting on questions of social justice, poverty, exclusion, and so on. Emergent messy governance is thus all the nodes of governance in their various forms, operating at different scales and concerning different circuits, socially productive systems, and institutions. It is a picture of the total number of self-reflective processes, a composite intelligence that emerges out of different forms of rationality and societal rule-making, for many purposes which often clash with one another, and through myriad forms of organisation and power relations. Each governance node is attached to one or more circuits of social reproduction at different scales, which it tries to steer in a particular direction.

It is clear that this emergent messy governance is marked by a dramatic failure to regulate and address the question of social reproduction. Given the fact that all four modes of governance – whether by markets, networks, command, or solidarity – could all in principle fail in given circumstances (Jessop, 2016), the actual failure of social reproduction, as expressed by spiralling social and ecological crises, has to do with the specific influence and combination of each of these different modes and their corresponding principles. In other words, it is a question of hegemony. The hegemonic role of capital and its principle of competition works in conjunction with hierarchies of control as they are embedded in both corporations and the state. This particular configuration maintains constraints (such as property laws) that are not conducive for resolving the problems that arise from the failure of social reproduction.

## 3. Governance and Complexity

In principle, in the light of failures of governance, it would be necessary to establish processes for redefining the mode of governance, which in the literature is called "meta-governance" (Jessop, 2016; Meuleman, 2008) or the regulation of self-regulation, if not a complete overhaul of the rules of the game (collibration). The problem we are faced with is not so much the failure of this or that form of governance in a given context, but rather its failure as an agent of social reproduction as a whole. For this reason it is useful to look at the relationship between complexity and its regulation, as studied by second-order cybernetics.

Complexity here is taken to refer to complex systems, that is, systems that are made up of different components, which themselves act as subsystems and interact with each other in a variety of ways. Two fundamental characteristics of complex systems are *self-organisation* and *emergence*. The self-organisation of components within a system is a character of complex adaptive systems, those biological, ecological, and social systems capable of adapting to their environment as a result of experience. Emergence, on the other hand, is a process whereby the system as a whole comes to be characterised by the interaction between its components and their self-organisation, in ways that were not foreseeable on the basis of the laws that govern those components themselves. For example, consciousness, language, or reflexive properties in human beings cannot be explained through the sum of the characteristics of neurons alone, just as the properties of a city are not reducible to the sum of its human or structural components. Instead, their emergence depends in large part on the type of interactions that their components give rise to. In this sense, a city is a complex entity, as is a market, an institution, a community organisation, the global economy, and social reproduction.

In this context, the question of governance acquires a further meaning as *coordination within complexity*. Indeed, Jessop (2016: 179) has defined governance as the "mechanisms and strategies of coordination in the face of complex reciprocal interdependence among operationally autonomous actors, organisations, and functional systems."

## 4. Complexity and Viability

A property of complex systems is variety: they are made of many different components which, in combination, produce diverse dynamics and effects. In the study of cybernetics, the relationship between variety and complexity is fundamental in order to define viable ways of regulating complexity. The greater the quantity and variety of elements within a system to be regulated, the greater its complexity. If this complexity of interactions generates phenomena that can be defined as "problems" (ecological destruction, poverty, precariousness), the greater the need to think and act in an accordingly complex manner.

In cybernetics, Ashby's law argues that in order for regulation (governance) to be viable, it is necessary for the regulator to possess the same degree of variety as the complex system it intends to regulate. The regulator will attempt to increase its variety in relation to that of the object of regulation through selective processes, which include a filtering of both the variety of its environment and of the processes that will allow it to achieve this aim. This will continue until the variety required to address the problem, and ensure the regulator's viability, is reached. This scheme may seem highly abstract, but it contains a very simple insight: that in order to deal with the diversity of the problems that one may face, a repertoire of responses with at least an equivalent level of nuance as those problems is essential. In the hegemonic structure of our cities and nations, this repertoire of responses is limited by the domination of statist and market-oriented responses within constellations of emergent messy governance. We need to increase the variety of responses to our socio-ecological crises. This, however, is constrained by current power structures. Indeed, there is an intimate relationship between power and variety. The primacy of certain power blocs within decision-making spaces stifles the variety of possible choices and solutions as a function of private interests. This stands in direct contrast to a deep democratic culture and organisational structure, favoured by autonomy and diffused governance, which is essential for helping the city to self-regulate (Espinosa, Harnden, and Walker, 2005: 577). For this reason, the role of commons movements could be decisive here.

## 5. The Need for a Diffuse and Participatory Model of Governance

The law of requisite variety should alert us to the fact that the failure of governance as a whole is a result of insufficient variety on the part of the regulator in relation to the system(s) to be regulated. A solution to this is to increase the variety of the regulator. An increase in localised, diffuse, and decentralised autonomy means a greater capacity for variety in the system as a whole. Distributed control or governance, with a highly autonomous network of local actors pursuing specific forms of social reproduction, would mean devolving "responsibility to already self-organised groups of people" (Espinosa and Walker, 2011: 85). This in turn would give way to a situation in which:

> the managers do not need to "absorb" an immense amount of variety – as it has already been dealt with at the lower levels of recursion. An immediate reflection for the sustainability of societies is that by each society addressing and solving the most urgent issues for its own sustainability locally, the need for top-down control at the national level would be reduced significantly.
> *(Espinosa and Walker, 2011: 85)*

Thus, the first point to be drawn from this discussion is that we need more distributed, polycentric governance systems (Savini, 2021) with increased participation. In other words, we need to govern the city as a commons.

Commons have always had a fundamental role in the metabolic function of the city (Brinkley, 2020: 131–132). The question for us is how to make this metabolic function central to the complex system that is the city today, within an overall framework of degrowth and deaccumulation. The commons cannot only be conceived of as an actual, physical site where certain forms of reproduction can take place (even if such centres may take on an important role for social reproduction in given contexts and scales), but also as a centre that emerges from the coordination and articulation of different kinds of reproduction, carried out in different places and across different scales. City commons should therefore be seen as an emergent system for coordinating social reproduction in its fullest form, starting with the transversal sphere of (re)production.

As with any commons system, the city as a commons comprises three elements: *common resources*, governed by a *community of commoners* who also regulate their own relations, and processes of *commoning*, of social cooperation or common doing (De Angelis, 2017). Reflexive city governance is carried out from different nodes of social cooperation, and the priority of (re)production over accumulation shapes the integration and reciprocal balances of these nodes. City governance, as a diffuse system, emerges at different scales from nodes that must integrate with one another to suit the overall aim of (re)producing a "good life" for all along social, distributive, and ecological lines.

In the context of this kind of governance, each node faces the problem of Ashby's law as described earlier. That is, each finds itself having to filter out a certain type of variety from the environment and amplify another. How do we integrate these nodes? How do we make sure that their different objectives do not contradict but support one another, and that they are aligned in the service of (re)production? Stafford Beer's viable system model allows us to posit such an integration.

## 6. The Viable System Model

The viable system model (VSM) was developed by organisational theorist and cyberneticist Stafford Beer (1981). It is based on the organisational structure of a given system (a firm, a city, a nation, and so on at different levels of recursion), and conceptualises that system as autonomous and autopoietic; that is, capable of (re)producing itself. This would make our city (as the system in focus) viable, organised in such a way as to be adaptable and meet the demands of surviving in a changing environment.

The key contribution of the VSM is an approach to designing a system so as to fully articulate the autonomy of its parts without compromising the cohesion of the whole, in relation to a common purpose. The VSM, when applied to the diffused governance of a city, requires us to consider two things: first, the importance of recognising, in any choice we make, that our city is co-evolving with the social and ecological environment to which it relates, and that any choice of governance would trigger effects and responses from such an environment; second, that the autonomy and self-regulation of any governance nodes must be matched by a mechanism that generates some degree of cohesion between different nodes. Whereas the first point is addressed by the VSM through the development of specific techniques for information management (Espinosa and Walker, 2011: 78–90), the second point can be explored through a discussion of the holon (Koestler, 1967), and the distribution of functions modelled by the VSM. It is this second point that I will now turn to.

At the bottom of a holon structure, we would find – whether at the level of a local neighbourhood or that of the whole city – those social nodes, organisations, institutions, or branches of institutions whose function it is to furnish their environment with activities for (re)production. These *operational* nodes (individuals, communities, organisations) must be empowered to take day-to-day decisions concerning the modes and objectives of their social cooperation, so that they can deal with the issues they face quickly and effectively. Empowerment includes both autonomy of decision making, and sufficient resources to meet needs. Such a diffused autonomy would also allow for a city to learn from its mistakes, a basic survival mechanism generally limited by hierarchical power structures, which prevent nodes of social cooperation from dealing with the complexity they face. Instead, learning and adaptation require a system to be both self-reflective, and able to analyse its interactions within its socio-ecological niche.

For any complex organisation to be viable it must ensure that, as well as providing enough autonomy to its embedded nodes, it also comprises a meta-systemic management structure in order to guarantee the cohesion of its constituent elements. Bureaucracy and managerial autocracy are the answers given by capital and the state to the problem of cohesion among different parts, but this reduces the variety through which one can relate to an environment. The solution offered by cybernetics, on the other hand, is to create layers of meta-management (or meta governance), or second-order governance, which permit distributed operational nodes to control day-to-day decisions. These meta-management functions would only intervene in day-to-day operations:

> when any of them has been out of control at the local level, and no solutions have been found to correct the situation for an agreed period of time (this is similar to what has been called "management by exception"). What it means is autonomy and self-regulation at the local level, while keeping cohesion to the embedding organisation.
>
> *(Espinosa and Walker, 2011: 84–85)*

It is important to highlight that these layers of meta-management are not positions that correspond to particular roles within a hierarchy, but should rather be understood as management/governance functions, taken on following principles of democratic participation and openness. Indeed, increased active participation in these layers of governance would further address the problem of the variety of the regulator. Now, the need to trust the operational levels to not only self-organise, but also control their operations as well as their relationship with the environment, implies that the city – as with any other VSM-based organisation – "requires development of a culture of respect, trust, transparency and reciprocity" as well as "proper mechanisms for monitoring and deciding on local accountability that the Metasystem can access all the time". Beyond this culture and mechanism then, within the VSM, each level's meta-system need only "deal with the 'residual variety'", that is, those issues that do not fall within the remit of the operational day-to-day but which are still crucial for the organisation of the city as a whole (Espinosa and Walker, 2011: 84–86). This reduces top-down control significantly, while amplifying the freedom and autonomy of the parts, and addresses social and environmental concerns through the pooling of knowledge at the local level.

## 7. The Basic Model

Stafford Beer's viable system model takes inspiration from how natural systems work, extracts some basic principles, and sees whether those same principles can be applied to human social organisations which could be characterised as "viable".

A viable system is one that is capable of independent existence, through its adaptation to a continuously changing environment (which requires maximum autonomy of its parts), while maintaining its identity or purpose (which requires overall cohesion of its parts). It is a holon, a system that is a whole whilst simultaneously containing subsystems, as well as being a part of a suprasystem (Koestler, 1967).

The basic model features the conceptual separation and re-articulation of three elements found in other kinds of system: a set of operational processes; an understanding of management as a function and not as a privileged group of hierarchs; and the environment, that is, the socio-ecological systems that it relates to at different levels of recursion. The system in focus here, the city, is a subset of the environment that it relates to.

Stafford Beer thus identifies five functions that any viable system should find ways to integrate, and to each function corresponds a particular system whose role is to serve that function. These functions and the corresponding systems of the VSM are:

Function/System 1: operations
Function/System 2: coordination
Function/System 3: cohesion
Function/System 4: intelligence
Function/System 5: purpose

Since these functions/systems are integrated as holons, the need for functional levels above them emerges as residual variety. In other words, there are issues not dealt with by lower functional levels, but that nevertheless remain crucially important for the cohesion of the whole, which still need to be met. The governance of the city system is functionally divided across the five systems (S1 to S5) and these – with their corresponding functions – are mirrored across social activity in a fractal manner at different scales (Espinosa, Harnden, and Walker, 2005: 577).

Figure 7.1 shows the three main elements: the operation (O), the management (M), and the environment (E). The operational ellipse is composed of a number of operational units (in this case, three). As we have seen, the operational units must be as autonomous as possible. This autonomy, or System 1 (S1), implies self-management or self-governance at the operational level, and corresponds to day-to-day management units (labelled 1a, 1b, and 1c). The job of higher levels of governance is to provide the "glue" which enables and coordinates this autonomy. The meta-management diamond is composed of four sub-systems (labelled 2, 3, 4, and 5) which I have already discussed in relation to their function. The various arrows represent the numerous and complex interactions between the five systems and the environment.

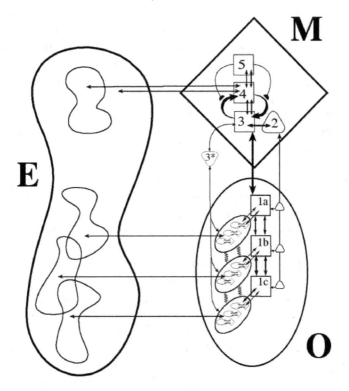

**FIGURE 7.1** Diagrammatic representation of a VSM

Source: Lowe, Espinosa, and Yearworth (2020: 1015)

## 8. VSM and the City: An Illustration

The first difficulty one comes across in attempting to define a city as commons has to do with establishing System 1, i.e. the operational units, those sites where the community of commoners can come together to address different issues of (re)production. In principle, the characteristics needed to define S1 depend on the objectives and actual context of the city in question.

As we have seen, social labour in a city (whether paid or unpaid) is performed through a variety of organisational forms and their corresponding systems of governance, giving rise to a state of emergent messy governance and its failures. In a developed city, from an ecological and a social point of view, improvements in quality of life and ecology can only occur by reducing the material impacts of social production, drastically increasing equity of distribution, and creating a context that is conducive to positive relational development.

With this in mind, a functional distinction would allow us to define the operational domain of the city as commons in terms of its different domains of (re)production (health, education, ecological preservation/regeneration, and so on), and to construct a diffused multiscalar VSM on this basis. We should not see these functions as closed silos, but interconnected and interdependent spheres. There are also institutions that tend to mix and integrate these functions at different scales. For example, the household is not only a site of education, but also of care, food production, emotional support, and so on. The same goes for many territorial associations as well, such as urban commons. Additionally, and fortunately, the division of the operational level into different functions through the VSM is open to integration with Systems 2 and 3, which can mix and articulate these different realms and help to develop synergies. Through the activity of commoning and boundary commoning (De Angelis, 2017), each of these local sites of (re)production may, in turn, also open up: clinics become educational spaces, and schools practise health care.

So the different operations in a city can be classified according to the functions of (re)production that are necessary and desirable. The scale at which social cooperation and the corresponding governance occur, however, is also important. For the sake of simplicity, scale here is taken to have three main layers: the locality/neighbourhood, districts, and the city as a whole. At each of these layers, institutions of (re)production are identified or created to play a role in governance, according to their main functions. These institutions are simultaneously a node of production, and a node of governance. Our city governance model (Figure 7.2) will therefore be constructed as follows: (re)production functions on the $x$ axis, and the scale of intervention on the $y$ axis. Note that at each scale, the different (re)production functions are integrated by Systems 2 and 3 of the VSM.

Let us now review how the governance of our city would be organised. System 1, and its corresponding set of subsystems, is the realm of *operation*, the process of provisioning and governing that which the system was designed for, (re)production.

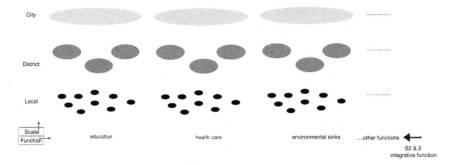

**FIGURE 7.2** Relationship between scale and (re)productive functions

Source: author

System 1 includes all realms of human cooperation that have to do with (re)production in a city: health services, education, care, culture, public spaces, food, ecological transition, and so on. It is the job of public debate to define the criteria and scope of these systems in their given contexts.

What should be kept in mind is that each of the subsystems (1a, 1b, 1c, etc.) corresponds to different functions of (re)production in the city, and that each has a democratic and participatory form of open governance/management, in order to achieve the necessary level of variety. Thus, for example, subsystem 1a – health care at the local level of recursion – would include all institutions or subsets of institutions based at that level which deal with health care in whatever form. The governance/management function of such a subsystem would be carried out by employees and user members of local clinics, trade unionists from workplaces, students and teachers from schools, groups of patients, and so on. The purpose of these would be to manage the health function on that scale in such a way as to explore and implement synergies, evaluate methods, carry out organisational experiments, coordinate critical responses, mobilise networks, and generally address needs.

As one moves up the vertical axis in Figure 7.2, for example to the level of district, city, province, region, and so on, the model is replicated but on a larger scale, for the purpose of addressing specific problems relating to coordination, organisation, resources, and structures. Action is needed, for instance, at the level of the district, city, or region to deal with issues across smaller scales, concerning the distribution of resources, or the reorganisation of health services, or the funding of a hospital serving the entire province, and so on. This is also true at a still smaller scale, below the neighbourhood level, where each organisation can be imagined to use the same VSM to structure its operations. This implies self-organisation on the part of both workers and users, along with a drastic reduction of managerial hierarchy, practices that are well documented (Laloux, 2014). Among these, the case of Buurtzorg is striking.

Buurtzorg is a care foundation established in 2006, in which 10,000 nurses divided into teams of up to 12 members deliver district care in a self-organised manner, even deciding their wages and what equipment to purchase. The foundation outperforms the privatised managerial care industry, drastically improving both the working life of the nurses and the care they provide, by simply throwing away rigid appointment schedules and giving nurses the time and freedom to build relationships with their colleagues and patients, as well as the latter's relatives and neighbours. Over ten years, the foundation has accounted for 80% of the district nurse sector in The Netherlands, and it is currently formulating a model for hospitals.

We have seen that the city produces and exports entropy to its environment as entropic debt. Given this, therefore, the governance of each functional node should be open to subjectivities in the city's environment. The relational links between each operational node of System 1 and its niche environment are essentially of two types: coordination (including the gathering of information) and provision.

System 2 in the VSM coordinates different domains in subsystem 1 such as health, education, culture, and so on. As System 1 is composed of several viable systems, each with its own specific aims and objectives, the task of System 2 is to deal with the inevitable conflicts or problems of coordination that emerge when a plurality of different actors, systems, or units interact. The role of System 2 is to make sure that there are ways to deal with such conflicts, rather than postponing them until they become a real problem. This can also be achieved by helping each operational unit in System 1 to develop a perspective on the needs of other operational units. This will require a variety of tools, such as creating shared vocabularies, information tools and systems, technical standards, and communication protocols.

The role of System 3 is to provide opportunities for seeking, integrating, and optimising synergies among the operational units in System 1. This is the system that continuously pursues a balance between a cohesion of the whole and an autonomy of the parts, so as to make sure that activities coordinated across different operational subsystems are more successful than if those subsystems had been working in isolation. System 3 also establishes a mechanism for resource bargaining and for auditing the components of System 1. It bridges the criteria for decision-making at the operational level with strategic criteria from higher organisational layers, in particular System 5. System 3 can be understood as the assembly of all of the co-producers in System 1 at different levels of recursion, divided into working groups for specific issues. In the case of the diffused governance of a city, System 3 may act as an institutional resource pool at a given level of recursion, where the resources would be allocated in an open and transparent way to reflect public debates about the priorities and goals of social reproduction.

Next, System 4 mobilises the collective intelligence necessary to orient the city in relation to its environment. It seeks to ensure that the whole can rapidly adapt to challenges by creating knowledge about its external/internal environments, formulating plans, strategies, and quality and technological standards, as well as alerting the overall system at different levels of recursion to changes that relate to organisational viability. Whereas Systems 1, 2, and 3 relate to issues that emerge at different scales from inside the city in an immanent temporality, System 4 looks to the outside in an anticipatory temporal framework, meaning, therefore, that the overall system adopts a Janus face (De Angelis, 2019). Its focus is the outside world, anticipating possible challenges as well as modes to which the system could adapt. It looks for threats and opportunities alike, and proposes plans to adapt to new circumstances. System 4 is, therefore, akin to "the steersman at the back of the boat who sees a storm coming and decides to change the rigging and plot a new course through safer waters" (Espinosa and Walker, 2011: 52). It represents the strategic component of collective intelligence.

Finally, System 5 is where the basic purpose, politics, ethos, and identity of the city are worked out and established. Since this purpose is grounded in (re)production, System 5 provides an organisational closure to the whole city system, on the basis of pursuing a transformation of the social and ecological conditions for living. It provides the meta-language necessary to oversee and regulate the interaction between Systems 3 and 4, and must make sure that there is a "balanced debate between S3 and S4 so that the core decisions on strategies and policies are both highly creative (S4 blue sky thinking) and feasible (S3 down-to-earth common sense)" (Espinosa and Walker, 2011: 54). In this sense, System 5 is the ultimate authority of the VSM, and its policies are put into practice as System 3 and System 4, in consultation with each other, carry out their functions.

## 9. The City as a Commons and the Perils it Faces

To posit the city as a commons is to take seriously the idea that its inhabitants can govern it, and that they do so for social and ecological purposes. But as there is no model which is totally impervious to the divisive and exploitative flows of capital, so the model presented here could in principle be used to contravene the very democratic and emancipatory ideas that inspired it. This is especially true in the case of weaker commons movements. The VSM, in particular, has two nodes of meta-management that are prone to the dangers of being co-opted by power. System 3 may turn into a "command and control" trap, which happens when domineering individuals and social forces coalesce in spite of the original purpose and ethos established in System 5, and at the expense of the networks of social cooperation in System 1. System 5, in turn, may be seen through the lens of autocracy. In autocratic organisations (such as corporations), System 5 comes to be taken over by a small privileged group of appointed senior managers. In democratic societies – as in the case of Allende's Chile where the VSM was first adopted (Medina, 2011) – System 5 was the "people" through the representation of the president, parliament, and the workings of the hierarchal state structure. In periods of transition, the city's commons movements may set up systems of governance that resemble the VSM as a shadow of existing governance structures, or as a manifestation of existing dual power, in which case System 5 for the city as a whole would be split between its priorities and purpose. When the politics of the city government is broadly aligned with the priority of social reproduction and democratic governance and participation, it is possible to conceive of commons movements and the city state working together towards a diffused form of city governance, in which case the organs of the municipal state may find suitable relationships with the different, layered systems of a VSM. As is the case for all levels of the VSM, the job of System 5 is to intervene only if meta-norms or agreed policies are being ignored, or are proving ineffective. Ultimately, a city's System 5 can be regarded as the combination of all of its components at different levels of recursion: a broad horizon of openness, nurturing always newer and interconnected forms of inclusive democracy; an assembly of the city's multitude.

## References

Barca, S (2020) *Forces of Reproduction. Notes for a Counter-Hegemonic Anthropocene*. Cambridge: Cambridge University Press.
Beer, S (1981) *Brain of the Firm*. 2nd edn. New York: Wiley.
Bhattacharya, T (2017) *Social Reproduction Theory. Remapping Class, Recentering Oppression*. London: Pluto Press.
Brinkley C (2020) Hardin's Imagined Tragedy is Pig Shit: A Call for Planning to Recenter the Commons. *Planning Theory* 19(1): 127–144.
Caffentzis G (2002) On the Notion of a Crisis of Social Reproduction: A Theoretical Review. *The Commoner* (5), https://thecommoner.org/wp-content/uploads/2020/06/C-Caffentzis-On-the-Notion-of-a-Crisis-of-Social-Reproduction.pdf [last accessed June 2021].
Dalla Costa M and James S (1975) *The Power of Women and the Subversion of the Community*. Bristol: Falling Wall Press.
De Angelis M (2017) *Omnia Sunt Communia: On the Commons and the Transformation to Postcapitalism*. London: Zed Books.
De Angelis M (2019) Social Reproduction and the Transformation at the Edge of Chaos. *South Atlantic Quarterly* 118(4): 747–766.
Espinosa A, Harnden R and Walker J (2005) Cybernetics and Participation: From Theory to Practice. *Systemic Practice and Action Research* 17(6): 573–589.
Espinosa A and Walker J (2011) *A Complexity Approach to Sustainability: Theory and Application*. London: Imperial College Press.
Federici S (2012) *Revolution at Point Zero: Housework, Reproduction, and Feminist Struggle*. New York: PM Press.
Fortunati L (1995) *The Arcane of Reproduction*. New York: Autonomedia.
Hardt M and Negri A (2009) *Commonwealth*. Cambridge, MA: Harvard University Press.
Jessop R (2016) *The State: Past, Present, Future*. Cambridge: Polity Press.
Koestler A (1967) *The Ghost in the Machine*. London: Hutchinson.
Laloux F (2014) *Reinventing Organizations. A Guide to Creating Organizations Inspired by the Next Stage of Human Consciousness*. Brussels: Nelson Parker.
Lowe D, Espinosa A and Yearworth M (2020) Constitutive Rules for Guiding the Use of the Viable System Model: Reflections on Practice. *European Journal of Operational Research* 287(3): 1014–1035.
Medina E (2011) *Cybernetic Revolutionaries. Technology and Politics in Allende's Chile*. Cambridge, MA: MIT Press.

Meuleman L (2008) *Public Management and the Metagovernance of Hierarchies, Networks and Markets*. Heidelberg: Springer.

Savini F (2021) Towards an Urban Degrowth: Habitability, Finity and Polycentric Autonomism. *Environment and Planning A: Economy and Space* 53(5): 1076–1095.

# 8

# HACKING THE LEGAL

The commons between the governance paradigm and inspirations drawn from the "living history" of collective land use

*Giuseppe Micciarelli*

## 1. The battlefield of governance behind the state and the market

When Elinor Ostrom was awarded the Nobel Prize in 2009, concepts such as "self-organisation", "decision-making", "horizontality", "self-regulation", "critique of hierarchy", "decentralisation", "cooperation" and "network" were already central to debates not only within economics, but also in political science (Mayntz, 1998). With the rise of neo-liberalism, these concepts came to be embedded within the paradigm of governance and applied to those interactions and exchanges between institutional networks and economic actors that fell outside of the legal and political borders of the state's authority.

The political theory of governance began to develop during the 1970s as a way of implementing public policies. Critiques of political power as a kind of hierarchical control focused on two lines of discussion around alternative forms of societal governance: "market principles and horizontal self-organization" (Mayntz, 1998: 11). The impacts of this paradigm on the global economy, specifically in building neo-liberal institutions, are well known and widely discussed. Less explored is the dimension of local self-government, where the so-called "third sector" of private, non-profit service organisations experimented with new ways of managing assets and services: this issue was quickly discarded from conceptions of "modern governance", despite also being a part of an anti-hierarchical matrix, or "the spirit of the times, which was set against all manifestations of hierarchical authority, whether by parents, teachers, or the state" (Mayntz, 1998: 12).

An important influence is to be found in the mobilisations of '68, which changed a part of left-wing perspectives: the criticism of hierarchies shed new light on the lexicon of power. For this reason, a certain stereotype has met little resistance when used to account for the market's capture of that culture of desire, immanence and

DOI: 10.4324/9781003160984-12

biopower that originated in those uprisings (an account occasionally corroborated by the uprisings' own leaders). In an equally summary manner, others have criticised the original sin of post-modern anti-statism as inevitably entailing a kind of "neo-liberal fascination" (Zamora, 2014). We cite these critiques because they are aimed at the core of social activism that inspired urban commoning (see, among others, Bollier, 2014; Stavrides, 2017). Indeed, these critiques share an intellectual terrain with those directed, albeit less overtly, at commons governance: given that such governance is built upon a relatively small number of homogeneous communities (Ostrom, 1990), it would run the risk of becoming a neo-liberal Trojan horse (Pennacchi, 2012; Gutiérrez, 2017), functioning to dismantle the state both theoretically and legally (Maddalena, 2020).

These are worthwhile criticisms, which are to be taken seriously. Their error, however, is perhaps in the implicit assumption which – albeit in very different terms – either advocates the "return of the state" or at least laments the lack of focus on power in its sovereign and transcendental form. The issue is that in the neo-liberal revolution, state and sovereignty never left the scene. The strength of neo-liberalism has been its success in fostering an anthropological vision that redesigns social life by shaping it entirely in the mould of valorisation (De Carolis, 2017), in remodelling the state's institutions and authorities according to its rationale (Dardot & Laval, 2015) and in creating a new institutional order that has a private normativity that comes from the world of private powers (Sassen, 2007: 40). This is just the challenge: to rearticulate the powers and tools of the state in other social contexts, and to put public powers at their service, providing them with guarantees and intervening in traditional systems of sanction where necessary (Jessop, 2015). Commons, despite still being a relatively limited experiment, represent a hybrid territory between the public and private realms, capable of transforming both. The epochal transition that undermined the traditional political frameworks of the statist left was the clear separation of public and private, and consequently the dialectic between political and economic, which had articulated how the former saw and handled the latter. Rather than condemning this fracture, we must take advantage of it, understanding not only the dangers, but also the potential of the commons that lies behind the state and the market.

## 2. The style of governance: from corporations to ex-places

Governance is a "new mode of governing", different from and more cooperative than hierarchical control and where state and non-state actors participate in mixed public/private networks (Mayntz, 1998). As a modality, it applies to different environments. Through their involvement, institutions and actors change not only its design and objectives, but also its meaning. Different styles of governance are therefore described by the adjective that qualifies them: "corporate", "good", "local", "participatory". So, governance will here be considered as a paradigm for the new balance of relations between public and private, where neo-liberal "common sense" is hegemonic today but not irreversible. Given this perspective, we will investigate the ways in which the governance of urban commons is either coherent with, or different from, those adjectives of governance aforementioned. It is argued that this may explain some overlooked reasons for why law has become such an important battleground in the claims of commoners, and why, in the legal translation of commons, there lies a narrow red line separating their co-optation by the market (De Angelis, 2010, 2017) from their potential to re-enchant the world (Federici, 2018). A key concept for understanding any system of governance is that of the "stakeholder". In corporate governance this notion meets the new needs of control and remuneration imposed by the increasing diversification of capital within the market. Indeed, corporate governance tends to develop "structures, processes, cultures and systems that engender the successful operation of the organisations" (Keasey, Thompson, & Wright, 1997), oriented to bring the interests of investors and managers into line, and to ensure that firms are run for the benefit of investors (Mayer, 1997).

In local governance, a key factor is the breadth of the group of reference actors. In this case, the "outputs" are the public policies – and the widening of stakeholder-status – targeted at:

> any person, group or organization that can place a claim on an organization's attention, resources, or output, or is affected by that output. Examples of a government's stakeholders are citizens, taxpayers, service recipients, the governing body, employees, unions, interest groups, political parties, the financial community and other governments.
> 
> *(Bryson, 1988: 74)*

The neo-liberal hegemony that also dominates local governance has then not led to a:

> diminishment or a reduction of state sovereignty and planning capacities but a displacement from formal to informal techniques of government and the appearance of new actors on the scene of government (e.g., NGOs), that indicate fundamental transformations in statehood and a new relation between state and civil society actors.
> 
> *(Lemke, 2016: 84–85)*

We can address governance as a subjectification process (Foucault, 1976), so in corporations and local government alike, and therefore when platforms for the distribution of powers developed, we can observe a twofold movement involving both sharing amongst and transformation of the actors involved.

We will consider here only the dimension of local governance. Regarding the public "side", it is argued that one of the peculiarities of local governance is that, since it has to do with the government of a territory, it requires the presence of at least one public actor, and often more. This contributes to disrupting the pyramidal architecture of public powers: municipalities, regions, federal departments, ministries, agencies and so on are intertwined in a definition of competencies that is not always clear. So governance can either act virtuously – by reducing bureaucracy and helping the different levels to develop common strategies – or it can overcomplicate procedures – by turning bargaining over competence into quicksand.

Regarding the private "side", it is clear that a diverse variety of subjects can be addressed as stakeholders. Placing them within the same conceptual frame entails rewriting the norms of political participation. Once again, we must understand this transformation as having both positive and negative effects. On the one hand, qualifying citizens as stakeholders has the consequence of shifting their status from the realm of "rights" to that of "utilities". This conceptual shift benefits those with more wealth and influence because they can claim to be the carriers of different interests, thus multiplying their voice at the expense of those who can "only" be considered as inhabitants of a neighbourhood. Moreover, the universal umbrella of citizenship does not help either: neighbourhood groups, associations and communities can self-organise according to antagonistic schemes, but in wealthy districts, such initiatives can have directly or indirectly market-oriented aims, such as defending investments in real estate (Harvey, 1998: 233). On the other hand, thanks to local governance, citizens have been involved in new decision-making platforms, which are usually only accessible to corporations and lobbies. In addition, citizens have gained access to a new kind of management of public real estate, green areas and in some cases local services. The urban renewal of abandoned premises and real estate is one of the fields where most attention has been paid to participation. In most cases, these are public buildings, which are abandoned because of their huge size and dilapidated condition, and which are very difficult to renovate.

It is on these premises that intense neo-liberal restructuring has been based, which since the 1990s has brought into being not only legislative reforms (Cozzolino, 2021), but also heritage management institutions: *Agenzia del Demanio* and *Patrimonio S.p.a.* are two of the most relevant examples in the Italian context (Settis, 2002). Their hybrid public/private nature has, however, for experts and others, proved difficult to interpret (Ferrari Zumbini, 2010). Neo-liberal literature invested seemingly common-sense concepts, such as rationalisation and valorisation, with meanings that are today known to be anything but neutral, even if they appear so.

This process of institutional replacement and "hetero-direction" by both public and private actors is not without precedent. It represents the application to Western cities of one of the first political dimensions of governance (Arienzo, 2004): the concept of "good governance", developed by the World Bank in its report entitled "Sub-Saharan Africa: From Crisis to Sustainable Growth" (World Bank, 1989). The term's origins are outlined with bewildering superficiality and couched in a paternalistic critique of apparent irresponsibility on the part of the regions described: inability to use foreign aid, criticism of public-sector institutions, poor investment decisions, expensive and unreliable infrastructure (Börzel, Pamuk, & Stahn, 2008). This delegitimisation apparatus, intended to pave the way for "good governance", incriminates not only institutions but the citizens themselves. It is easy to see how similar toxic narratives about the role of the public prepare the ground not only for the sale of its property, but also for the cancellation of its participatory role. Moreover, the equation that links the degradation of ex-places to social decline is a racist device that can be applied simultaneously to parts of Africa and Southern Europe, as well as to the inhabitants of the suburbs (Vesco, 2020).

In these highly unfavourable conditions, participatory regeneration of abandoned spaces is a terrain serving multiple rationalities with multiple legal tools, but they share one element of governance: public and private regulatory co-production (Dardot & Laval, 2015: 372). Italy provides a wealth of examples. Its hermeneutical cornerstone is the "principle of subsidiarity", which presumes that the institutional level closest to the issue at hand is the most appropriate one. Its origin is the so-called "vertical dimension", which originates in the field of European governance as an ordering principle for relations between the Union and the member states. Italy's constitutional reform of 2001 recognised the constitutional principle as a "horizontal" dimension: horizontal subsidiarity means that autonomous initiatives by individuals and associated citizens represent the first level potentially capable of satisfying the general interest, and must therefore be supported by state bodies which nevertheless respect their independence. The application of this principle has, however, also had distorting consequences (Marella, 2013). Nevertheless, the implications of the principle are relevant because they contradict the binary public/private logic:

> [the subsidiarity principle] denies the belief that only the public sphere can take the responsibility to look after collective interests, and, at the same time, disavows the idea that private subjects act only to protect and to guarantee their own egoistic interests.
>
> *(Donati, 2013: 138; my translation)*

## 3. Hack the legal, empower the political

The previous section has illustrated the contest – where neo-liberal local governance uses civic participation for other aims – from which the lexicon of the "urban" commons arises. Now, it is crucial to understand the ways in which commons governance is relatively unique in the framework of participatory policies and, more broadly, its relation to the paradigm of governance as a whole.

First of all, we need to agree on what constitutes urban commons. Unlike in the Common Pool Resources studied by Ostrom, we consider urban commons to be characterised by heterogeneous communities. Furthermore, they are goods wherein the exclusion of potential beneficiaries is the result of a political choice of management, rather than (mainly) of their physical structure. Urban commons are ex-places collectively used by community-based organisations where principles of non-excludability are a political priority linked to a non-rivalistic cooperative governance of rival premises (Micciarelli, 2017a). These are frequently very large, where shared management is an almost rational choice.

Given this perspective, commons governance differs from public and private framings (as well as from civic-based and associative ones): it is a particular form of collective management and action. This means multiple and equal rights of use. So, in the same space, whether simultaneously or in different areas, there might be a theatre, cinema, craft workshops, co-working spaces, and even mutual community centres for education, medical care and legal aid (Stavrides, 2017; Kioupkiolis, 2020).

One of the problems with the many theories on commons is that they have tended to prioritise a socio-economic focus, or dilemmas of political community-making, overlooking the legal instruments that translate them. The law is not merely a container, it shapes the content; it is performative. This means that not only are the rules that commoners (formally or informally) give themselves important, but their compatibility or incompatibility with the more general legal framework is also very relevant. When commoners are legally translated into "private subjects", this also impacts their position as such. Let us draw on an example for clarification. If a collective wants to legally manage an urban space, citizens are almost always forced to set up an association and ask for an assignation. This means an entire system of rules which, as we have observed, has consequences for the process of subjectification: a president must be elected, even if there is no desire to have one; a legal responsible must be identified, even if there is widespread and differentiated responsibility for the type of activities carried out; a system of voting and a quorum must be established even if assemblies are held by consensus and are immediately open to newcomers. This is not to bracket such practices as better or worse forms of governance, but to observe the substantial impacts such differences can have.

It is not the legal instrument that qualifies an urban commons as such; however, the application of different legal tools will necessarily condition those commons. In this way, a private law-based style of governance could incubate a proprietorial mentality instead of deconstructing it, and this would represent a major defeat for commoning.

What is needed is a "creative use of law", or in other words to "hack" the legal proposals made by local authorities or private owners. "Hack" comes from "to cut", "to shred", and when applied to software it shows how a gap can be exploited to change, even in one step, a decisive part of the overall functioning, if not the entire device itself. Hacking is much more than computer expertise: it is a logic, an approach and can be applied to any field, including astronomy as explained in the "Jargon file", a "comprehensive compendium of hacker slang illuminating many aspects of hackish tradition, folklore, and humor" (Jargon File, 2000). To paraphrase, a legal hacker is an expert or enthusiast who enjoys the challenge of creatively overcoming or circumventing legal limitations in order to repair the gaps that can produce ineffective rights. Unlike most people, who only read the law according to the binary logic of compliance or violation, a legal hacker uses law to create access spaces of self-government and people's empowerment. This last stipulation is a significant departure from the "original" Jargon file statement, because it grounds the activity in the construction of a political objective much more than in the personal satisfaction of overcoming software barriers with one's own genius and wit. However, a legal hacker also differs from a traditional lawyer or jurist, who use their expertise for a client. In truth, this approach is a hybrid method that a generation of scholars, not only in law, pursues when engaging in battles involving the civil, social and political rights they care about. Their legal-political activity, which lies in a specific middle ground between advocacy and professional consultancy, has been profoundly changed as one of the corollaries of the new relationship between public and private powers. First, because contemporary rule of law is "court-centred", and therefore in the "litigious explosion" of "judicial governance" (Ferrarese, 2014), many gaps are opened for claiming rights in which even a jurist can act to create leading case and conquer rights. But this is also an era of governance-centred institutions, which has opened regulatory co-production zones that were previously unthinkable. Soft law-making is already an established space for law firms and legal experts to rewrite the rules that characterise the metamorphosis of contemporary law (Catania, 2008).

In this context, hacking the law means making creative use of it to produce selective changes within the legal system, and to implement certain (in this case participatory) processes. Opening a breach between the lines of its own code, it becomes possible to cut and sew norms so that a legal system is forced to recognise actions and powers capable of subverting its "normal" order. Such an expertise thus makes use of multiple skills, both within and outside of the law. Legal hacking is therefore a collective and multidisciplinary approach: at the same time, it is a practice of critical analysis and of co-designing institutions.

Consider the case of the hacking of the administrative system of the city of Naples, where a new legal tool for the collective governance of urban commons was created by activists, citizens and legal hackers: a "collective urban civic use".

The first normative space hacked was inside the field of definitions. One of the main issues regarding the legal translation of the grammar of the commons is that if on the one hand any legal taxonomy which lists them is deficient, there is the risk that existing exclusions will be retained and carried over, thus obstructing, rather than fostering, the emergence of new goods as such. On the other hand, a precise categorisation is juridically essential to defend them, because if everything is a common good, then effectively nothing is (Rodotà, 2012). This also applies to the political dimension of the commons; failing this, we will leave them exposed to legalitarian repression, to co-optation by market demands and to the political benevolence of the administration in power.

On these grounds important attempts have been made, such as those of the so-called Rodotà Commission. Although they had the merit of identifying the connection between common goods and fundamental rights, they also proposed an inadequate taxonomy, underestimating the issues of governance. Instead of disempowering the role of state property as proposed by the Rodotà Commission, which would have exposed the public commons to spoliation through private management (Maddalena, 2020), the best strategy would have been to leverage the opportunities of governance to broaden the range of management: the commons can be considered as state property strengthened by popular participation, and their governance should therefore be withdrawn from the exclusive competence of state bureaucracy.

So, any participatory structure depends on the type of common and on a cooperative structure (Coriat, 2011). The challenge is to conceptualise a cooperative approach that brings benefits not only to the cooperators, but also exponentially to other parts of society as a whole (which I have called one of the "reasonable aporias of the commons", see Micciarelli, 2018). Inserting fragments that bring radical changes to the entire functioning of a system can be qualified thus as a legal hack. Although laws cannot always be changed, they can be interpreted. Article 822 of the Italian Civil Code distinguishes between state property and contingent state property. That is, there are assets that are state property ("demanio necessario") by virtue of the general principles of the legal system, and others that are considered eventual-legal state property ("demanio eventuale") only if and insofar as they belong to the state (roads, motorways, aqueducts, artistic and museum collections etc.). What if we try to substitute the subjective perspective of sovereign state ownership with another subjective perspective, founded on popular control-use? That way, we can qualify as *necessary commons* goods that *must* be rendered (or remain) common for their connection with the exercise of fundamental rights. Their governance must therefore be public in an even wider sense, such as participated in by citizens. There are however also *emerging commons*, or goods that *can be* considered commons, if and insofar as there is a specific governance that qualifies them as such. An abandoned building, for example, is not a common because of its heritage or intrinsic architectural value.[1] It can be qualified as a common if it emerges as such, because it is managed by a particular cooperative governance, aimed at satisfying social and civil rights in a "direct social action", like that which characterises contemporary social movements (Zamponi & Bosi, 2019; Della Porta, 2020). The distinction between necessary and emergent commons enables us to concretise the role of commoners by identifying their powers within the bundle of property rights. Here, too, we use the changes underway in a strategic manner, taking advantage of the studies and practices that in corporate governance have focused on the distinction between ownership and management (Berle & Means, 1932). So, the commons do not need a third ownership regime, but to affect the governance of the public and private spheres.

The "dangerous relations" between governance and the commons are a field to be crossed in a "counter-governance" strategy (Micciarelli, 2014; Napoli, 2015), but how can these be translated? First, we should avoid the language of stakeholders: commoners are citizens (whether formal or migrants) entitled to political participation and the care of collective interests. Second, in urban areas we are dealing with polycentric governance, where citizens, local public entrepreneurs, and public officials are engaged in different ways (Ostrom, Tiebout, & Warren, 1961: 831–832; Ostrom, 2010). The challenge is therefore not to build archipelagos of private commons, but to use patterns of local autonomy to constitute "home-rule", thereby also exerting influence on the functioning of other centres of power, as well as services and spaces of political and economic decision-making. Third, this means avoiding, where possible, assigning real estate to a single legal entity, and instead encouraging multi-stakeholder management or, better still, assembly ecosystems as themselves bodies of self-governance. This last scenario is not a simple option. Legal systems display a certain reluctance in recognising assembly bodies as tools of governance, or at least they do not recognise their effective central role. Of course, there are good reasons for identifying those tasked as responsible and decision-makers in a traditional manner. But these must be balanced against other values and rights, as opposed to discounting everything that such formalism destroys by cutting off practices and experiences in the very social contexts where they are most needed. Consider the assignment of a public use licence to a civic association for the management of a public site. The principles of transparency can be fulfilled (and hacked) in a different way, not through a call for tenders to select the best party (in competition with others), but by legally recognising the rules produced by the commoners as a public-community regulatory co-production. This perspective should also change the relationship between citizens and public officials, who would be accountable not only to the political democratic bodies, but also to the citizen bodies, in a collaborative and anti-authoritative framework. In this way, a new perspective can be brought to Murray Bookchin's extraordinary insights into municipalist democracy. I believe it is this invisible (and very difficult to realise) thread that links the commons to the theoretical framework of neo-municipalism.

## 4. The precious seed under the land (governance)

The hacking method is focused not only on law, but also on the institutional system. The reorganisation of the micro-levels of corporate governance has been the driving force behind a new level of governance brought about by the neo-liberal hegemony creating what I have elsewhere referred to as "free trade governance" (Micciarelli, 2017b). Now it is our turn to pioneer the creation of something different. This approach intersects both diachronically and synchronically with the places and times of different cultures' legal practices, learning from their *ratio legis*. The differences between various legal systems are normally a problem, but for the hacking approach they are an opportunity. Indeed, one can exploit numerous systems of governance by adapting them to different contexts, which often have advanced autochthonous legal tools.

It is in this light that we should look to an ancient living history: rivers and forests operate, in a different scenario, very similar collective and communitarian governance strategies to those discussed here. The importance of such communities is not in the number of agents they are capable of involving, because they might be few, but in their amount and reach. We can propose that they be taken to elucidate some elementary physics of political aggregation.

In the Italian legal framework, civic uses ("usi civici") and collective domains ("domini collettivi") are two names which bring together different institutions for the collective governance of natural resources. More specifically, civic uses designate the rights of use and direct appropriation of benefits that come from natural resources, like collecting wood mushrooms, using water and so on (Nervi, Caliceti, & Iob, 2019). They are accorded and known to each member of a community settled on a specific territory near that resource, e.g. a forest, where they have the right to extract a certain amount of timber, water, mushrooms etc. Civic uses can arise on private, public or collective property and express a qualified relationship between community and resource. The particularity of the rights of civic use lies therefore in the collective character of how each right is imputed. What is interesting, and often underestimated, is that the right of use and the collective governance of land resources are not only "another way of possessing" (Grossi, 1977), but also "another way of governing". Indeed, collective uses have generated "ante litteram local institutions" (De Martin, 1990). So, we may say that urban commons generate "prefigurative institutions" for other models of society, relationships and even economic production.

In Naples, the right of use has been translated as a collective right with a new legal tool: collective urban civic use, employing a constitutionally oriented hermeneutics of substantial equality (De Tullio, 2020) and social function for the right of use which breaks down the monotony of property rights (Capone, 2019). This "legal hack" was designed during the art workers' occupation of the Asilo Filangieri, which started in 2012 and is still ongoing. To achieve this before the law, commoners challenged the approach of two traditional social movements: the form of the collective as avant-garde, and the position that one of the communities should be bound on affinity circuits, which Bookchin called "lifestyle anarchism" (1995). This open governance system was experimented with for three years, during which commoners set up a "declaration of rights", which can be seen as a median path between a "civil constitution" and regulations on the use of a park or other public space. This "in-house" rule-writing is a political matter before it is a legal one. The hacking process is a collective research into the issues that lie behind all assembly practices: who is entitled to use the spaces, how decisions are made, who has the right to propose activities or work inside, taking a position in the public debate, what political actions to support, what are the borders of a community, what is a broader meaning of violence and safe space: elements of political self-reflexivity that are aimed at addressing more than just the efficient management of a property. In the emerging process of this constituency, the draft proposed by commoners is publicly discussed and recognised by public authorities. Instead of attributing a concession to an association, the Neapolitan municipality has, with different administrative acts, recognised this structure as an "emerging commons", considering first the non-exclusive right of the inhabitants to use them. The assembly ecosystem therefore performs the dual function of an organisational-relational mode and is recognised by the municipality as the management body. In this case, both collective land governance systems and commons remind us that the priority is not to identify one or more juridical subjects that hold governance powers, but the governance system itself.

This governance structure does not erase the role of the public, but gives it another function, with very different functions and language compared to the authoritative perspective; it is oriented to ensure that the governance system is not discriminatory or undemocratic, and to set up possible guarantee systems. This latter function, in the concrete experience of Naples, has been assigned to a special body: the "Permanent Citizen Observatory on the Commons, participatory democracy and fundamental rights of the city of Naples", which plays a crucial counter-expertise role in opposing the parallel neo-liberal ideology, and has an advisory function both for the administration and for commoners. Commons, therefore, require special governance, neither public nor private, but in reality more public than private, because they serve collective interests (Marotta, 2013). The public authorities are those which should be participating to support the commoners, and not vice versa.

Collective and urban civic use has now been adopted by eight spaces in the city (constituting about 50,000 square metres overall) and in several others within and outside of Italy: Torino, Alghero, Chieri and Montevideo among others. Moreover, it is claimed to be nationally adopted by many groups in the "emerging commons and civic uses Italian national network".

I will end with two more considerations. First, collective properties are far from exclusive to Western societies. It is interesting to note that urban commoners interpret collective use not from the perspective of property-sovereignty, but as custodians or guardians, a term with echoes in several indigenous legal cultures, from Brazil to New Zealand (Kawharu, 2000). Here lies the importance of redistributing institutional knowledge, and of power within decision-making systems, which the West has erased by colonising the imaginary of democracy.

Second, in the neo-liberal age, self-regulation is not an absolute value. Focusing on alternative land tenures is an attempt to face the challenge of the time, or "the crazy-quilt nature of modern interdependence. And such is the staggering challenge of global governance" (Rosenau, 1995: 15). It gives us the chance to widen our conception of interdependence. I am not just referring to the material interdependence of common pool resources, nor to the economic meaning that binds us within the global economy. The commons indicate the political, social and ecological dimensions of interdependence. I think this issue runs through modernity, even though this point is rarely made explicitly.

The neo-liberal promise of an empowered and self-governing individual unrelated to others is not only illusory, intimately founded on and sustained by inequalities, but it is also untenable if we see it within a system of interdependent relations which encompasses all other living beings. Reconnecting with the land and sharing a post-growth perspective also means taking a step back from the anthropocentric, which in turn would perhaps allow us to better reflect upon humanity. Nature dictates the "governance" of the harvest. It is up to human beings to choose: to ponder how to better relate to nature, for example by rotating the crops so as to make them more productive, or to focus only on their own desires and bring about a "tragedy" which would certainly not be limited to the commons. In these days of pandemic, this should be abundantly clear.

## Note

1 Therefore, in the case of a cultural value that can be connected with the exercise of fundamental rights it can be considered a necessary common if its governance experiments with new agreements between citizens' community and property.

## References

Arienzo A (2004) Dalla corporate governance alla categoria politica di governance. In Borrelli G (ed) Governance. Controdiscorsi. Napoli: Dante & Descartes: 125–162.

Berle A and Means G (1932) The Modern Corporation and Private Property. New York: Commerce Clearing House.

Bollier D (2014) Think Like a Commoner: A Short Introduction to the Life of the Commons. Gabriola Island, BC: New Society Pub.

Bookchin M (1995) Social Anarchism or Lifestyle Anarchism: An Unbridgeable Chasm. Chico, CA: AK Press.

Börzel T A, Pamuk Y and Stahn A (2008) Good Governance in the European Union. Berlin: Working Paper on European Integration.

Bryson J (1988) A Strategic Planning Process for Public and Non-Profit Organizations. Long Range Planning, 21(1): 73–81.

Capone N (2019) L'esperienza dei beni comuni a Napoli e l'inaspettata riscoperta degli usi civici e collettivi. Itinerari amministrativi e nuove prospettive. In Rosati S (ed) Dalle leggi liquidatorie degli usi civici al riconoscimento costituzionale dei domini collettivi. Viterbo: Edizioni Archeoares.

Catania A (2008) Metamorfosi del diritto: Decisione e norma nell'età globale. Rome and Bari: Laterza.

Coriat B (2011) From Natural Resource Commons to Knowledge Commons: Common Traits and Differences. LEM Papers Series 2011/16. Pisa: Laboratory of Economics and Management, Sant'Anna School of Advanced Studies.

Cozzolino A (2021). Neoliberal Transformations of the Italian State: Understanding the Roots of the Crises. London: Rowman & Littlefield.

Dardot P and Laval C (2015) Common: On Revolution in the 21st Century. London: Bloomsbury.

De Angelis M (2010) Crises, Capital and Cooptation: Does Capital Need a Commons Fix? In Bollier D and Helfrich S (eds) The Wealth of the Commons: A World beyond Market and State. Amherst, MA: Levellers Press.

De Angelis M (2017) Omnia Sunt Communia: On the Commons and the Transformation to Postcapitalism. London: Zed Books.

De Carolis M (2017) Il rovescio della libertà: tramonto del neoliberalismo e disagio della civiltà. Macerata: Quodlibet.

De Martin G C (1990) La riscoperta e l'attuale rilevanza delle comunità di villaggio. In De Martin G C (ed) Comunità di villaggio e proprietà collettive. Padua: Cedam.

De Tullio M F (2020) Uguaglianza sostanziale e nuove dimensioni della partecipazione politica. Naples: Editoriale scientifica.

Della Porta D (2020) How Social Movements Can Save Democracy: Democratic Innovations from Below. Cambridge: Polity Press.

Donati D (2013) Il paradigma sussidiario: interpretazioni, estensione, garanzie. Bologna: il Mulino.

Federici S (2018) Re-enchanting The World: Feminism and the Politics of the Commons. Oakland, CA: PM Press.

Ferrarese M (2014) Sulla governance paragiudiziaria: arbitrati e investimenti esteri. Politica del diritto, 3: 375–402. DOI: 10.1437/78909.

Ferrari Zumbini A (2010) L'amministrazione dei beni pubblici dalla conservazione alla valorizzazione. In Mattei U, Reviglio E and Rodotà S (eds) Invertire la rotta. Bologna: il Mulino: 189–246.

Foucault M (1976) La volonté de savoir: l'usage des plaisirs et Le souci de soi. Paris: Gallimard.

Grossi P (1977) Un altro modo di possedere: l'emersione di forme alternative di proprietà alla coscienza giuridica postunitaria. Milan: Giuffrè.

Gutiérrez B (2017) Pasado mañana. Viaje a la España del cambio. Barcelona: Arpa Editores.

Harvey D (1998) L'esperienza urbana (1989). Udine: il Saggiatore.

Jargon File (2000) The On-Line Hacker Jargon File, version 4.2.2. 20 August. Retrieved from https://vanderworp.org/wp-content/uploads/2019/06/jargon.pdf.

Jessop B (2015) The State: Past, Present, Future. Hoboken, NJ: John Wiley & Sons.

Kawharu, M. (2000). Kaitiakitanga: A Maori Anthropological Perspective of the Maori Socioenvironmental Ethic of Resource Management. The Journal of the Polynesian Society, 109(4): 349–370.

Keasey K, Thompson S and Wright M (1997) Introduction: The Corporate Governance Problem – Competing Diagnoses and Solutions. In Keasey K, Thompson S and Wright M (eds) Corporate Governance: Economic and Financial Issues. Oxford: Oxford University Press.

Kioupkiolis A (2020) The Common. Final Report. 'Heteropolitics. Refiguring the Common and the Political' (ERC-COG 2017–2020). Retrieved from http://heteropolitics.net/wp-content/uploads/2020/12/The-Political-1.pdf.

Lemke T (2016) Foucault, Governmentality, and Critique. Abingdon and New York: Routledge.

Maddalena P (2020) La rivoluzione costituzionale. Alla conquista della proprietà pubblica. Reggio Emilia: Diarkos.

Marella R (2013) Pratiche del comune: per una nuova idea di cittadinanza. Lettera Internazionale 116: 24–29.

Marotta S (2013) La via italiana ai beni comuni. Aedon: Rivista di arti e diritto online 1. Retrieved from www.aedon.mulino.it/archivio/2013/1/marotta.htm.

Mayer F (1997) Corporate Governance, Competition, and Performance. In Deakin S & Hughes A (eds) Enterprise and Community: New Directions in Corporate Governance. Oxford: Blackwell Publishers.

Mayntz R (1998) New Challenges to Governance Theory. Jean Monnet Chair Papers. Florence: The Robert Schuman Centre at the European University Institute.

Micciarelli G (2014) I beni comuni e la partecipazione democratica. Da 'un altro modo di possedere' ad 'un altro modo di governare'. Jura Gentium, XI(1): 58–83.

Micciarelli G (2017a) Introduzione all'uso civico e collettivo urbano. Munus, 1: 135–161.

Micciarelli G (2017b) CETA, TTIP e altri fratelli: il contratto sociale della post-democrazia. Politica del diritto, 2/2017: 231–266. DOI: 10.1437/87301.

Micciarelli G (2018) Commoning. Beni comuni come nuove istituzioni. Materiali per una teoria dell'autorganizzazione. Naples: Editoriale Scientifica.

Napoli P (2015) Il comune: un'appartenenza non proprietaria. Alfabeta2. Retrieved from www.alfabeta2.it/tag/yan-thomas/.
Nervi P, Caliceti E and Iob M (2019) Beni e domini collettivi: la nuova disciplina degli usi civici. Milan: Key.
Ostrom E (1990) Governing the Commons: The Evolution of Institutions for Collective Action. Cambridge: Cambridge University Press.
Ostrom E (2010) Beyond Markets and States: Polycentric Governance of Complex Economic Systems. American Economic Review, 100 (June): 641–672. DOI: 10.1257/aer.100.3.641.
Ostrom V, Tiebout C and Warren R. (1961) The Organization of Government in Metropolitan Areas: A Theoretical Inquiry. American Political Science Review, 55(4): 831–842. DOI: 10.1017/S0003055400125973.
Pennacchi L (2012) Filosofia dei beni comuni: crisi e primato della sfera pubblica. Florence: Donzelli.
Rodotà S (2012) Il diritto di avere diritti. Rome and Bari: Laterza.
Rosenau J (1995) Governance in the Twenty-First Century. Global Governance, 1(1): 13–43.
Sassen S (2007) A Sociology of Globalization. New York and London: W.W. Norton & Company Inc.
Settis S (2002) Italia S.p.A: l'assalto al patrimonio culturale. Turin: Einaudi.
Stavrides S (2017) Common Space. The City as Commons. London: Zed Books.
Vesco A (2020) Case Studies in Italy. Final Report. 'Heteropolitics. Refiguring the Common and the Political' (ERC-COG 2017–2020). Retrieved from http://heteropolitics.net/wp-content/uploads/2020/12/Case-Studies-in-Italy.pdf.
World Bank (1989) Sub-Saharan Africa: From Crisis to Sustainable Growth. Report. Washington, DC: World Bank. Retrieved from https://documents1.worldbank.org/curated/en/498241468742846138/pdf/multi0page.pdf.
Zamora D (2014) Critiquer Foucault, Les années 1980 et la tentation néo-libéral. Brussels: Aden.
Zamponi L and Bosi L (2019) Resistere alla crisi. I percorsi dell'azione sociale diretta. Bologna: il Mulino.

# PART 5
# Regulating

# 9
# PLANNING BEYOND THE BACKWASH OF A GROWTH NODE

Old and new thinking in Cambridgeshire, England and Skåne, Sweden

*Yvonne Rydin*

## 1. Introduction

Planning systems have their origins in the management of urban growth. This was true of nineteenth-century Europe and North America and is still true of countries facing rapid urbanisation today. The reliance of planning systems on growth derives from the interface of several arguments: market-led urban development delivers economic growth; such growth delivers public benefits; planning should therefore facilitate urban development; and planning can, at the same time, shape that development to deliver public benefits. The emphasis within planning thus falls on promoting but also regulating urban development to ensure that it contributes to environmental and social sustainability. This approach has been particularly prevalent within the United Kingdom where local authorities have to rely on private sector development to deliver urban change, given the long-term decline in local authority powers and resources since the 1980s. However, it has become increasingly the case that the tools and resources available to local authorities in different national contexts have been curtailed and diminished. This covers the use of public landbanks, public investment in key urban infrastructure and the legitimate use of regulatory powers by public bodies. As a result, local authorities are having to rely more and more on private sector developers for delivering urban change and are less able to influence that change.

Furthermore, the reliance on so-called "planning gain" to deliver a wider range of benefits to the community – from nursery provision to nature reserves, from enhanced landscaping to an element of affordable housing, from high energy and water efficiency measures to local construction employment commitments – this is all increasingly dependent on the market profitability of the development. This alters the power relationship between planners and urban developers and it pushes planning authorities to become reliant on growth for meeting their broader goals.

130  Y Rydin

As we shall see, this embeds a pro-growth stance in local plans. Market-led growth is seen as the solution to the many social problems. However, the spread of growth within a region is neither even nor guaranteed. This is very apparent within the two regions studied in this chapter, Cambridgeshire in eastern England and Skåne in southern Sweden, when considering the ripples of growth outwards from the cities of Cambridge and Malmö.

Figure 9.1 provides a schematic illustration of how growth can be unevenly dispersed from a growth node into the surrounding region. It draws on key features of the two case studies, but does not represent these cartographically; it is a generalisation. In the figure, there are areas of growth and development within the city (represented by the largest circle). This spreads locally through multiplier effects associated with increased local income and employment. However, the figure also

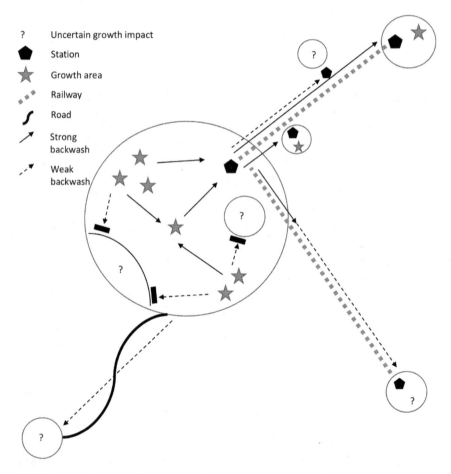

**FIGURE 9.1** A schematic illustration of the limited backwash of local economic growth

Source: author

shows intra-urban areas where these effects do not reach (indicated by?). Blockages (the solid bars) could be the result of poor labour market skills, racism and other prejudices and/or other sources of weak social integration. But the possibilities for the spread or backwash of growth to the surrounding area are also heavily influenced by transport infrastructure, whether rail or road. The figure illustrates a couple of smaller settlements to the top-right where growth arises from business and commuter links with the main city; however, it also indicates a station on this rail link, a settlement on a rail link to the bottom-right and one on a road link to the bottom-left, all of which fail to experience those growth pressures. Where market development pressures are weak, this creates a planning vacuum.

What can a system that is oriented towards planned urban growth do when faced with reduced pressures for such growth? And what lessons does this give us for a post-growth future? This chapter addresses this question by drawing on the experience of Cambridgeshire and Skåne. The analysis relies on a close reading of policy documentation and plans in the two areas, together with contextual research and field knowledge. The purpose of the two cases is to highlight similarities but also contrasts in a way that enhances our understanding of this problematic. The following sections look at the dominance of growth-dependent planning within the growth nodes of Cambridge and Malmö, before going on to consider the implications for the broader county or region. The fourth section considers alternative approaches that emerged in some of the low-growth areas, and the final section uses this to draw out some lessons for post-growth planning.

## 2. The influence of growth-dependent planning

Cambridge is a historic university-dominated town, with limited manufacturing traditionally and within commuting distance of London to the south. The City of Cambridge District Council is tightly drawn around the historic city and its suburbs, and is completely surrounded by the district council of South Cambridgeshire so that the effective urban area spreads out into this neighbouring territory, leap-frogging a green belt in places. Since the 1980s the city has been the focus of the "Cambridge Phenomenon" based on high-tech business spin-offs, with major global technology companies recently locating there alongside multiple smaller start-ups (Baker, 2010; Simmie, 2012; Boddy and Hickman, 2016; Cooke, 2018). In the 1950s and 1960s, local planning for the city embedded the view that the qualities of Cambridge could be best preserved by limiting the growth of the city, and a green belt of about 5 miles' depth was created in 1965. However, from 1969 onward, Cambridge University increasingly questioned this stance. By the mid-1980s the growing importance of research and development (R&D) activities to the economy of the city was recognised (While et al., 2004) and planning strategies began to accommodate some growth, releasing some land from the green belt for R&D activities and proposing two new settlements outside Cambridge.

In 1996 a network of key stakeholders in the city was formed, Cambridge Futures, which produced an influential report: *Cambridge 2020*. The Cambridge

Local Plan of that year made modest shifts towards accommodating growth. Cambridgeshire County Council then commissioned a study on the capacity for new development, the Cambridge Futures Study, and by 2000 the planning agenda had moved to being clearly pro-growth. In 2001 a Greater Cambridge Partnership was formed, a Cambridge Sub-Region Study was commissioned and Cambridge University announced plans for a new development on land it owned in the green belt in north-west Cambridge, now called Eddington (Morrison, 2013). By 2003, the Cambridgeshire and Peterborough Structure Plan actively planned for growth in a new settlement and urban extensions, and the 2006 Cambridge Local Plan then identified land releases from the green belt for five sites, complemented by the South Cambridgeshire District Council Local Development Framework of 2008. From this point, work moved forward on developing a number of different sites around the city; science and business park development also proceeded. The City of Cambridge and the surrounding district of South Cambridgeshire have continued to work together to create local plans that reinforce each other in providing for considerable growth.

Turning to Malmö, the history is one of late-nineteenth-century industrialisation, late-twentieth-century decline and twenty-first-century regeneration. In contrast to England, industrialisation and urbanisation happened much later in Sweden (Goldfield, 1986). Industrial suburbs were built in the larger cities at the end of the nineteenth century with blocks of very small, low-quality flats (kåkstader). In the early twentieth century, the cooperative housing movement, together with municipalities and Municipal Building Companies, became significant housing providers. After World War II, there was a functional separation of land uses (Qviström and Bengtsson, 2015), with a heavy emphasis on car-based urbanisation (Lindelöw et al., 2016). The Million Programme during 1965–74 saw massive housebuilding led by the municipalities, often in slab form and on the outskirts of cities. Examples of this are found in the suburbs of Malmö.

Until the 1970s, the city continued to be characterised by heavy industry, focussed around shipbuilding and the port, but shipbuilding and other key industries closed down and, from the 1970s to the mid-1980s, Malmö lost 36,000 residents and, in the 1990s, 30,000–40,000 industrial jobs. The city then underwent a remarkable transformation. The Öresund bridge/tunnel was constructed connecting the city with Copenhagen by road and fast train services. This supported major urban regeneration efforts in the old shipbuilding area of the Western Harbour and, more recently, at Hyllie to the south. "The transition of Malmö from a city in decline to a city of growth has been acknowledged internationally, and the city has won recognition for its successful urban policy" (Nylund, 2014: 43). Malmö's vision, as expressed in the current Comprehensive Municipal Plan, is to be dense, green and connected, with major development planned within the existing city and also at the major extension of Hyllie.

Most commentators see Swedish municipalities as able to exercise considerable discretion and control in their local planning (Söderholm and Pettersson, 2011), and to adopt flexible but rapid decision-making (Hrelja et al., 2012). Relationships between tiers of government are interactive rather than hierarchical (Balfors et al., 2018) so that Hrelja et al. argue that Swedish local authorities "hold a powerful position in relation to the national Swedish goals" (2012: 126). This contrasts with the situation in England where local plans must comply with central government guidance in the National Planning Policy Framework. Furthermore, Malmö, in common with many larger municipalities in Sweden, has the benefit of significant landownership to help fulfil this vision (even if this has reduced compared to the twentieth century; Barlow, 1990). It has been estimated that 11% of Swedish municipalities own all the land where housebuilding is planned in their areas and 75% of municipalities own some land, although this varies considerably with municipal ownership being higher in the three main metropolitan areas of Stockholm, Gothenburg and Malmö (Caesar, 2016). This contrasts with the situation in England where, for over four decades now, public authorities including local authorities have been encouraged to sell off their landholdings and often forced to do so due to fiscal pressures.

Although both cities have examples of well-designed, functional and environmentally sustainable new urban areas, there have been concerns in both places over how the different social groups within the cities have fared. In Cambridge, much of the new build is occurring in a rising housing market with limited provision of affordable housing. This is in the context of Cambridge having an affordability ratio of 12.97 compared to the national average of 7.72 (house prices to annual workplace-based earnings, 2016). The latest report updating the Quality Charter used to guide design and planning of new major developments recommends a maximum of 30% affordable housing within any development and that this should be oriented towards key workers including an element of owner-occupation (Falk, 2019). But the definition of key workers has proved contentious in the Cambridge context. Nationally this term is used to cover health, education and other public service workers where average salaries adversely affect access to housing. However, with the new settlement of Eddington, Cambridge University successfully argued that research workers within the university counted as key workers, so that this development caters heavily to postgraduates, postdoctoral fellows and research staff (Morrison, 2013).

Similar concerns have been raised about developments in Malmö. Policy shifts since the 1980s have led to development for higher-income residents being prioritised over housing equality (Soneryd and Lindh, 2019) and income gaps have increased faster than the national average (Nylund, 2014). This is in the context of weak social integration within the city. The city has received many international migrants over recent years and the share of foreign-born residents in Malmö doubled over 1995–2012. Malmö Stad acknowledges the problems of spatial segregation, inequality and uneven employment, with fears for a negative impact on the city's economic fortunes (Nylund, 2014: 49). Planning policy has, since 2012, used densification, public transport and the design of public places as key strategies to deal with these social problems, focussing on connectivity across the city and promoting "a whole city".

In both cases, the influence of developers and landowners in pro-growth local planning is apparent. The English planning system is highly reactive, responding to development proposals put forward by developers and landowners. There is limited public landownership to direct development and although local plans identify sites for development this does not preclude other sites coming forward. There is a strong presumption in favour of development arising from central government guidance and the requirement to demonstrate a 5-year land supply for housebuilding. In Cambridge, the local authorities have been involved in key stakeholder networks, including major developers, to guide the growth of the city and have a long-running engagement with Cambridge University, as a major local landowner who is supportive of such growth. In Sweden, as indicated already, there is the scope for municipal landownership to play a larger role; however, Caesar (2016) has outlined how land allocation agreements between the developer and the municipal landowner now link the creation of development rights through drawing up a Local Detailed Plan with a land transfer, encouraging the involvement of developers in the preparation of this plan (see also Metzger and Zakhour, 2019). Nylund notes that local plans emphasise that, "it is important to have an open and positive attitude to initiatives emanating from property owners and developers" (2014: 54) and Koglin and Pettersson (2017) also suggest that the need to discuss building projects with private developers limits the formal power of the local planning monopoly and that Swedish planners have less power than 10–15 years ago.

## 3. Regional implications of relying on growth nodes

If Cambridge and Malmö exemplify growth-dependent planning, how does this impact on the wider region within which they are located? In examining this area, the research covered all 6 district councils within Cambridgeshire (East Cambridgeshire, South Cambridgeshire, Huntingdonshire, Peterborough and Fenland, in addition to Cambridge); in Skåne, there are 33 municipalities so the focus was on those that were benefitting less from growth, specifically 7 municipalities where the unemployment rate was at or above the regional average (Helsingborg, Landskrona, Eslöv, Burlöv, Åstorp and Perstorp, in addition to Malmö), together with 2 of the geographically larger municipalities (Kristianstad and Hässleholm). The English districts covered range from 88,000 (East Cambridgeshire) to just over 203,000 (Peterborough) in population, whereas the Swedish *kommuner* ranged from over 330,000 (Malmö) to as low as 7,500 (Perstorp).

In Cambridge, rail links are an important part of the growth plans. The existing guided bus system passes by the main railway station before heading south to the new developments alongside the medical and research campuses or north-west to the science and business parks and then on to Huntingdon. There is a relatively new station on the main route to the north of the city, again near science and business parks, and another planned for the major developments to the south, on the Cambridge–London section. However, this leaves areas not served by rail or the guided busway less connected to the city and its growth overflow. In Malmö, there is also a major north–south rail route, here going south to Copenhagen and north to Gothenburg, via the university city of Lund and the major international port of Helsingborg. There are other rail routes into the centre of Skåne and to the northeast, heading to Stockholm, but this still leaves areas that are not well-connected and less able to benefit from the backwash of Malmö's growth pressures.

The nature of regional planning varies between the two contexts. In England there are no elected regional bodies; however, the county council of Cambridgeshire is long-established and in 2017 a Combined Authority was created from Cambridgeshire County Council and Peterborough City Council. This has provided a planning framework for the whole county – *Towards a Sustainable Growth Strategy to 2050* – which recognises the significant patterns of inequality in the county (Cambridgeshire and Peterborough Combined Authority, n.d.: 7):

> More deprived areas cluster to the north and within Cambridge and Peterborough themselves (indeed, Cambridge is ranked as the least equal city in the UK based on income and wealth). Peterborough and Fenland each contain areas that are among the 10% most deprived nationally.

However, the response remains growth-oriented, albeit termed inclusive growth. The aim is "healthy, thriving and prosperous communities" and there are three strands to this strategy: improved accessibility by bus and rail; new development in certain settlements, including the small market towns; and better training and education of the labour force. Commercial development is encouraged in two Enterprise Zones (where fiscal incentives and a relaxed planning consent regime operate) and, in the longer term, there are hopes for the ARC project developing a whole arc of development from Oxford to Cambridge via Milton Keynes, again based partly on a rail link.

In Malmö, a similar pattern can be found. The region of Skåne has the most fertile agricultural land in Sweden and an economy where agriculture and tourism are significant, but Skåne's unemployment rate in 2018 was 4.9% compared to 3.7% for Sweden as a whole. Sweden has a system of regional governance with 21 elected regions in place. Region Skåne was formed in 1995, supplementing a local federation of municipalities in South West Skåne. It has promoted transport-oriented development as the main strategy for regional development (Qviström and Bengtsson, 2015). The railway has been of historic importance in Skåne (Qviström, 2012), but this strategy also reflects a desire to tie in more of the region to the urbanisation in Malmö; Qviström and Bengtsson, when discussing the small rural municipality of Skurup, noted the desire to promote access to a "pulsating city life" (2015: 2528). There are currently two key documents setting out a vision for the region: *Open Skåne 2030* (Region Skåne, 2015) and *The Structural Picture for Skåne* (Region Skåne, 2010), itself a combination of other documents and plans. Both of these seek to combine a commitment to growth with goals of sustainability and equality and use the term "growth motor" to describe the vision of Skåne. Polycentric patterns of urban development are planned, which it is argued will deliver more sustainable mobility, areas where quality of life can be enhanced and economic-environmental win-win options. Although *Open Skåne 2030* mentions the importance of creating "tomorrow's welfare service", the main way to generate better social outcomes is through economic growth.

Turning to the district level and moving to the north of Cambridge, both the districts of Huntingdonshire and Peterborough aim straightforwardly for market-led growth with increased housebuilding and business development. Again, the aim is for this development to be high quality, well designed, locally distinctive and sustainable and the social goals are to rebalance the local population (which is skewed towards the elderly) and give people opportunities for healthy lifestyles, active community participation and high quality of life. Although laudable, it is not clear how the market-led development will deliver this. Once one moves to the east and north-east of Cambridge, the social problems increase and the levels of economic activity fall. The local plan for Fenland, a rural and sparsely populated district, begins with a litany of the severe health problems that the local population face: low life expectancy for men, childhood obesity, and high levels of diabetes, road injuries/deaths and alcohol-related hospital stays. This is Cambridgeshire's most deprived district, ranking 94th of 326 nationally (1st being most deprived). Yet the local plan still sees growth – with market-led urban development – as the solution to a variety of economic and social problems: jobs, labour market participation, infrastructure provision, health inequalities, education, service provision for an elderly population and out-migration. The proposed development is to be concentrated on the existing market towns but a flexible attitude to development elsewhere is also proposed. The challenges of attracting such development to a low-income area are not fully addressed.

In Sweden, the municipality of Burlöv, which is contiguous with Malmö, plans to build new mixed-used areas around the three railway stations within the municipality; they see themselves sharing in the regional growth emanating from Malmö and foresee a more cosmopolitan character for the area. In Helsingborg, the plan sets out the vision for spatial planning and urban development which has almost become a planning orthodoxy in Sweden: a polycentric urban structure; a dense mixed-use, multi-functional urban form; transport-oriented development; improved connectivity across the area; and high-quality development and public realm. Taken together these are intended to attract residents, visitors and businesses, and also promote sustainable patterns of urban development. A similar vision can be found in the paired plans for Hässleholm and Kristianstad, who see themselves as a joint growth-engine in the east of Skåne for the wider region, and in Eslöv, which frames itself as a "regional star" due to its central location in the region. There are a few municipalities where the emphasis is mainly on enhancing connectivity through the rail system. Landskrona seeks to promote new development between the city centre and the station to cater for those commuting between Malmö and Helsingborg; Perstorp takes a similar line. Here there is less emphasis on attracting economic growth but rather a reliance on commuting to attract residential growth. These Swedish plans reinforce the point made by Hrelja et al. (2012) that private developers and commercial interests have a strong, even increasing influence on urban planning because the perception of fierce competition between cities leads to municipalities being reluctant to turn down any development proposals.

Thus, the planning system beyond the growth nodes in both areas continues to rely on urban growth and development, led by market signals, to resolve problems of unequal economic and social development. Many of these plans look frankly implausible, waiting for market interest in new development which may never come. And once it is recognised that market demand is weak and land values are low, then the potential for negotiating community benefits also weakens. In the review of the Cambridgeshire Quality Charter, Falk (2019) argues that affordable housing requirements should be reduced in such low-demand areas, even though these are often the areas with greatest needs.

## 4. Beyond the backwash of growth nodes

The problem of planning being dependent on urban growth and market-led development extends from the growth nodes themselves out into the urban hinterland, and this is linked to the role that private sector developers and landowners play in both promoting urban development projects and shaping local or municipal plans that set out visions for these local areas. In both cities, this does result in high-quality new urban developments with environmental sustainability features. However, it does not help address the social problems of housing need, inequality and social segregation that both cities and their hinterlands experience. Nor does it contribute to a new model of local economic development, which remains heavily reliant on exogenous investments into local areas. There are some alternatives present, though, and these suggest pathways that are less growth-dependent. Although small-scale and tentative, they may suggest lessons for post-growth planning.

East Cambridgeshire District Council stands out from the other Cambridgeshire local authorities in this respect. It also proposes new development; however, it gives a key role to community-led development through Community Land Trusts (CLTs). A CLT involves joint community ownership of a development site. As landowner they are able to exercise more control over the development and benefit from future increments in land values. The key feature here is the creation of a long-term landownership right in local development. East Cambridgeshire has a CLT structure supported by East Cambridgeshire Community Housing, which is now part of the Combined Authority. Under an umbrella CLT there are nine active local CLTs across the county, seven of which have developments completed or at an advanced stage. For example, the Swaffham Prior CLT was set up expressly over concerns at the village becoming a dormitory settlement reliant on commuting and with a lack of affordable housing. In partnership with Hundred Houses Housing Association and Iceni Homes (a private developer) they have built 20 dwellings, 8 of them affordable. The Stretham and Wilburton CLT (SWCLT) aims for 30% of its Camp's Field development to be held by the CLT in perpetuity for local households. Other CLTs go beyond housebuilding: SAVE aims to protect and enhance the Soham Community Theatre and the Manor Farm development by SWCLT includes a doctor's surgery and flexible units for small and medium enterprises (SMEs).

This approach is not without its limitations. It is not a solution to the most severe housing needs; rather it provides for local people to live and work locally. Communities typically favour lower-density developments that combine market and affordable housing to create a social mix. The mix of housing also allows for cross-subsidisation of affordable by market housing but works best in relatively higher-value areas. The ability to bargain with landowners for lower land prices is partially dependent on the planning system being able to demonstrate a five-year housing land supply elsewhere; i.e. market development occurring elsewhere in the district. But it does offer an alternative to reliance on market-led development.

A rather different use of landownership was highlighted in Sweden, showing the importance of using municipal land to provide subsidised premises for SMEs as a way to support the local economy through endogenous growth; this provides a different model of local economic development to a reliance on inward investment. Rents are set by the council rather than the market and sometimes premises are tailored to the specific needs of a business. Land is also sometimes available for sale, connected to land use policies set out in the municipal plan. This approach was evident in Eslöv's municipal plan and also in tiny Åstorp, which sought to reduce the level of commuting by diversifying the local economy. The significance of this approach is that it seeks to meet the needs of SMEs and new local start-ups, rather than enabling commuting to urban growth nodes. It was particularly notable in the smaller municipalities and was often combined with other forms of local business support such as networking, training and mentoring, crowdfunding, guidance on regulation and tax reductions. Kristianstad has developed an Incubator and Science Park as a municipality-owned business in connection with the local university. Unlike the Cambridge science parks, this was linked to the local agricultural hinterland through a focus on food, environment and health; it had over 100 tenants and connections with over 1,500 firms in the food industry. Of course, business support was also found in Cambridgeshire but this was much less well integrated into the local planning system and less focussed on using public land and premises.

## 5. Implications for post-growth planning

This chapter has illustrated the continued dependence on growth as a driver for delivering wider community benefits and the associated limitations, particularly with regard to ensuring social equity and cohesion. It acknowledges the need for strong planning action in areas where there is sufficient market demand to drive such growth, action which uses the resources of municipal landownership and regulation to ensure the availability of affordable housing, as well as measures that contribute to environmental sustainability. However, even in such high-demand areas, there remain concerns. First, such development involves major resource use and thus a sustainability perspective demands attention to how such resource use can be minimised, say through circular economy or lean design principles and/or a greater emphasis on re-use of the existing built stock. Second, it is notable how arguments about housing need are often misused in the context of growth-dependence, relying on tropes about trickle-down within the housing market and the need for tenure and social mix in the name of social cohesion. This fails to recognise the urgency of providing sufficient low-cost housing to meet needs and ensuring that it will remain low-cost over time. Limiting the extent of low-cost housing, emphasising owner-occupation or shared ownership as a tenure, and using gentrification as a measure of success all contribute instead to inequitable social outcomes.

This chapter also emphasised the importance of looking beyond the areas subject to growth pressures and considering how to plan for well-being here. The two areas studied showed the continued reliance on links to growth areas for a planning solution, either hoping to draw some of that growth to the low-demand area or relying on commuting into the growth area. These proposals either exacerbate the problems of growth-reliance or, frankly, seem unrealisable. However, the two cases also point to other possible ways of working. In Skåne, the value of municipality landownership was clear, particularly in terms of providing premises for local SMEs. In Cambridgeshire, the role of CLTs provides a new way of developing housing and business premises for local residents and SMEs. The first conclusion this draws us to is the importance of landownership and how it is used. It is possible to use municipal landownership to support endogenous growth rather than inward investment and ensure the provision of services. It can also be used to support common forms of ownership as exemplified in the CLTs. This suggests that local planning in post-growth conditions needs to engage directly with landownership issues, seeking to diversify such ownership and link the planning of new development for housing, local businesses and services to how land is owned, by whom and to what ends. Public sector landownership can be a vital local resource to support this. In lower-growth locations, land will be cheaper and thus municipalities could look to retaining and/or building their land banks so as to be able to be proactive in such support.

This implies a form of governance that works across sectors but in a different way to the municipality–developer nexus of pro-growth planning. Rather connections between civil society and developers, with the support of local authorities, were central to the efficacy of CLTs in Cambridgeshire; and connections between local authorities and the smaller business community were central to supporting endogenous growth of local economies outside the influence of the growth nodes. Both these forms of governance need to supplement or even replace the corporatism involving larger-scale economic and ownership interests that is more typically found. This reinforces the importance of working with small-scale local stakeholders and asserting the value of small-scale initiatives. Local plans tend to focus on the major urban developments that will accommodate growth rather than looking to the smaller-scale ways that well-being can be promoted. Post-growth planning needs to look beyond the control and management of new urban development to forms of urban management, i.e. management of existing (often smaller) places for the well-being of local residents and businesses. This would be a significant re-orientation as many urban planning systems have seen their raison d'être in the management of growth pressures.

It would also imply a shift away from conventional indicators of success in terms of rising property prices and increased value-added as measured by economists for several reasons. First, there may be a need for an element of subsidy, at least initially, to support post-growth local initiatives. Second, such initiatives typically involve considerable non-monetary resources in the form of the time, labour and expertise of local civil society and business communities. These in-kind resources are not directly valued by the market but should be recognised for their essential contribution. Third, there is a need to delink local government finance from the direct or indirect monetary benefits of urban development, suggesting a fundamental reform of how local government is financed. In England, local authorities get about half their income from central government grants, with the rest coming from council taxes (a property tax paid by local residents) and a share of Business Rates, the property tax on local commercial property. It has been recent government policy to increase the share of Business Rates revenue that stays with the local authority; this, of course, encourages them to permit more and higher-value commercial development in order to get more funds, further feeding into the growth-dependent paradigm. By contrast, in Sweden municipalities have a quite considerable tax base; they can levy a tax on the income of local residents and currently this is around 33%, about two-thirds of which goes to the municipality. This provides financial scope for supporting the smaller-scale well-being measures, provided the political will is there.

Finally, what are the implications of such a shift in emphasis for the regional scale? The polycentric model of regional growth has become widely embedded in planning culture, as has the value of enhancing accessibility across a region for the benefits to economic development. These models explicitly connect the well-being of low-growth areas with the growth of selected nodes. Regional planning needs to go beyond this and consider that the "holes" in the polycentric structure are not just absences – not-yet-connected to the growth nodes – but rather areas with the potential for an innovative form of management through planning, harnessing local resources and meeting local needs. This would mean a more central role for models of endogenous growth within regional planning rather than using connectivity at the regional scale to try to drive more inward investment to areas.

## References

Baker ARH (2010) Controlling the Growth of Cambridge (UK): Challenges to Planning Its Built Environment. *Annales de Géographie* 119(673): 293–304.

Balfors B, Wallström J, Lundberg K et al. (2018) Strategic Environmental Assessment in Swedish Municipal Planning. Trends and Challenges. *Environmental Impact Assessment Review* 73: 152–63.

Barlow J (1990) Owner-Occupier Housing Supply and the Planning Framework in 'Boom Regions': Examples from Britain, France, and Sweden. *Planning Practice & Research* 5(2): 4–11.

Boddy M and Hickman H (2016) The 'Cambridge Phenomenon' and the Challenge of Planning Reform. *The Town Planning Review* 87(1): 31–52.

Caesar C (2016) Municipal Land Allocations: Integrating Planning and Selection of Developers while Transferring Public Land for Housing in Sweden. *Journal of Housing and the Built Environment* 31(2): 257–75.

Cambridgeshire and Peterborough Combined Authority (2018) Towards a Sustainable Growth Strategy to 2050. https://naturalcambridgeshire.org.uk/wp-content/uploads/2018/10/cpca-strategic-spatial-framework.pdf (accessed 6 January 2022).

Cooke P (2018) Generative Growth with 'Thin' Globalization: Cambridge's Crossover Model of Innovation. *European Planning Studies* 26(9): 1815–34.

Falk N (2019) *Refreshing the Cambridgeshire Quality Charter for Growth*. London: Urbed Trust.

Goldfield DR (1986) Metropolitan Planning in Sweden, 1890–1945: The European Context. *History of European Ideas* 7(4): 335–51.

Hrelja R, Isaksson K and Richardson T (2012) IKEA and Small City Development in Sweden: Planning Myths, Realities, and Unsustainable Mobilities. *International Planning Studies* 17(2): 125–45.

Koglin T and Pettersson F (2017) Changes, Problems, and Challenges in Swedish Spatial Planning—An Analysis of Power Dynamics. *Sustainability* 9(10): 1836.

Lindelöw D, Koglin T and Svensson Å (2016) Pedestrian Planning and the Challenges of Instrumental Rationality in Transport Planning: Emerging Strategies in Three Swedish Municipalities. *Planning Theory & Practice* 17(3): 405–20.

Metzger J and Zakhour S (2019) The Politics of New Urban Professions: The Case of Urban Development Engineers. In Raco M and Savini F (eds) *Planning and Knowledge: How New Forms of Technocracy Are Shaping Contemporary Cities*. Bristol: Policy Press: 181–96.

Morrison N (2013) Reinterpreting the Key Worker Problem within a University Town: The Case of Cambridge, England. *The Town Planning Review* 84(6): 721–42.

Nylund K (2014) Conceptions of Justice in the Planning of the New Urban Landscape – Recent Changes in the Comprehensive Planning Discourse in Malmö, Sweden. *Planning Theory & Practice* 15(1): 41–61.

Qviström M (2012) Contested Landscapes of Urban Sprawl: Landscape Protection and Regional Planning in Scania, Sweden, 1932–1947. *Landscape Research* 37(4): 399–415.

Qviström M and Bengtsson J (2015) What Kind of Transit-Oriented Development? Using Planning History to Differentiate a Model for Sustainable Development. *European Planning Studies: European Creative Regions* 23(12): 2516–34.

Region Skåne (2010) Structural Picture of Skåne – Future Challenges. https://utveckling.skane.se/siteassets/publikationer_dokument/strukturbild_future_challenges.pdf (accessed 6 January 2022).

Region Skåne (2015) Open Skåne 2030. https://utveckling.skane.se/publikationer/strategier-och-planer/the-open-skane-2030---skanes-regional-development-strategy/ (accessed 26 February 2021).

Simmie J (2012) Learning City Regions: Theory and Practice in Private and Public Sector Spatial Planning. *Planning Practice & Research* 27(4): 423–39.

Söderholm P and Pettersson M (2011) Offshore Wind Power Policy and Planning in Sweden. *Energy Policy* 39(2): 518–25.

Soneryd L and Lindh E (2019) Citizen Dialogue for Whom? Competing Rationalities in Urban Planning, the Case of Gothenburg, Sweden. *Urban Research & Practice* 12(3): 230–46.

While A, Jonas AEG and Gibbs DC (2004) Unblocking the City? Growth Pressures, Collective Provision, and the Search for New Spaces of Governance in Greater Cambridge, England. *Environment and Planning A: Economy and Space* 36(2): 279–304.

# 10
# PLANNING LAW AND POST-GROWTH TRANSFORMATION

*Jin Xue*

## 1. Introduction

Degrowth scholars have exposed and scrutinized the many inherent structural driving forces for the current growth dependency and fetishism (Fotopoulos, 2007; Foster, 2011; Jackson, 2009). Apart from offering a critique of existing structures, degrowth scholars have in recent years explored and proposed structural changes to facilitate the emergence of a post-growth economy (Dietz and O'Neill, 2013; Jackson, 2009; Raworth, 2017; Victor, 2018). Among these contributions, very few studies have been undertaken on what role legal structures may play in either maintaining the growth economy or providing the necessary conditions for post-growth transformation (see overviews by Cosme et al., 2017; Kallis et al., 2018; Weiss and Cattaneo, 2017). When it comes to planning as a potentially essential, yet underexplored, institution to drive post-growth transformation, an emerging scholarship has begun to discuss the implications of a post-growth society paradigm for planning (Lehtinen, 2018; Wächter, 2013; Xue, 2018, 2021). Nevertheless, this engagement has not yet discussed the legal dimension of planning.

Against this background, the chapter seeks to address the role of the legal structure of planning in driving and hindering societal transformation towards post-growth. The chapter will contextualize the investigation within the Norwegian planning practice, i.e. the Building and Planning Act 2008 (PBA 2008). Norway is a relevant case to the post-growth debates given its high affluence level. In addition, as a traditional welfare state being gradually neoliberalized over the past few decades, its planning institutions may indicate both potentials for and obstacles to the transition to post-growth. Specifically, the chapter investigates the following core questions:

(1) How do the structure and contents of the planning system as regulated in the PBA 2008 provide hindrances and potentials for post-growth transformation?
(2) What are the ideological bases underlying the PBA 2008 and their conditioning effects on post-growth transformation?

Section 2 will attempt to spell out the foundations for planning law in light of post-growth thinking, so as to provide a framework to assess the potentials and barriers in the planning law. The analysis in section 3 will focus on the structure and contents of the Norwegian planning system as regulated in the act and evaluate the extent to which they, through regulating planning practices, preserve the continuity of the growth society and provide potentials for change in social orders towards post-growth. In section 4, the analysis will move from the written to the unwritten in the act and address the ideology underlying the planning law. Here, law is understood, to some extent, as a reflection of social values and moral imperatives which justify and legitimate certain planning rationalities and principles while silencing others. Section 5 brings in a broader reflection on the essences of a post-growth planning law and briefly reflects on the relation between reconstruction of law, culture and agency.

## 2. Post-growth, law and planning

### 2.1 Post-growth and legal structures

Although legal structures are an essential and complementary element of a systematic change towards post-growth, they have not drawn much attention within the degrowth debates. Compared to studies focusing on the political, economic and cultural structures, very little has been written on what role legal structures can play in providing conditions for transition beyond growth capitalism. A few exceptions include discussions on implications of degrowth for ecological law (Garver, 2013), human rights law (Candiago, 2013) and public international law (Vandenhole, 2018). These studies indicate that the existing legal frameworks in the aforementioned fields have deficiencies when being scrutinized from the post-growth perspective, and suggest that new foundations for the laws should be set according to post-growth principles. Rather than focusing on the law per se, Alexander (2013) directs attention to the necessary forces that can effectively drive the reformation of legal structures. He argues that the structural change of law beyond growth is dependent on the realization of the emergence of a post-consumerist culture. Alexander perceives law, though not purely, but to a significant extent, as a reflection of the dominant culture and values. As such, the mobilization of law reform towards post-growth can only be possible if social movements lead to a cultural revolution of simplicity and sufficiency in consumption.

### 2.2 The foundations of post-growth planning law

So, what grounds does a radically different starting point of post-growth provide for the planning law?

## Finity – the ontology about the world

Acknowledging the existence of ecological constraints, a new ontology of a stratified world introduces a hierarchal structure between the ecological, social and economic, where the social is a sub-system of the ecological and the economic is only part of the human society. Although the social and economic systems are dependent on and constrained by the ecological system, there is not a vice versa relationship. Based on this ontology, post-growth gives prominence to the ecological over the social, and the economic is seen as a means to achieve the social goals and is constrained by ecological limits (Schneider et al., 2010). The legal structures should therefore reflect and be based on how the ecological, social and economic systems function. The perception of a stratified world should underline the ontological foundation to planning law. Furthermore, this ontology on finity necessitates downscaling of human economic activities in terms of the levels of production and consumption, which sets the normative ground for making planning decisions. Associated with this is the priority of satisfying basic needs (food, clothing, shelter, water supply, sanitation, healthcare, jobs) rather than promoting higher consumption and living standards. A post-growth planning law requires the promotion of values that encourage consumption standards that are within the bounds of the ecologically possible.

## Justice – the ethical premise

Post-growth further argues the ethical premises of downscaling, that is the justice within and between generations and across species (Martinez-Alier, 2012). Humans' moral obligations over time, across spaces and species constitute the ethical grounds for the need of reducing consumption (Arler, 2006). Substantial reduction in consumption of natural resources and generation of wastes and scraping unsustainable lifestyles and values in rich countries are necessary, if ecological space is to be left for poor countries, future generations and non-human species. This sets a new ethical ground for planning law that should offer protection against failures in the satisfaction of basic needs and a ceiling on inequality (i.e. the allowed gap between the rich and poor). The former is a negative obligation (to prevent dissatisfaction of basic needs) and the latter is a positive obligation (to fulfil equality) (Vandenhole, 2018), and the former alone cannot guarantee a just outcome.

## Redistribution – the approach to justice within limits

To achieve justice and meanwhile stay within planetary boundaries can only be possible by redistributing resources and wealth. The importance of redistribution in the post-growth society necessitates a multi-scalar strategy and a certain level of power centralization. There are several reasons for this (Strand and Næss, 2016; Xue, 2014): (1) the centralized power can set limits and higher-order constraints for actions taken by local regimes; (2) balancing and coordination from a centralized power are necessary to avoid the development of inequalities among communities and to deal with externalities generated by decisions on the local scale; (3) the centralized power is essential to provide common goods that cannot be achieved locally. All these suggest the crucial role the state needs to play in order to achieve redistributive justice. Arguably, power centralization is even more crucial in a post-growth society where the trickle-down mechanism through which the benefits of growth finally fall onto the poor (albeit disproportionately) is absent.

### Non-materialistic quality of life – the goal of development

Post-growth shifts the goal of development from growth to welfare and repositions the economy as a means to enhance welfare and quality of life. Post-growth confronts the meaning of "the good life" based on the possession of material wealth and argues that people can live meaningfully and happily by maintaining a minimally sufficient material living standard, in exchange for more time and freedom to pursue non-materialistic and non-consumerist sources of satisfaction and meaning (Alexander, 2015). These non-consumerist sources of satisfaction can be about giving, sharing and caring, community engagement, creative activities, family life, political engagement, artistic projects, etc. This sets one ground for planning that aims at promoting a non-materialistic and non-consumerist quality of life.

### Democracy – as a moral imperative and a process

Post-growth engages in democracy on two fronts. One arises from an aspiration for deeper democracy through autonomy and self-determination, with the intention of reclaiming citizens' power from global capital and repoliticizing social choices. Democracy per se is seen as a moral imperative, like justice, that needs to be pursued. Criticizing the liberal representative democracy, post-growth scholars advocate direct forms of democracy, e.g. deliberative democracy and participatory democracy (Asara et al., 2013). The realization of direct democracy requires widespread public participation. Associated with this perception of democracy as something inherently good, there is no doubt that the pathway to post-growth should be democratic. In other words, the realization of downscaling and implementation of redistributive strategies cannot be imposed on people but must be carried out in a voluntary and democratic way. This second engagement in democracy therefore addresses the democratic process.

### Summary

To sum up, the post-growth reconceptualization of the ecological, social, political and ethical provides new grounds for planning. Generally speaking, post-growth addresses equally both outcome and process (Table 10.1). These new grounds will have significant implications for planning law.

**TABLE 10.1** Post-growth grounds for planning law

| | |
|---|---|
| **Outcome** | • Prominence of the ecological over the social and the economic<br>• Downscaling of production and consumption<br>• Satisfaction of basic needs<br>• Ceiling on inequality<br>• Promotion of non-materialistic and non-consumerist quality of life |
| **Process** | • Certain level of power centralization<br>• Multi-scalar strategy<br>• Widespread public participation<br>• Democratic process |

Source: author

In the following sections, they will be employed to inform the assessment of the existing planning law and exploration of a post-growth planning law.

## 3. Hindrances and potentials for post-growth transformation provided by the PBA 2008

Although planning activities in Norway started long before 1965, the first planning law dated from 1965, which made planning obligatory for all municipalities (Aarsæther, 2018). In 1985, the second generation of the planning act was adopted. Since then, new challenges and problems had arisen which outdated the law. Increasing demand and pressure led to the production and adoption of the third generation of the planning law: the Planning and Building Act 2008. Planning law sets out the ground rules for managing land use. Consequently, it makes some planning intentions, practices and decisions easy to realize and others difficult or impossible. The PBA 2008 organizes planning at three levels: the national, the regional and the municipal. The analysis will follow these three levels.

### 3.1 Purpose of the act

Compared to the two previous planning acts, the PBA 2008 introduces an innovative and radical change by stating that, "the Act shall promote sustainable development in the best interests of individuals, society and future generations" (Ministry of the Environment, 2008). The introduction of "sustainable development" to the act as an overarching purpose is considered as innovative, as PBA is in nature a process law which remains neutral on different sectoral interests (Hanssen et al., 2018), whereas the sustainability goal lends the act a substantive dimension. In principle, that means planning at all levels should be evaluated against its contribution to sustainable development. The emphasis on sustainable development opens the space to address a post-growth conceptualization of sustainability. Since the post-growth foundations put strong weight on the outcome or substantive dimension of development, the move from a pure process law to the inclusion of limited concern on substantive goals represents a potential for the act to be utilized for post-growth transformation.

## 3.2 National planning

National planning expectations should be prepared every four years when a new national government is elected. Being obligatory for every government, the major role of the national planning expectations is to promote sustainable development, which follows the overarching purpose of the act (Ministry of the Environment, 2008). So to speak, sustainable development should be pursued and safeguarded regardless of the political standpoint of the government. Although the national planning expectations are not legally binding, they shall be followed up by regional and municipal planning and shall serve as the basis for the central government's participation. The potential for the post-growth enterprise lies in the substantive focus in the national planning expectations and its intended influence on the regional and municipal planning. Thus, it gives the national planning authority an opportunity to make objections to regional and municipal planning proposals based on the substantive goals of sustainability, if the proposals are in conflict with national interests. The criteria to make objections shall put more emphasis on the compliance of regional and municipal planning with the substance or outcome of planning rather than the process. However, one barrier to promoting post-growth is the ambiguous understanding of sustainable development. Although every government, regardless of its political ideology, must oblige itself to promote sustainable development, there is a lot of room to conceptualize it. Indeed, studies have found out that the two generations of national planning expectations since 2008, issued by the social democratic government and the right-wing government respectively, have framed rather differently the understanding of sustainable development (Aarsæther and Strand, 2018).

Another national planning type is central government land-use plans. This type of plan is not obligatory, and the Ministry can decide when such plans need to be prepared. According to PBA 2008, the Ministry can request such plans, "when the implementation of important central government or regional development, construction or conservation projects so requires, or when it is justified by other social considerations" (Ministry of the Environment, 2008). As such, there is a large amount of discretion of the state to prepare national land-use plans. Seen from the post-growth perspective, this planning type has a potential to provide a framework to set up land-use boundaries and caps, balance and coordinate national territorial development, and provide infrastructure and facilities that are beyond the capacity of regional and municipal authorities. It can be a significant tool to strengthen a centralized planning power that is essential to realizing downscaling, redistribution and inequality reduction. For instance, the central government land-use plans fit well with the development of large-scale transport infrastructure, cabins and key public facilities.

## 3.3 Regional planning

PBA 2008 regulates two planning types at the regional level: regional planning strategies and regional master plans. PBA 2008 has initiated a strategic turn in regional planning and downplayed its comprehensiveness as a tool of land-use planning (Higdem and Kvalvik, 2018). This is done through several law regulations. First, the regional planning strategies are the only obligatory planning type at the regional level, to be prepared within one year after the new regional authority is constituted. Second, instead of preparing an overall and comprehensive regional master plan, the regional master plans, as regulated in PBA 2008, shall only need to target and address the issues identified in the regional planning strategies. The weakened comprehensiveness of regional planning is seen as a barrier to post-growth transformation. The regional planning is supposed to be a bridge between the state and municipalities, which can assume an important role in safeguarding national interests and implementing national strategies. In addition, it is supposed to be an effective instrument for coordinating local development. Arguably, a regional planning that is more targeted to certain issues cannot fulfil these assumed functions. In addition, there is a lack of instruments in the law that can secure an effective cooperation and dialogue between the state, region and local. In practice, this has resulted in low commitment of the regional and municipal authorities to regional planning.

## 3.4 Municipal planning

Planning at the municipal level includes three types: planning strategy, master plan and zoning plan. The municipal planning strategy is, according to the PBA 2008, supposed to be a form of strategic planning that is politically anchored. The act states, "the planning strategy should comprise a discussion of the municipality's strategic choices related to social development…" and "the municipality should also promote broad public participation and general debates as a basis for the municipal council's consideration of the strategy." It is therefore the intention of the act that the strategic choice of a municipality should be politically debated. Although in practice the planning strategy has so far failed to function as a political governance instrument other than an administrative tool (Kvalvik, 2018), it provides a platform for different political perspectives and the wider public to engage in debates on future strategic development. This means planners and/or post-growth advocates can employ such a planning instrument to initiate discussions and imaginaries on different alternatives of development beyond growth-dependency and -orientation.

The municipal master plan is composed of a social element and a land-use element. The social part plays a central role in the municipal planning, as it should determine long-term challenges, goals and strategies, function as a basis for other sectoral plans, and coordinate municipal activities. What is very interesting in the light of post-growth transformation is that the social part should also contain "a description and an assessment of alternative strategies for development in the municipality". This is a recognition of potentially different perspectives on futures, providing an opportunity to raise discussions on post-growth possibilities including long-term goal setting and development of strategies. Planners can present scenarios of development which contain, among others, post-growth alternatives and assess the pros and cons of these different future choices. In addition, the PBA makes it possible to link the social development part with the land-use part and the municipal economic plan. That is to say if a post-growth future is envisaged and formulated in the social part, it will be better implemented through a consistent land-use plan and allocation of financial resources. However, the social element of the master plan, though obligatory, is not legally binding. Unlike the social element, the land-use element of the master plan has a legal effect. It is considered as the most important planning type that directs municipal development.

The land-use element employs two planning tools to steer development: land-use objectives with provisions, and designation of zones requiring special consideration. The former allocates mutually exclusive functions to land, whereas the latter sets requirements on land use. Therefore, different zones can overlap with each other on a piece of land. From a post-growth perspective, the limitations of these land-use tools lie in three aspects: constraining land development of mixed use, limited possibility to secure social justice, and lack of tools to secure climate concerns. Designation of land based on one function hinders the possibility of achieving compact urban development in the form of mixed land use. Multiple functions of land use at the local level are necessary in order to localize residents' activities. In addition, the act's requirements on planning provisions related to land use do not give planners the right to influence the type, tenure form and financial model of housing projects. This makes it very hard to secure the access of vulnerable groups to affordable housing and to limit overall housing consumption. Furthermore, there is no legal basis that can enable planners to set requirements on climate mitigation.

The zoning plan is the planning platform that makes most visible the dilemma between planning's intentions to regulate land use for the public good and safeguarding the private sector's right to initiate planning. The PBA 2008 aims to alleviate this tension by designing two types of zoning plan: the area zoning plan and detailed zoning plan. Although technically speaking the two plans have no differences, they differ in their intentions, planning objects and initiators. The main difference is that the area zoning plan is initiated by the municipality covering a larger area, whereas the detailed zoning plan is privately initiated (by private bodies, developers, organizations and other authorities) with the purpose of materializing development projects. The hindrance to post-growth transformation lies in the lack of tools for public planners to regulate the developers who are primarily profit oriented. The fact that local authorities do not own municipal land constrains their ability to regulate development, especially when it comes to the fulfilment of social goals. Moreover, it hinders the development of commons due to the unavailability of common land for such land-use intentions.

## 4. Ideological underpinnings of the PBA 2008

As the foregoing analysis shows, within the existing legal framework there lie potential planning instruments and opportunities to bring in post-growth thinking. In this section, it will be argued that the opportunities provided by the law for pursuing a post-growth transformation are rather constrained, given the embedded, hidden norms and values in the planning law.

### *4.1 Property right as the foundation of planning law*

PBA 2008 sets a legal framework that aims to balance between the public and private interests. The legal provisions that allow the proposing of plans and development projects by private sector actors as well as the compensation scheme to landowners are premised on the private ownership of land. Here, the private ownership of land or property is "ideologized as an instrument of the owners' power to exclude" (Davy, 2020: 38). Such an exclusion-based ideological conception of private property has dominated the field of planning in Western countries over a long history. Exactly because of the understanding of private property as a right to exclude others, it can potentially generate tensions between the public and private interests. The impacts of this ideology of private property cannot be underestimated, as it sets the foundation for framing the rationales of the planning law. Planning law therefore attempts to find a good balance between the interests represented by different stakeholders. On one hand, it has to respect the freedom to develop projects initiated by private sector actors; on the other hand, the law needs to secure wider public interests through following certain planning processes and employing planning tools.

The problematic of the exclusion-based property right as the foundation of planning has been reflected upon by some planning scholars (Blomley, 2017; Savini, 2021). In light of post-growth thinking, the private property rights constitute an essential element of market-driven growth through speculative investment in land and real estate. It also constrains public planning's capability to safeguard social and environmental concerns, such as securing affordable housing, reducing social segregation, etc. Effective planning instruments have to be offered by the law in order to counteract these socially and environmentally negative tendencies. However, in PBA 2008 there is a lack of such instruments (Hanssen and Aarsæther, 2018). In addition, urban communing, which is often advocated as a post-growth practice, can be hampered if the land property rights structure does not provide support.

Davy (2020) called the hegemonic understanding of private property an unreflected and anti-social ideology of planning. Instead, drawing on several philosophers' work, he proposed an alternative ideology of property as a social function. Owning a property therefore means allowing the best use to fulfil its social functions. Only if the property is used for fulfilling its social functions, will it be protected by property rights. In this sense, designating functions for land through planning can be understood as defining the social function of that land, which landowners or developers need to fulfil. Such an ideological underpinning of property arguably provides planners with the room for action to designate land use based on use values and to better secure social and environmental interests.

## 4.2 The primacy of process over outcome

As stated earlier, PBA 2008 as a process law keeps a neutral position and provides an arena for different sectoral interests to negotiate. As a law that sets up the overall rules of the game for key actors involved in land use-related issues, it has a high legitimacy. Although the law prioritizes the process, it is not value neutral. It is the first time in the history of Norwegian planning law that "sustainable development" has been explicitly formulated as one of the purposes. The adding of this purpose to the act expands the scope of the law from a sole focus on process to embracing the outcome. This means that any development has to contribute to or at least not violate sustainable development. The question, however, is if the primary focus on process and the planning instruments offered in the act are appropriate and sufficient to secure the achievement of sustainable development.

Post-growth has strong ethical premises and is normative in the sense that it aims to achieve a just society with more equitable distribution of resources and wealth within a finite planet. Both distributive justice and keeping within the ecological limits are concerned with outcomes. As such, post-growth gives a sharper and more accurate meaning to the concept of sustainable development. The law, which addresses procedural justice and democratic process, cannot make sure that the outcomes will be in line with post-growth. To make the planning law an effective social structure for promoting post-growth, more tools and instruments must be provided in order to facilitate the materialization of the substantive post-growth goals. For instance, PBA 2008 cannot effectively counteract a growing social inequality in health and housing (Hanssen and Aarsæther, 2018). Specifically, there is a lack of tools for planners to secure a certain amount of affordable housing in residential development. The point is that, although the law itself has a primary focus on the process, it cannot get away from the substantive dimension. Arguably, post-growth needs to reinforce the substantive norms. This suggests that the framework of the planning process has to be designed in such a way that these substantive norms can be better articulated, embedded and integrated.

## 4.3 The principle of decentralization

The planning system according to PBA 2008 follows a multilevel governance approach, nevertheless with the main principle of decentralization. The primary planning authority lies at the municipal level where the only legally binding land-use plans are made, whereas national and regional planning authorities with an intention of safeguarding broader social and environmental interests constitute the departure point of their intervention. Generally, local politicians have a strong say in the field of planning with very limited influence from national and regional governments. The decentralization is also strongly reflected in the law that opens up for private planning initiatives. Privately initiated planning has a long tradition in Norway, and nationwide, more than 70% of detailed zoning plans are initiated by the private sector (Børrud, 2018). As stated by Andersen and Skrede (2017), the *de facto* city makers are business enterprises who can organize, make or shape the urban spaces and their cultural, material and social features according to their own interest. The decentralization principle in law is partly a consequence of the neoliberalization of the Norwegian planning and governance system (Falleth et al., 2010).

Scrutinizing from a post-growth perspective that requires a stronger planning power to direct or even constrain development for the sake of environmental and social sustainability, it can be challenging for a decentralized planning and governance system to serve these functions (Strand and Næss, 2016). As argued earlier, regional planning can assume an important role in, e.g. setting limits, balancing and coordinating cross-municipal development or providing common goods (cf. section 2.2). This is particularly applicable to fields such as land use, climate change, nature protection, resource management, cross-municipal transport and other infrastructure, landscape protection, and development in the coastal zone and mountain areas (Holth and Winge, 2016). This is because these fields particularly need a holistic plan to trace, manage and control the accumulated effects generated from development in individual municipalities. Take biodiversity as an example. Regional planning can be essential in protecting the integrity of habitats for species and avoiding the fragmentation that can result from local land-use planning. However, the decentralization principle has weakened the role of regional and national planning in intervening in development. Under PBA 2008, regional planning is struggling with gaining legitimacy, commitment and compliances, which undermines the planning system's capability to steer development towards being socially and environmentally sustainable.

## 5. Conclusion

This chapter has attempted to address one of the social structures, i.e. the legal structure, and its links to post-growth. This is based on an acknowledgement of the powerfulness of legislation as a means of societal transformation. The scrutiny of the Norwegian Planning and Building Act indicates that the legal framework provides both opportunities and constraints for striving for a post-growth society. The chapter further argues that, more deeply, the values and norms embedded in the law constitute ideological barriers to post-growth transformation. Therefore, only if planning law undergoes a paradigmatic shift in its ideological underpinning, may it keep transformative potential towards a post-growth society.

The study of the Norwegian planning act inspires a broader reflection on the relation between law and post-growth. What can a post-growth planning law look like? What can be the essential elements in and underlying the law that make it distinguishable from the existing one? Here, I attempt to spell out tentatively some insights. First, the planning law has to build on an ontology of finity. This will renounce the idea of balancing different interests from different spheres (usually economic growth and environmental sustainability) represented by different actors. This is because the new stratified ontology falsifies the idea of reconciling economic growth and sustainability. Respect for the environment has to prevail over the other concerns. Second, there is a need to normativize the planning law by incorporating the outcomes and substantive values. Redistributive justice and respect for environmental limits need to be visible, which fleshes out the overarching goal of sustainable development. The legal framework should also design effective tools to facilitate the achievement of the substantive goals. Third, a post-growth planning law will build on an understanding of property as a social function which replaces the conventional exclusion-based conception. This alternative notion of property undermines the micro-level driving forces of economic growth derived from exchange values in land and instead reinforces the use values of land. Fourth, a post-growth planning law should revisit the decentralization principle, build a planning system that distributes more equally the power among different planning authorities and arguably strengthens the hierarchy of power in planning.

An intriguing question is how these fundamental changes that post-growth planning law is required to make can happen. Following the argument of Alexander (2013), the reconstruction of law will not happen unless a post-growth ethics is embraced and mainstreamed at the cultural level. As the analysis shows, even though the existing legal framework provides potentials to pursue a post-growth agenda, the materialization of these planning potentials is premised on the intentions, initiatives and striving of conscious post-growth planners and actors. The reconstruction of a social structure, such as the law, is a consequence of human transformative agency. Meanwhile, the reforms in the law will have an impact on public opinions, affect cultures and norms, and lead to the building of a new social order.

## References

Aarsæther N (2018) Plan- og bygningsloven 2008 – "i et nøtteskall". In: Hanssen GS and Aarsæther N (eds), *Plan- og Bygningsloven – en lov for vår tid?* Oslo: Universitetsforlaget, pp. 25–36.

Aarsæther N and Strand A (2018) Nasjonale forventninger – stive og fleksible? In: Hanssen GS and Aarsæther N (eds), *Plan- og Bygningsloven – fungerer loven etter intensjonene?* Oslo: Universitetsforlaget, pp. 81–94.

Alexander S (2013) Voluntary simplicity and the social reconstruction of law: degrowth from the grassroots up. *Environmental Values* 22(2): 287–308.

Alexander S (2015) Simplicity. In: D'Alisa G, Demaira F and Kallis G (eds), *Degrowth. A vocabulary for a new era.* Abingdon: Routledge, pp. 133–136.

Andersen B and Skrede J (2017) Planning for a sustainable Oslo: the challenge of turning urban theory into practice. *Local Environment* 22(5): 581–594.

Arler F (2006) Ethics of large-scale change. *Geografisk Tidsskrift – Danish Journal of Geography* 106(2): 131–144.

Asara V, Profumi E and Kallis G (2013) Degrowth, democracy and autonomy. *Environmental Values* 22(2): 217–239.

Blomley N (2017) Land use, planning, and the "difficult character of property". *Planning Theory & Practice* 18(3): 351–364.

Børrud E (2018) Detaljregulering – planlegging i spagaten. In: Hanssen GS and Aarsæther N (eds), *Plan- og Bygningsloven – fungerer loven etter intensjonene?* Oslo: Universitetsforlaget, pp. 267–284.

Candiago N (2013) The virtuous circle of degrowth and ecological debt: a new paradigm for public international law. In: Westra L, Taylor P and Michelot A (eds), *Confronting ecological and economic collapse: ecological integrity for law*. Abingdon: Routledge, pp. 215–225.

Cosme I, Santos R and O'Neill DW (2017) Assessing the degrowth discourse: a review and analysis of academic degrowth policy proposals. *Journal of Cleaner Production* 149: 321–334.

Davy B (2020) "Dehumanized housing" and the ideology of property as a social function. *Planning Theory* 19(1): 38–58.

Dietz R and O'Neill DW (2013) *Enough is enough: building a sustainable economy in a world of finite resources*. Abingdon: Routledge.

Falleth EI, Hanssen GS and Saglie IL (2010) Challenges to democracy in market-oriented urban planning in Norway. *European Planning Studies* 18(5): 737–753.

Foster JB (2011) Capitalism and degrowth: an impossibility theorem. *Monthly Review* 62(8): 26–33.

Fotopoulos T (2007) Is degrowth compatible with a market economy? *The International Journal of Inclusive Democracy* 3(1).

Garver G (2013) The rule of ecological law: the legal complement to degrowth economics. *Sustainability* 5(1): 316–337.

Hanssen GS and Aarsæther N (2018) Pbl (2008) – en lov for vår tid? *Plan* 3: 2–7.

Hanssen GS, Aarsæther N and Winge NK (2018) Lovens intensjoner. In: Hanssen GS and Aarsæther N (eds), *Plan- og Bygningsloven – fungerer loven etter intensjonene?* Oslo: Universitetsforlaget, pp. 27–39.

Higdem U and Kvalvik KJ (2018) Regional planstrategi – strategi for planleggingen eller ny fylkesplan? In: Hanssen GS and Aarsæther N (eds), *Plan- og Bygningsloven – fungerer loven etter intensjonene?* Oslo: Universitetsforlaget, pp. 107–118.

Holth F and Winge NK (2016) Juridisk betenkning. Styrking av regional plan og regionale styringsmidler i plan- og bygningsloven. Betenkning utarbeidet for KS. www.ks.no/contentassets/8a7948cbf1fd4ed892183e3fa1034c98/juridisk-betenkning-fredrik-holth-og-nikolai-k.-winge.pdf.

Jackson T (2009) *Prosperity without growth: economics for a finite planet*. Abingdon: Routledge.

Kallis G, Kostakis V, Lange S, Muraca B, Paulson S and Schmelzer M (2018) Research on degrowth. *Annual Review of Environment and Resources* 43: 291–316.

Kvalvik KJ (2018) Kommunal planstrategi – frå politikk til administrasjon? In: Hanssen GS and Aarsæther N (eds), *Plan- og Bygningsloven – fungerer loven etter intensjonene?* Oslo: Universitetsforlaget, pp. 141–155.

Lehtinen AA (2018) Degrowth in city planning. *Fennia – International Journal of Geography* 196(1): 43–57.

Martinez-Alier J (2012) Environmental justice and economic degrowth: an alliance between two movements. *Capitalism Nature Socialism* 23(1): 51–73.

Ministry of the Environment (2008) Planning and Building Act (2008).

Raworth K (2017) *Doughnut economics: seven ways to think like a 21st-century economist*. White River Junction, VT: Chelsea Green Publishing.

Savini F (2021) Towards an urban degrowth: habitability, finity and polycentric autonomism. *Environment and Planning A: Economy and Space* 53(5): 1076–1095.

Schneider F, Kallis G and Martinez-Alier J (2010) Crisis or opportunity? Economic degrowth for social equity and ecological sustainability. Introduction to this special issue. *Journal of Cleaner Production* 18(6): 511–518.

Strand A and Næss P (2016) Local self-determination, process-focus and subordination of environmental concerns. *Journal of Environmental Policy and Planning* 19(2): 156–167.

Vandenhole W (2018) De-growth and sustainable development: rethinking human rights law and poverty alleviation. *Law and Development Review* 11(2): 647–675.

Victor PA (2018) *Managing without growth: slower by design, not disaster*. Cheltenham: Edward Elgar Publishing.

Weiss M and Cattaneo C (2017) Degrowth – taking stock and reviewing an emerging academic paradigm. *Ecological Economics* 137: 220–230.

Wächter P (2013) The impacts of spatial planning on degrowth. *Sustainability* 5(3): 1067–1079.

Xue J (2014) Is eco-village/urban village the future of a degrowth society? An urban planner's perspective. *Ecological Economics* 105: 130–138.

Xue J (2018) Housing for degrowth: space, planning and distribution. In: Nelson A and Schneider F (eds), *Housing for degrowth: principles, models, challenges and opportunities*. Abingdon: Routledge, pp. 185–195.

Xue J (2021) Urban planning and degrowth: a missing dialogue. *Local Environment*: 1–19. DOI: 10.1080/13549839.2020.1867840.

**PART 6**
# Nurturing

# 11
# NURTURING THE POST-GROWTH CITY
Bringing the rural back in

*Julia Spanier and Giuseppe Feola*

## 1. Introduction

It is widely acknowledged that cities are destructive to the environment and the natural resources that sustain human and non-human life (Næss et al., 2020). Any planning for post-growth cities must take on the challenge of resolving the currently prevailing dissonance between urban societies and the ecosystems on which they draw to survive.

Urban sustainability scholarship has put forward numerous proposals to resolve the dissonance between cities and their natural environments, and their ideas can greatly inform post-growth visions of ecologically sound cities. However, rather than over-hastily choosing from these proposals the perfect blueprint for ecologically sound post-growth cities, we would like to use this chapter to slow down and take a step back. Looking at proposals for ecologically sustainable cities, we find a shared excitement about and predisposition to the concept and socio-natural reality of the city. There is no drastic break with the idea of cities as compatible with, or even crucial for, the achievement of ecologically sound futures. This belief in cities is certainly not always shared in more radical contributions, but even in those cases, we find an optimistic idea of the city as a space of disruption and revolution.

However, is it sufficient to solely enquire into ecologically sound post-growth *cities*? Are the notions of the 'city' and the 'urban' able to accommodate and prefigure post-growth futures in which humans and more-than-humans thrive? Or might planning for post-growth cities need to extend the frame beyond the urban?

To engage with these questions, we embed the problem of urban unsustainability in the history and present of capitalist societies. Marxist and political ecologist accounts of the evolution of capitalism provide useful insights into the relationship between capitalism's environmental destructiveness and the rift between the rural and the urban. Building on these understandings, we review academic debates

DOI: 10.4324/9781003160984-17

on ecologically sustainable cities, enquiring how they consider the relationship between the nature/society and urban/rural divides. From this, and building on feminist and postcolonial urban studies and the diverse economies agenda, we draw lessons for a post-growth vision for urban sustainability planning that contributes to the mending of these binary rifts. We propose conceptual lenses and empirical foci to extend post-growth urban sustainability planning beyond the frame of the city. We use the case of the Colombian movement *Territorios Campesinos Agroalimentarios* to illustrate our proposal.

## 2. Capitalism and the rift between the rural and the urban

Marx (1981) drew a direct link between the ecological destructiveness of capitalism and the urbanization of society. Foster (1999) further developed these observations into the concept of the metabolic rift, which posits that the fundamental connection between nature and society was disrupted by the onset of capitalist development and the accompanying urbanization process, namely the introduction of capitalist wage labour, the commodification of land, the development of large-scale industry, the industrialization of agriculture, the expropriation of smallholders and the consequent de-peasantization and forced migration into industrializing cities (Foster, 1999; McClintock, 2010). These processes have engendered the virtually complete subjugation of the rural to the urban. Planetary urbanization theorists observe that '[t]he rural[,] this supposedly non-urban realm[,] has now been thoroughly engulfed within the variegated patterns and pathways of a planetary formation of urbanization' (Brenner and Schmid, 2015: 174). As Brenner and Schmid (2015) argue, capitalist urbanization has eroded any foundation for speaking about rural and urban as independent categories.

Ironically, it has similarly become commonplace to speak of a global 'urban/rural divide' (Andersson et al., 2009), which refers to the difference in 'economic development' between cities and countrysides (Gopinath and Kim, 2009). At present, the majority of the global poor live in the countryside (CFS, 2016), and rural communities are lacking much-needed investments into education, health, small-scale agriculture and infrastructure (FAO et al., 2013). At the same time, the notion of the urban/rural divide represents the purification of these concepts as discrete categories in modern capitalist societies (McClintock, 2010), which is manifested in the disconnection of city dwellers from the countryside and that between urban consumers and the mostly rural places where their food is produced (Kneafsey et al., 2008). It is similarly represented in current cultural discourse, in which the rural has become synonymous with the past (Woods, 2012). The cultural disconnection between the rural and the urban—and the livelihoods of their dwellers, the obfuscation of the countryside as a crucial *agent* in the continuous making of the world, serves to conceal the ongoing subjugation and material plundering of the rural by the urban.

In the framework of the metabolic rift, the breaking off of the 'dialogue between humans and nature' is directly tied to the cultural divide between the rural and urban.

Originally, this linkage was explained with reference to the disruption of nutrient cycles through planetary urbanization—the idea that nutrients (food) flowing from rural areas into cities are not 'recompensated' by a reflow of nutrients (waste) back from cities, leading to a degrading quality of soils (Moore, 2000). However, we consider the *socio-cultural* dimension of the metabolic rift most instructive. Schneider and McMichael (2010) as well as McClintock (2010) interpret the metabolic rift to manifest at the societal and individual levels as well as ecologically. Human–nature relations were disturbed by the onset of urbanization because 'the proletarianization of rural populations who flood into urban centres in search of work' alienated humans from land and labour and instilled in humans 'the perception of self as external to the environment' (McClintock, 2010: 196, 201). Peasants' migration to cities and their transformation from autonomous farmers into agricultural labourers disrupted the 'production and reproduction of knowledges about agricultural practice and local ecosystems' (Schneider and McMichael, 2010: 477), thereby rupturing the cultural bond between humans and nature. This alienation is understood to sit at the root of the false belief in the possibility of human mastery over and decoupling from nature (Moore, 2017), a core tenet of modern Western societies that must be overcome in order to find a way out of the current ecological crisis.

What does the foregoing imply for creating cities that form a symbiosis with the ecosystems on which they depend? We propose that it signals the need to pay tribute to the historically entangled evolution of the nature/society and rural/urban rifts as well as the ways in which the cultural obfuscation of the links between human and nature might be effected through imposing a divide between the urban and the rural—and vice versa. It implies that we need to reconfigure the exploitative relations between the urban and the rural and emancipate the latter both materially and culturally. Thus, we are presented with the difficult task of *both* unmaking the cultural rift between city and countryside by insisting on their hybridity and interlinkage *and* empowering the rural as a liberated agent in planning for sustainable futures.

## 3. Visions for ecologically sustainable cities: which role for the rural?

This section engages with the heterogeneous field of urban sustainability studies through two questions: (i) Which concepts and ideas used in the urban sustainability studies community explicitly engage with the rural and its relations to the urban? (ii) Which visions for sustainable cities offer solutions to the difficult task we have described?

To address the first question, given the rather technical, solution-oriented approach of many urban sustainability studies, it is unsurprising that only a few concepts and ideas explicitly consider rural–urban relations as a structural underpinning of urban sustainability. Although urban studies, in particular urban political ecology, has long criticized the concept of the city as being insufficient to understand global and multi-spatial urbanization processes that reach beyond the 'boundaries' of the city (Brenner and Schmid, 2015), the debate around urban sustainability seems broadly untouched by these developments. As Angelo and Wachsmuth (2020) diagnose, 'dominant forms of urban sustainability planning and thinking focus too narrowly on cities' (13). Most discussions of urban sustainability exclusively focus on greening the city space, including proposals for nature-based solutions in cities (e.g. Frantzeskaki et al., 2019). However, even perspectives that extend beyond the city space mostly limit themselves to implicit considerations of the rural as 'that which is outside the city'. Recent reviews of the role of cities in achieving sustainability fail to meaningfully examine the rural and the role of rural–urban relations for urban sustainability (e.g. Bayulken and Huisingh, 2015; De Jong et al., 2015; Heymans et al., 2019; Roggema, 2017; Wolfram and Frantzeskaki, 2016).

The undervaluation of the rural leads directly to a second tendency that can be identified across the literature on urban sustainability, namely that 'everyone now thinks cities can save the planet' (Angelo and Wachsmuth, 2020: 2202). Designs for dense urbanism, or the 'compact city', are now considered the most ecologically sustainable settlement forms versus smaller settlements interspersed with rural and green spaces (Bayulken and Huisingh, 2015; Næss et al., 2020). Cities have become key players in the governance and mitigation of global warming in the climate change discourse (e.g. Bulkeley et al., 2014; van der Heijden et al., 2019). Likewise, in the sustainability transition and innovation debate, cities are quite broadly seen as 'incubators and catalysts of socio-economic and environmental change' (Wolfram, 2018: 11).

Similar pitfalls sometimes appear in radical visions of sustainable cities. Although far from committing the fallacy of perceiving the urban phenomenon as constrained to the spatial form of the city, Harvey (2012: 120) reproduces the idea of urban exceptionality when he insists that it 'is inherently worth asking' if 'struggles within and over the city [should] be seen as fundamental to anti-capitalist politics'. Other anti-capitalist urban studies similarly reproduce the cultural idea of the city's dominance by restraining their research to grand, structuralist theories of capitalist urbanization, as observed by Roy (2016a, 2016b), Derickson (2018) and Jazeel (2018). Theorizing urbanization in the Global South, Roy (2016a) highlights how Brenner and Schmid's (2015) universal narrative of a planetary urbanization leaves limited space for those realities, places and stories in which urbanization is a messy entanglement of rural and urban performances.

Post-colonial and feminist urban scholarship has provided valuable contributions on the urban that can be mobilized for this chapter's task. However, even if we restrict our search to the literature on sustainable cities, we can identify starting points for an explicit consideration of rural–urban relations. For example, Martin et al. (2018) criticize proponents of the smart-sustainable city for their limited consideration of 'the extra-urban ecosystems that supply resources to the city' (271). The landscape approach used in urban planning implicitly grasps the interrelation of rural and urban lives, as evinced in its demand for a consideration of the 'connectivity of landscapes between multiple geographical scales' (Heymans et al., 2019: 11). In a similar vein, Haughton (1997) distinguishes types of cities according to their 'relations to their environmental hinterlands' (Roggema, 2017: 7), including 'self-reliant cities', which resemble other proposals for sustainable, circular city-regions such as the 'regenerative city' or 'bioregionalism' (Sale, 1985).

Still, considerations of cities' metabolic relations to countrysides do not automatically capture the political processes and power-laden realities in which the rural and urban are embedded. Although the concept of urban metabolism, or circulatory metabolic flows, has been discussed both in urban studies accounts that do not talk about capitalism (e.g. Bayulken and Huisingh, 2015; Céspedes Restrepo and Morales-Pinzón, 2018; Kennedy et al., 2007) and in those that critique it (Gandy, 2004; Swyngedouw, 2006), this does not mean that their analyses of sustainable urbanisms are aligned. Beyond agreeing that cities depend 'on spatial relationships with surrounding hinterlands and global resource webs' (Kennedy et al., 2007: 43), the two debates are quite at odds with each other. Non-radical scholars have largely ignored their Marxist colleagues' writings. Gandy (2004) finds in those accounts of urban metabolisms a 'functionalist impetus [that] has consistently failed to grasp the way in which urban space is historically produced' (364). With their apolitical and ahistorical analyses of material flows in and out of cities and limited assessments of cities against a blueprint of a sustainable, circulatory urban system, non-radical accounts of urban metabolisms neglect the circulatory processes that unsustainably and unjustly *produce*, *constitute* and *transform* urban and rural socio-natures and cultures under capitalism (Gandy, 2004; Swyngedouw, 2006).

Although radical urban scholarship has also failed to sufficiently grapple with their reproduction of some aspects of the rural–urban divide, it proves useful for the task of meaningfully reinserting the rural into planning for post-growth urbanities. Howard's (1902) early concept of the 'garden city' could be understood as a design-based proposal for how to achieve some kind of 'marriage of town and countryside' (Clark, 2003). Bookchin's (1974) monograph on 'the limits of the city' recounts the development of the city through the lens of transformations in rural–urban relations. Grounded in this analysis, Bookchin formulates a vision of a better urbanism as one 'that go[es] beyond the city as such and produce[s] a new type of community, one that combines the best features of urban and rural life in a harmonized future society' (5). More recently, Angelo and Wachsmuth (2020) have reiterated calls for studies on urban sustainability that extend beyond the boundaries of the city.

Bookchin's (1974) imagination of eco-communities is presently being taken up by post-growth scholarship, which has implicitly begun to break with the cultural dominance of the city in advancing what Mocca (2020) even describes as an 'anti-urbanist view' (86). The post-growth debate has put forward alternative types of human settlements, such as demoi, urban villages or bioregions (Cato, 2011; Mocca, 2020; Xue, 2014). Emphasizing a re-grounding of communities in the 'local' and the 'territory' and demanding some kind of disconnection from the global market and a reconnection of production and consumption within localized economies (Latouche, 2016), these alternative settlement types not only explicitly question the cultural hegemony of the city as a symbol of the future, they also offer (largely unembraced) opportunities to rethink the relations between the rural and the urban. However, while representing important opportunities, these ideal types of post-growth settlements have been contested for their romanticization of local communities (the local trap), for reproducing a global–local binary and for their disputed environmental sustainability as decentralized settlement forms (Mocca, 2020; Xue, 2014).

Other proposals in the radical urban literature can help us further reconfigure the rural and the urban. Envisioning the 're-earthing of cities' through 'rurbanization', among other means, Escobar (2019) highlights Martínez Espinal's architectural designs, which reconnect the rural and urban by 'introduc[ing] a peasant view of the soil into the city' (136). Moreover, extending beyond the too easily maintained simplification of 'the rural' as synonymous to the agricultural, Escobar (2019) takes inspiration from Roy's (2016a, 2016b) work, which, as described, has crucially shaped the critique of the urban fetish within urban theory. Roy (2016a) carves out the many ways in which the rural is an agent in itself and proposes a research agenda capable of capturing historical difference due to its engagement in a 'non-totalizing' theory of the urban.

## 4. Rural-inclusive planning for urban sustainability

In our proposal for a post-growth vision for urban sustainability, we follow Roy's call for an approach that takes difference seriously and thus build on post-structuralist, feminist and post-colonial scholarship that has suggested ways to look for difference in the economy and the urban. These insights inform a perspective that can contribute to the reconfiguration of the exploitative relations between the rural and the urban while not reproducing a cultural rift between them. In fact, this perspective invites a reconsideration of the usefulness of speaking about *urban* planning. We nonetheless retain this terminology for the following reasons. This chapter is intended as an explicit contribution to the urban planning community whereby we advocate for the integration of the rural into the discipline's thinking. Similarly, acknowledging the persistent cultural force of the concepts of rural and urban in our society, we did not wish to casually propose an alternative concept. In the same way as calls for abandoning the human/nature binary do not abolish the need to call for a consideration of *societal* issues in *nature* protection policies, it is still useful to remind us that urban policies must consider the rural.

Post-colonial and feminist scholarship on the urban has brought the non-European urban, non- and not-fully urban and rural into the theorization of urbanization (Derickson, 2018; Jazeel, 2018; Roy, 2016a, 2016b). Referring to her research on Calcutta, Roy acknowledges that 'trying to read [the maps and histories of Calcutta] using the conventional dualisms of urban analysis: city and countryside; formal sector and informal sector; state and civil society; household and firm' impeded her from grasping the realities and social relations forming the subject of her study, and she had to 'dramatically reshape the social and spatial categories in which [she] had been trained' to understand the places she was researching (2016b: 2). As an urban theorist, Roy does not aim at prefiguring urban sustainability. Nonetheless, her work can be instructive for our project of bringing the rural back into urban sustainability planning. She teaches us to let go of the 'general' or 'universal' concept of the urban, the city, the rural, the countryside (Roy, 2016b), and thus also of the sustainable city or the sustainable countryside. We become able to see the city, the urban and the project of urban sustainability as an 'experience … negotiated at spatial scales that implode the city' (Roy, 2016b: 7).

We thus begin our engagement with the question of urban sustainability within a relational ontology of space, seeking ways forward without being constrained by inherited rural/urban dichotomies or cultural expectations of urban dominance in the variegated and local performances happening on the ground. This attention to diverse performances is particularly emphasized by the diverse economies agenda. Based on a feminist and post-structuralist critique of structuralist analyses of capitalism, the diverse economies agenda put forward by Gibson-Graham (2008) engages in an 'ontological re-framing' of the economy; rather than seeing capitalism as a monolithic entity whose logic now reigns over every action taking place, this agenda perceives the economy as a hybrid, contingent performance in need of constant re-production. Capitalist practices and relations co-exist with a variety of non-capitalist practices and relations which together comprise a diverse economy. This perspective helps to open up urban sustainability planning to the rural when we apply ontological reframing to capitalist urbanization and stop perceiving urbanization as a monolithic and finalized project. We can then perceive the diversity of performances—some rural, some urban, some in-between—that are shaping rural–urban space, and we start seeing that *not all* of them reproduce the material and cultural relations of power and exploitation that are dominant in capitalist society (Spanier, 2021). Seeing these hopeful performances of difference should not be misunderstood as ignoring patterns of dominant performances—the performances currently driving the dominant process of capitalist urbanization (Tsing, 2017). The performances attempting to reconfigure power relations between rural and urban have not yet shaped a new pattern; however, they are important starting points for the transformation towards different, sustainable rural–urban relations in a post-growth society.

In building on these two debates, our proposal for post-growth planning for urban sustainability particularly focuses on two questions. First, which lenses and concepts should planners use to enquire what post-growth urban sustainability could look like? Second, with which practices and cases should planners engage? The focus on these two questions rests on the idea that by engaging with certain concepts and cases, we contribute to the performance of a certain world. If we want to focus on the rural–urban dimension of post-growth sustainability, we require a research approach that does not in itself reinforce the cultural dynamics at the root of the problem. Similarly, we need an approach that pays attention to initiatives from which we can learn how to overcome these cultural and material dynamics. As such, our proposal consists of the following four elements.

*Reading for diversity and difference.* Post-colonial urban theory and feminist re-framings of the economy direct our attention to the local, practical performances that produce difference within our capitalist economy and its production of rural and urban space. Rather than working with predefined concepts or designing prototypes of sustainable urban living and thereby neglecting existing difference, we start from concrete places and performances and their experiences in prefiguring sustainable post-growth societies within a world currently dominated by performances of capitalist growth and urbanization.

Taking this as a general guiding principle, the following elements should be understood as specific ways of enacting this reading.

*Refraining from prioritizing the urban and the city.* While Marxist scholarship on the urban has successfully taught us to study the urban beyond the boundaries of the city, post-colonial urban theory gives us the tools to similarly refrain from starting our research with the idea of an urban-dominated future. The diverse economies agenda motivates us to actively look for non-urban, not-fully-urban or rural performances when exploring pathways and experiments prefiguring post-growth sustainability. Even when envisioning ecologically sustainable cities, we may find inspiration in rural reconstruction movements (Alcock, 2019), back-to-the-landers (Calvário and Otero, 2015), or other 'radical rural' initiatives (Halfacree, 2007). A myopic occupation with imagining post-growth urban sustainability might obscure that creating a sustainable post-growth society could require an extension of urban planning beyond the urban and an engagement with alternative notions capable of countering the marginalization of the rural. This call for a diversity of concepts leads directly to the third element of our proposal.

*Complicating the categories of the urban and the rural.* Conventional categories of rural and urban reproduce a cultural separation that is not representative of the multiplicity of relations that fundamentally connect and hybridize the two spheres. Such cultural purification conceals the ongoing subjugation and material plundering of the rural to and by the urban. Post-growth planning for urban sustainability should refrain from reproducing the urban/rural binary just as it should abolish the conceptual binary between nature and society. We propose that a greater openness to the many performances towards post-growth sustainability that occur across rural–urban boundaries and syncretize the rural and the urban will enable us to take into account performances that trouble expected rural/urban binaries, including those that shed these categories altogether.

*Looking for performances that reconfigure the material, cultural and power relations between the rural and the urban.* As the urban metabolism framework shows, scholarship on urban sustainability already includes the non-urban in conceptualizations of ecologically sustainable cities. We agree that it is critical to look into initiatives and practices that aim at establishing equitable, circular and fundamentally non-exploitative material flows between urban centres and the rural resources on which they draw. However, planning for post-growth urban sustainability requires more; we need to look for performances that not only reconfigure material flows between rural and urban but also unmake the ways in which these spheres interact, relate and constitute each other materially *and culturally* within capitalist society. This means exploring performances and practices that unmake the unequal power relations between rural and urban—in which the rural is rendered as inferior and passive in contrast to the superior and active urban—as well as those practices that reconfigure the socio-natural assemblages through which these injustices unfold. Which performances unmake the capitalist cultural, material and power relations between rural and urban and how does this unmaking contribute to the construction of ecologically sustainable post-growth futures?

To illustrate the four elements of this proposal, in the next section, we present the case of the *Territorios Campesinos Agroalimentarios* (TCA) in Colombia as an example of rural–urban agri-food grassroots movements that challenge the industrial food system. Agri-food grassroots movements gather a range of capitalist, alternative capitalist and non-capitalist practices (Koretskaya and Feola, 2020) and include oppositional global, regional and local peasant movements; alternative food networks such as direct farm sales, farmers' markets, community-supported agriculture or permaculture; and urban gardening collectives or food policy councils (Goodman et al., 2012; Rivera-Ferre et al., 2014).

## 5. From the post-growth city to the post-growth territory: the *Territorios Campesinos Agroalimentarios* movement

The *Territorios Campesinos Agroalimentarios* (TCA) movement is an example of concrete, ongoing socioecological transformation towards a post-growth society at the territorial level (Coordinador Nacional Agrario [CNA], 2017). Through the lens proposed in this chapter, we observe how this case, like many others that remain too often overlooked in urban sustainability studies, challenges established categories of rural and urban and the primacy of the city in the pursuit of an ecologically viable post-growth society.

The first TCA, *Territorio Campesino Agroalimentario del Macizo del norte de Nariño y sur del Cauca*, was officially declared on 25 November 2016. Local communities from 15 municipalities, encompassing 3 community meetings in each municipality, various local mayors, and more than 3,000 peasants from the region, actively participated in the collective discussion and elaboration of the declaration.

TCA is a Colombian peasant movement motivated by the defence of human and non-human life and the assertion of peasant identity against capitalist appropriation and exploitation. As such, it cannot be reduced to a mere backward-looking defence of a supposed pre-existing peasant culture. Rather, TCA constructs a post-growth society at the territorial level by organizing novel and dignified social and political relations as well as ecologically and socially re-embedding economic practices, thereby improving the well-being of the local population and ensuring ecological sustainability. TCA structures and consolidates the performance of this post-growth society through institutions constructed through autonomous community-led planning (*Plan de Vida Digna*), which aims at conducting collective processes for the creation of visions of possible futures as well as at empowering communities to govern, decide and legislate over their territory, ways of living, economy and culture (CNA, 2017). *Plan de Vida Digna* is informed by principles of solidarity, justice, dignity, autonomy and sovereignty, a holistic view of human and non-human life, and collective participation (CNA, 2015).

TCA's performance of a territorial post-growth society entails the reconfiguration of material flows, cultural relations and power relations. First, TCA reconfigures material flows between rural and urban spaces. It expels extractive industries from the territory, thereby putting a halt on resource transfer from rural to urban spaces at high ecological and social costs for the former. Furthermore, it envisions—and to an extent already practices—a re-localization of the territorial economy and an exit from market exchanges. Peasants are expected to first produce for themselves, and initial surpluses go to the local market before any engagement in trade with the rest of the nation and potentially other countries. TCA practices agroecology, which combines traditional and academic knowledge in support of an agriculture that works with and regenerates ecological cycles regardless of any administrative or symbolic (including rural–urban) borders.

Second, linked to the reconfiguration of material flows, TCA reshapes cultural representations of the rural and the urban. Peasants conceive of and represent TCA as a territorial rather than rural movement. The construction of peasant territoriality encapsulates the essence of the sustainability transformation pursued by TCA. While it refrains from employing the binaries of rural and urban (as well as human and nature), its use of the territory as a pivotal spatial category realizes peasants' relational ontology, supporting their holistic understanding of place-based, historically rooted socio-natural relations.

Lastly, the reconfiguration of material flows and cultural representations of the urban and the rural are elements of the reconfiguration of power relations. Although it is a grassroots peasant movement, TCA is not limited to local or rural struggles, but rather proposes and concretely performs an alternative to capitalist development that has broader significance. It reverts deeply seated historical legacies of peasant exploitation and marginalization in Colombia by affirming its members as autonomous agents capable of determining how the territory and the human-non-human community living within it will develop. Peasants reject inferior identities of labourers or food producers (or, at best, agricultural entrepreneurs), who solely exist to supply the city. They claim, construct and perform the social role of citizens and agents of change who can inform dignifying and ecologically sustainable approaches for the development of not only their local community but also society at large. In effect, the TCA model is already informing the performance of diverse economies in various Colombian cities through community gardens and urban agriculture, among other initiatives (Feola et al., 2020).

## 6. Conclusion

How should we tackle the task of resolving the current dissonance between urban societies and the ecosystems on which they draw in post-growth urban planning? In this chapter, we presented conceptual lenses that planners can use to enquire what post-growth urban sustainability could look like. We proposed to look out for difference and diversity rather than constraining ourselves to inherited categories (such as the urban and the rural) and structural expectations (such as the dominance of the urban). We also advocated to not prioritize the city or the urban so that we can learn from non-urban cases that might be relevant for the prefiguration of urban sustainability, keeping the question open if a post-growth vision of sustainability should stick to the categories of the urban and the city. Third, we encouraged planners to complicate the categories of the rural and the urban, both as a performative act of not reproducing the cultural purification of these concepts and as a way to grasp the diversity of prefigurative performances that occur across imagined rural/urban boundaries. Lastly, we suggested looking out for performances that reconfigure the material, cultural and power relations between the rural and the urban as part of the performance of urban sustainability.

Where does this proposal lead? In this chapter, we identified lessons for a post-growth urban–nature symbiosis in a peasant movement far removed from the culturally expected boundaries of the city. TCA exemplifies emerging rural–urban agri-food movements that inspire us to think differently about urban sustainability by transcending the concept of the city. TCA constructs a post-growth society at the territorial level, ecologically and socially re-embedding economic practices in ways that advance the well-being of the local population and non-human life. We argue that this performance of a territorial post-growth society contributes to urban sustainability. By resisting resource extraction from rural to urban spaces, strengthening their territorial economies, transgressing any imagined rural/urban or nature/society boundaries and emancipating peasant identities and innovations as agents of transformations that concern society at large, TCA engenders the unmaking of unequal material, cultural and power relations between the rural and the urban. This movement proposes an alternative spatial concept—the territory—to prefigure post-growth sustainability that does not neglect the rural. In doing so, it reminds us that the rural also constitutes the urban; that envisioning post-growth *urban* sustainability is impossible without asking which role the rural plays in there—and which role it plays in *getting there*.

## Acknowledgements

The section on TCA elaborates as yet unpublished empirical material originally collected by Danika Moore and analysed by Danika Moore, Olga Koretskaya and Giuseppe Feola. This chapter has benefited tremendously from several reviews by Ellen Moors and Marion Ernwein as well as the constructive feedback provided by Guilherme De Sa Pavarini Raj, Leonie Guerrero Lara, Laura van Oers and Jacob Smessaert. We are grateful for the feedback received during the book authors' symposium and for Federico Savini's, António Ferreira's and Kim Carlotta von Schönfeld's excellent editorial work. This research was funded by the European Research Council (Grant 802441).

## References

Alcock R (2019) The New Rural Reconstruction Movement: a Chinese degrowth style movement? *Ecological Economics* 161(April): 261–269.

Andersson K, Eklund E, Lehtola M et al. (2009) Introduction: beyond the rural–urban divide. In: Andersson K, Lehtola M, Eklund E et al. (eds) *Beyond the Rural–Urban Divide: Cross-Continental Perspectives on the Differentiated Countryside and Its Regulation.* Bingley: Emerald Group Publishing, pp. 1–21.

Angelo H and Wachsmuth D (2020) Why does everyone think cities can save the planet? *Urban Studies* 57(11): 2201–2221.

Bayulken B and Huisingh D (2015) A literature review of historical trends and emerging theoretical approaches for developing sustainable cities (part 1). *Journal of Cleaner Production* 109: 11–24.

Bookchin M (1974) *The Limits of the City.* New York: Harper & Row. Available at: https://theanarchistlibrary.org/library/murray-bookchin-the-limits-of-the-city.

Brenner N and Schmid C (2015) Towards a new epistemology of the urban? *Urban City* 19(2–3): 151–182.

Bulkeley H, Castán Broto V and Edwards G (2014) *An Urban Politics of Climate Change: Experimentation and the Governing of Socio-Technical Transitions.* Abingdon; New York: Routledge.

Calvário R and Otero I (2015) Back-to-the-landers. In: D'Alisa G, Demaria F and Kallis G (eds) *Degrowth. A Vocabulary for a New Era.* Abingdon; New York: Routledge.

Cato MS (2011) Home economics: planting the seeds of a research agenda for the bioregional economy. *Environmental Values* 20(4): 481–501.

Céspedes Restrepo JD and Morales-Pinzón T (2018) Urban metabolism and sustainability: precedents, genesis and research perspectives. *Resources, Conservation and Recycling* 131(16): 216–224.

CFS (2016) Urbanization, rural transformation and implications for food security and nutrition: key areas for policy attention and possible roles for CFS (including draft decision). Rome: Committee on World Food Security. Available at www.fao.org/3/mr205e/mr205e.pdf.

Clark B (2003) Ebenezer Howard and the marriage of town and country. *Organization and Environment* 16(1): 87–97.

Coordinador Nacional Agrario (CNA) (2015) *Los Planes de Vida Comunitarios Para Los Territorios Agroalimentarios.* Available at https://cnagrario.files.wordpress.com/2015/07/cna_ta_planes-de-vida-comunitarios.pdf.

CNA (2017) *Territorios Agroalimentarios.* Available at www.indepaz.org.co/wp-content/uploads/2017/12/territoriosagroalimentarioscna_0.pdf.

De Jong M, Joss S, Schraven D et al. (2015) Sustainable-smart-resilient-low carbon-eco-knowledge cities; making sense of a multitude of concepts promoting sustainable urbanization. *Journal of Cleaner Production* 109: 25–38.

Derickson K (2018) Masters of the universe. *Environment and Planning D: Society and Space* 36(3): 556–562.

Escobar A (2019) Habitability and design: radical interdependence and the re-earthing of cities. *Geoforum* 101(February): 132–140.

FAO, Federal Ministry of Food and Agriculture and EXPO Milano (2013) Second International Expert Meeting: 'Territorial Approach to Food Security and Nutrition Policies: Empirical Evidence and Good Practices' (December). Available at https://www.fao.org/documents/card/en/c/00f62edd-5e66-4019-a08c-72145ec1f015/.

Feola G, Suzunaga J, Soler J et al. (2020) Peri-urban agriculture as quiet sustainability: challenging the urban development discourse in Sogamoso, Colombia. *Journal of Rural Studies* 80: 1–12.
Foster JB (1999) Marx's theory of metabolic rift: classical foundations for environmental sociology. *American Journal of Sociology* 105(2): 366–405.
Frantzeskaki N, McPhearson T, Collier MJ et al. (2019) Nature-based solutions for urban climate change adaptation: linking science, policy, and practice communities for evidence-based decision-making. *BioScience* 69(6): 455–466.
Gandy M (2004) Rethinking urban metabolism: water, space and the modern city. *City* 8(3): 363–379.
Gibson-Graham JK (2008) Diverse economies: performative practices for 'other worlds'. *Progress in Human Geography* 32(5): 613–632.
Goodman D, DuPuis EM and Goodman MK (2012) *Alternative Food Networks: Knowledge, Practice, and Politics.* Abingdon, UK: Routledge.
Gopinath M and Kim H (eds) (2009) *Globalization and the Rural-Urban Divide.* 1st edn. Seoul: Seoul National University Press.
Halfacree K (2007) Trial by space for a 'radical rural': introducing alternative localities, representations and lives. *Journal of Rural Studies* 23(2): 125–141.
Harvey D (2012) *Rebel Cities: From the Right to the City to the Urban Revolution.* London: Verso.
Haughton G (1997) Developing sustainable urban development models. *Cities* 14(4): 189–195.
Heymans A, Breadsell J, Morrison GM et al. (2019) Ecological urban planning and design: a systematic literature review. *Sustainability* 11(13): 3723.
Howard E (1902) *Garden Cities of To-Morrow.* London: Faber and Faber.
Jazeel T (2018) Urban theory with an outside. *Environment and Planning D: Society and Space* 36(3): 405–419.
Kennedy C, Cuddihy J and Engel-Yan J (2007) The changing metabolism of cities. *Journal of Industrial Ecology* 11(2): 43–59.
Kneafsey M, Cox R, Holloway L et al. (2008) *Reconnecting Consumers, Producers and Food.* 1st edn. London; Oxford: Bloomsbury.
Koretskaya O and Feola G (2020) A framework for recognizing diversity beyond capitalism in agri-food systems. *Journal of Rural Studies* 80: 302–313.
Latouche S (2016) Degrowth as a territorial-landscape project. *Journal of Research and Didactics in Geography (J-READING)* 1(5): 89–94.
Martin CJ, Evans J and Karvonen A (2018) Smart and sustainable? Five tensions in the visions and practices of the smart-sustainable city in Europe and North America. *Technological Forecasting and Social Change* 133: 269–278.
Marx K (1981) *Capital,* Vol. 3 *(1863–65).* New York: Vintage.
McClintock N (2010) Why farm the city? Theorizing urban agriculture through a lens of metabolic rift. *Cambridge Journal of Regions, Economy and Society* 3(2): 191–207.
Mocca E (2020) The local dimension in the degrowth literature. A critical discussion. *Journal of Political Ideologies* 25(1): 78–93.
Moore JW (2000) Environmental crises and the metabolic rift in world-historical perspective. *Organization and Environment* 13(2): 123–157.
Moore JW (2017) The Capitalocene Part II: accumulation by appropriation and the centrality of unpaid work/energy. *Journal of Peasant Studies* 45(2): 1–43.
Næss P, Saglie IL and Richardson T (2020) Urban sustainability: is densification sufficient? *European Planning Studies* 28(1): 146–165.
Rivera-Ferre MG, Constance DH and Renard MC (2014) Convergence and divergence in alternative agrifood movements. In: Mooney PH, Tanaka K and Ciciurkaite G (eds)

*Alternative Agrifood Movements: Patterns of Convergence and Divergence*. Bingley: Emerald Group Publishing, pp. 313–322.

Roggema R (2017) The future of sustainable urbanism: society-based, complexity-led, and landscape-driven. *Sustainability* 9(8): 1442.

Roy A (2016a) What is urban about critical urban theory? *Urban Geography* 37(6): 810–823.

Roy A (2016b) Who's afraid of postcolonial theory? *International Journal of Urban and Regional Research* 40(1): 200–209.

Sale K (1985) *Dwellers in the Land: The Bioregional Vision*. San Francisco, CA: Sierra Club Books.

Schneider M and McMichael P (2010) Deepening, and repairing, the metabolic rift. *Journal of Peasant Studies* 37(3): 461–484.

Spanier J (2021) Rural futurism: assembling the future in the countryside. *ACME: An International Journal for Critical Geographies* 20(1): 120–141.

Swyngedouw E (2006) Circulations and metabolisms: (hybrid) natures and (cyborg) cities. *Science as Culture* 15(2): 105–121.

Tsing AL (2017) *The Mushroom at the End of the World: On the Possibility of Life in Capitalist Ruins*. Princeton, NJ: Princeton University Press.

van der Heijden J, Bulkeley H and Certomà C (2019) Promises and concerns of the urban century. In: van der Heijden J, Bulkeley H and Certomà C (eds) *Urban Climate Politics*. Cambridge: Cambridge University Press, pp. 1–20.

Wolfram M (2018) Cities shaping grassroots niches for sustainability transitions: conceptual reflections and an exploratory case study. *Journal of Cleaner Production* 173: 11–23.

Wolfram M and Frantzeskaki N (2016) Cities and systemic change for sustainability: prevailing epistemologies and an emerging research agenda. *Sustainability* 8(2): 144.

Woods M (2012) Rural geography III: rural futures and the future of rural geography. *Progress in Human Geography* 36(1): 125–134.

Xue J (2014) Is eco-village/urban village the future of a degrowth society? An urban planner's perspective. *Ecological Economics* 105: 130–138.

# 12

## TOWARDS A POST-GROWTH FOOD SYSTEM

The Community as a Cornerstone? Lessons from Two Amsterdam Community-Led Food Initiatives

*Beatriz Pineda Revilla and Sarah Essbai*

### 1. Introduction

> The place remains in my memory as a grey landscape with little vegetation, a clouded sky hovering over dark buildings, and an atmosphere that suddenly made breathing a conscious act. I remember especially one smokestack with dense rust orange vapour rising like a solid column far into the sky before it dissipated. We always saw it there, every year, and it signalled our entrance into The City.
>
> *William Cronon (1991: 5)*

In his work *Nature's Metropolis: Chicago and the Great West*, Cronon (1991) describes how, as a child, he used to see the city and the country as two distinct separate realities: Chicago, the city, transformed by the effects of humans and its hinterland, the country, detached from it and radiating an almost bucolic and "natural" fragrance. This perception of separation continues nowadays in the imaginary of many urban and rural dwellers when in fact, city and country are intimately connected and both are influenced by humans' actions. Cronon makes a distinction between "first nature", the original, prehuman nature and "second nature", the artificial, human-manipulated nature. He points out that the country, with its rural farmlands and picturesque villages, has also been transformed by human hands and therefore it is as "second nature" as suburban and urban places are. Using the example of Chicago and its metropolitan region, he explains how the capitalist market system, developed in the nineteenth century, linked city and country. The country had the material resources, the means of production, and the city was in charge of transforming them into tradable commodities through labour (Harvey, 1982). This connection, as the case of the Chicago region illustrates, was made possible thanks to the rapid expansion of the railroad system. All of a sudden, country products and material

DOI: 10.4324/9781003160984-18

resources such as grain, lumber or meat could arrive fast and easily into the city. This reciprocal dependence and connection paved the way for our current lifestyles and associated patterns of consumption, which have, paradoxically, accentuated the divide between the city and the country.

This deep urban–rural rift remains nowadays and characterises contemporary Western societies, as high economic growth rates became the only sought-after measure of development. After decades of living with their backs to the countryside, urban dwellers have increasingly grown detached from what happens in the country and the impact it has for their urban lives. Food comes from the supermarkets, the lights turn on when we press the switch, and clean water runs from the tap in the blink of an eye. Generation after generation, there is an increasing loss of awareness of the indispensable ecosystem services that the country provides to the city. This divide between the urban and the rural is making natural resources something taken for granted, almost invisible to the urban eyes. Reconceptualising the city and the country as both "second nature", as our second nature, would contribute to re-establishing a missing link that is indispensable for the sustainability of our society. Cronon's words from 30 years ago have never been so up-to-date: "We are consumers all, whether we live in the city or the country. [They] are not two places but one" (Cronon, 1991: 384):

> We all live in the city. We all live in the country. Both are second nature to us [and therefore we need to be] "responsible" [for both,] we can only take them together and, in making the journey between them, find a way of life that does justice to them both.
>
> *(Cronon, 1991: 385 in Cutcliffe, 2010: 730)*

No matter how "smart" societies become, a balanced relationship between city and country can re-establish broken linkages at the ecological and social levels but also at the individual level (McClintock, 2010). This will provide current and future generations with pathways towards different ways of producing and consuming, enabling prosumption practices that empower citizens to be active players in all matters that regard their lives. Prosumption practices build upon an increasing awareness of the interdependencies between the rural and the urban, therefore reconfiguring their power relations and, in turn, establishing the basis for a shift towards post-growth. This chapter analyses an increasingly popular prosumption practice: purchasing food from alternative food networks (AFNs). This practice is reconnecting the natural processes of production and consumption with their societal, health and environmental impact, and challenging assumptions of continuous growth.

Prosumption practices lean heavily on the principles of participation, community building and engagement, and therefore, flourish within community-led initiatives. We find that community-led food initiatives deserve further exploration in the context of shifting towards a post-growth food system despite the criticism by a strand of the literature (Brown et al., 2012; Cook and Swyngedouw, 2012) accusing them of shifting the focus to small-scale and pragmatic actions, whereas systemic and radical change is necessary. We argue that community-led food initiatives can be seen as "microcosms of hope" (Bailey et al., 2010) that increase diversity in the current capitalist system (Callon, 1998; Gibson-Graham, 2006; MacKenzie et al., 2007), which is a necessary step towards its transformation.

In this chapter we address the following questions. Which role do community-led food initiatives play in the institutionalisation of emergent food prosumption practices, such as purchasing food from AFNs? And how do they contribute to unmaking capitalist cultural, material and power relations between the urban and the rural, paving the way towards a post-growth food system?

In order to analyse the aforementioned practice, we present the experiences of two community-led food initiatives in the Amsterdam region: "FoodCoopNoord", a food cooperative located in Amsterdam North; and "Pluk! Groenten van West", a Community Supported Agriculture (CSA) farm located in the western part of the city. The authors are both long-term members of these initiatives and have therefore first-hand access to up-to-date information. In addition, one semi-structured interview with a key member was conducted for each initiative, as well as desk research and policy document analysis.

This chapter is structured as follows. Section 2 sketches the context in which these community-led initiatives are emerging, the "Amsterdam food scene", as referred to by some of the interviewed members. In Section 3, we present the notion of "community capacity", setting up the structure for the analysis of the chosen community-led initiatives, which will happen in Section 4. Finally, the chapter's conclusion outlines some remarks on the role that communities play in enabling the institutionalisation of the prosumption practice at hand, and how community-led initiatives potentially contribute to a post-growth food system.

## 2. Amsterdam's Food Scene

The development of new forms of food production and food provision in the Amsterdam region can be explained to a large extent by the increasing emergence of AFNs in the last few decades. AFNs aim to "diversify and transform food provisioning by connecting ethical producers and consumers in more local, direct ways" (Edwards, 2016: 1). They appeared in the 1990s as a reaction against the agro-food system which stands for globalisation, industrialisation and unethical practices. The Netherlands, where the agro-food sector is an important economic base, played a pioneering role in the industrialisation and the transformation of agriculture into a highly intensive and technology-advanced sector. But the ongoing intense exploitation of its farmland is taking a toll on the country's scarce natural resources and fragile ecosystems (de Vries et al., 2016). The country is also increasingly experiencing the effects of the challenges posed by global climate change and by the poor dietary choices and habits, developed post-war, of its inhabitants (Bouma et al., 2020).

These challenges have prompted action at multiple levels of the Dutch government. The transformation of the food production and consumption systems is at the head of the priorities of the government 2050 circular economy program (Nederland Circulaire in 2050). In 2017, 16 national, regional and municipal Dutch government entities signed the Food on the Urban Agenda agreement (City Deal Voedsel op de Stedelijke Agenda) to consolidate their efforts in the area of food policy. Further efforts are being deployed also from networks of researchers and community-led initiatives, to support the development of policies, education and knowledge dissemination around the food transition. These developments have been, undoubtedly, instrumental in spurring the growth and multiplication of community-led food initiatives in The Netherlands in the last decade (van Kampen, 2020).

Amsterdam published its first integrated municipal food strategy (Voedselvisie) in 2014. Food appears also as a recurrent component of the city's health, sustainability, spatial planning, economy and poverty alleviation policies. Moreover, multiple policy instruments, including a subsidy program (Gemeente Amsterdam, 2019), are used to foster the development of food-related start-ups and community projects (Sibbing et al., 2019).

These municipal policy developments are forerun by a thriving movement of food-related community-led initiatives in Amsterdam. A number of civic organisations, non-profits and local businesses are actively working to advocate, educate, research and implement solutions for a local sustainable food ecosystem in the city and its region. On its ground, the city counts 212 urban farming projects and 75 worm hotels (Gemeente Amsterdam, n.d.). In addition to small-scale organic food production, composting, and their educational, recreational and innovative dimensions, these projects and spaces constitute the backbone of the city's green structure (Groenvisie 2050).

A growing demand and interest of consumers in the quality and provenance of their food is another defining aspect of the Amsterdam food scene. These consumers belong to the growing highly educated middle-class demographic segment of the city (Centraal Bureau voor de Statistiek, 2019). DeLind (2010) describes them as a group of committed individuals who feel that, through their personal behaviour and choices, they are able to address global issues, and therefore belong to a historically privileged elite responsible for "changing the world". This demand has been fuelling the booming market of organic food products and even challenging the existing food supply chains, but it has also been an opportunity for food-related prosumption practices to gain traction and visibility within a capitalist economy.

Amsterdam houses a growing number of options for consumers seeking alternatives to buying food outside the conventional system. These range from organic supermarkets, organic farmers' markets, organic specialty stores and organic food box subscription, to growing food in individual allotments or community gardens, CSA subscriptions and food cooperative memberships for the more civically engaged consumer. In this chapter we focus on the last two, where the community plays a central role, for their twofold potential: to bridge the urban–rural gap and to contribute to a post-growth food system.

## 3. Community Capacity: Understanding the Role of the Community in Enabling Food Prosumption Practices

What role do community-led food initiatives play in enabling prosumption practices such as purchasing food from AFNs, and how do they contribute to building the foundation of a post-growth food system? Before delving into these key questions, we will first explore the notion of community, as used in this chapter. It is important to state that there is no clear consensus about a definition of "community" (Cohen, 1985; Crow and Allan, 1994; Delanty, 2003 in Peters et al., 2010: 7601). A community is, conventionally, considered a social group whose members share similar interests, regardless of online or offline environments (Carroll, 2012; Rheingold, 1993), and develop forms of togetherness around these shared interests (Mosconi et al., 2017). In this chapter we understand community as a relational space shaped by social interactions (Massey, 2005), which actively construct the community in time. The space of the community is not a container or something fixed. It is always in flux and is constantly being shaped by the interactions of its members (Crang and Thrift, 2000).

The shift towards a post-growth food system requires a substantial lifestyle and cultural change that shapes the way we produce and consume goods and services, including food. We argue that the relational space of the community can contribute to this cultural change, by shaping understandings of what is considered "normal" regarding how we relate to food through prosumption practices. We look at these practices, as both constitutive and transformative factors of social change, instead of only at performances, in order to overcome the structure–agency dichotomy. In that sense, aiming at transforming practices implies addressing the issue not only from an agentic but also from a structural perspective, which is crucial to construct new understandings of normality in a post-growth society.

Acknowledging that "the very notion of community engagement goes against [current] existing socio-cultural norms that promote individualism" (Mulugetta et al., 2010: 7545), we explore, in this chapter, the notion of community capacity in order to go beyond romanticised and positive connotations (McCarthy, 2005) of community and to elucidate what is realistic when claiming that community-led initiatives can contribute to a post-growth food system. We understand community capacity as the "ability of the community in question and its members to make changes by drawing on the resources available to them individually and collectively" (Middlemiss and Parrish, 2010: 7561). The following community capacity indicators listed by the aforementioned authors will structure our analysis of the chosen Amsterdam-based initiatives:

- *Social capital* is defined as "the ways in which a community builds capacity for action through increased and strengthened network connections between individuals" (Evans et al., 2005 in Middlemiss and Parrish, 2010: 7560). This is what Woolcock and Narayan (2000) call "horizontal" social capital.[1]
- *Infrastructural capacity* refers to the specific physical facilities and assets available for a community, for example based on the established built environment

stock (buildings and roads), transport (vehicles), energy (power supplies), communications (platforms) etc. When applied to community-led initiatives that support food prosumption practices, infrastructural capacity refers to all the facilities that make an alternative food system possible, from production, processing and distribution through to consumption and disposal of food waste.
- *Organisational capacity* refers to how the community deals with the aforementioned resources and the support available to maintain the initiative and make it thrive. This includes the internal organisation of activities, volunteers' time schedules and division of roles and responsibilities, among other aspects.
- *Institutional capacity* refers to the ways in which a community participates in the established regime (Healey et al., 2003), i.e., to which extent current regulatory frameworks apply to the initiative and to which extent these initiatives remain "niches" or are able to scale up and become "mainstream", more normalised, in order to have a large impact in the current (food) system.

## 4. Purchasing Food from AFNs: Lessons from Two Amsterdam Community-Led Initiatives

### 4.1 FoodCoopNoord

FoodCoopNoord is a food co-op in North Amsterdam that offers local residents the opportunity to purchase local, seasonal and (mostly) organic products. FoodCoopNoord buys produce directly in bulk from local farmers and producers within the Amsterdam region, avoiding the extra costs of intermediaries. This allows the co-op to pay a fair price to the farmers while getting high-quality affordable products.

FoodCoopNoord was founded in 2011 by a small group of residents who, at the time, missed a more sustainable, conscious and healthy alternative to purchasing their food. Even if its members call it a food cooperative, FoodCoopNoord is legally an association. Its board of directors and members gather at least twice per year in a general meeting to discuss and vote on decisions regarding the association's organisational matters. This status provides the initiative with a base for its institutional capacity and an organisational framework, although the initiative remains at a niche level. The choice of using "FoodCoop" in the name of the association shows the importance that its members confer to a collective way of organisation and their commitment to building a community.

Anyone can become a member by creating an account on the food co-op website[2] and paying an initial amount of 10 euros. There is no formal contract; members commit, however, to volunteering a minimum of four (pick-up) days a year, approximately 20 hours in total, to sort out the bulk produce received from the local farms, and prepare the members' individual weekly orders. The food co-op relies heavily on the availability of both the local farmers, who weekly drive their products from Amsterdam's hinterland into the city, and the community volunteers, who need to receive them or pick them up at arranged locations. Volunteering members can also contribute to other tasks necessary to sustain the food co-op, such as coordinating the members' orders, communicating with the local producers, posting website and social media updates and organising community activities and workshops. Thanks to an online platform, members can check products' availability and prices, select their desired quantities and place their orders. The good functioning of the online platform plays a key role in strengthening the community's fragile infrastructural capacity.

FoodCoopNoord has, currently, 130 members, with approximately 50 who are active. Upon registration, members designate on a spreadsheet the days on which they are available to volunteer. This system has not been working as well as intended. Many members order regularly, but do not volunteer sufficiently, putting the burden on a core group of active members, who compensate with their time in order to keep the food co-op running. The lack of volunteers results in the cancellation of the weekly order from time to time. This has brought some complaints and has made many members disappointed to the point of leaving the initiative. In September 2020, during a general meeting, it has been decided to change the way volunteering is organised. A shift was made from a more individualistic approach towards a collective way of organisation. Six teams of ten members each, including a coordinator, were subsequently formed, and will rotate weekly to successfully perform the co-op duties. The goal is to hold members responsible for their teammates while allowing them to get to know each other and, in that way, strengthen the organisational capacity and the members' social capital all at once.

One of the main reasons behind the different levels of commitment in this initiative is that there are two different groups with different intrinsic motivations: there is a small group of active and long-standing members (approximately ten) driven by a strong will to contribute to a fairer and more sustainable food system by shortening the food chain and supporting local farmers and producers. Many of them are entrepreneurs and are long-time residents of North Amsterdam. This subgroup is characterised by high levels of social capital. The second group, which is the majority, is composed of members, mostly in their late 20s and early 30s, who are driven by the idea of eating local and healthier (organic) food and who like "playing supermarket" (according to one of the members). Many of the members of this last group moved to North Amsterdam in the last few years, and their busy urbanite lifestyles leave them with little time to invest in the food co-op. They usually start very enthusiastically but their motivation wears rapidly over time. These two groups do not mingle much, and the organised community engagement efforts and social events end up being attended mostly by the same group of dedicated members. The fact that the food co-op has changed its pick-up locations three times (always within the North district) in the last ten years can be seen also as an indication of its fragile infrastructural capacity, and is detrimental to building a strong community. Despite all these challenges, the co-op community spirit remains intact as shown by the unanimous rejection, during the last general meeting, of the idea of "selling volunteering shifts" to solve the problem of members' lack of commitment: "That does not suit the standards of a cooperative," as argued by one of the members.

## 4.2 Pluk! CSA Groenten van West

Pluk! Groenten van West is one of three urban CSA projects located within Amsterdam's city boundaries. It was founded in 2017 by three members of Cityplot,[3] a European collective of urban farming professionals, educators and permaculture designers. The collective has been active since 2008 in Amsterdam, organising educational workshops and activities, as well as supporting and managing community, school, rooftop and restaurant gardens. Pluk! CSA operates as part of the Cityplot Foundation and is the latter's first large-scale farming enterprise in the city. The project stemmed from its founders' belief in the necessity of transforming the current food production and consumption patterns and making concrete steps towards self-sufficiency and a sustainable food production system.

The CSA model[4] offers Pluk! an entrepreneurial structure but acts also as a community engagement and participation framework within the farm, anchoring the community's institutional and organisational capacities. Pluk! members pay an annual sliding scale fee and receive a weekly or bi-weekly share of the harvest from May to November. The CSA started with 54 members in its first year and has grown to a 100-strong community in its fourth year. The farmers and the CSA members are bound by individual harvester contracts which outline both parties' commitment, the farm permaculture growing practices and each member's annual contribution.

Pluk! is located within Fruittuin van West, a Demeter-certified[5] biodynamic orchard and free-range chicken farm in Amsterdam West – in Tuinen van West, a multifunctional urban farming and recreational area in the Osdorper Binnenpolder Noord. On half a hectare of ground spread around the perimeter of the farm, Pluk! grows more than 95 varieties of organic vegetables, herbs and edible flowers for its members using permaculture design principles. Fruittuin van West provided Pluk! with the critical infrastructure to start up, by leasing parts of its ground to the CSA. Fruittuin van West provides also a symbiotic environment for Pluk!, as it hosts other complementary projects and facilities that fit the farm's vision of a sustainable and circular food business (e.g., an organic supermarket, a cafe, a cheese dairy, educational tours, children's workshops).

During its start-up phase, Pluk! has benefitted from the "Subsidie Stadslandbouw en Voedselinitiatieven" (Agriculture and Food Initiatives Subsidy) awarded by the Municipality of Amsterdam. Furthermore, crowdfunding campaigns and benefit dinners were also organised to fund the purchase of a water pump and the installation of two greenhouses. In its fifth year, the CSA successfully applied for another grant from the municipality of Amsterdam for the right to use and expand its farming activities on an additional plot of land, in the Luktemeerpolder, a few minutes' bike ride from its current location, therefore increasing substantially its infrastructural capacity, but especially showcasing its institutional capacity.

The focus on the community is a core foundation of Pluk!'s organisation and is a pillar of its social capital. In addition to growing food, the farmers also play the roles of educators and community coordinators. Pluk! members receive regular updates and information about the farm, its produce and events via a weekly newsletter and are connected online through a Facebook group. The CSA relies on its members to weekly self-harvest which creates regular meeting and interaction opportunities between the harvesters and the farmers. Harvesters are encouraged, but not required, to participate in farming tasks, enquire about production methods and operations, proactively organise activities and events and exchange recipes. Members are also expected to provide feedback on the annual crop planning and budgeting through a written survey and during the annual members' dinner.

In its fifth year, Pluk! has five farmers and five interns onboard. The main source of income of the CSA consists of its members' subscription fees, but the collected amount is still not sufficient to fully cover the farming operation expenses and offer the farmers fair compensation. This organisational challenge makes volunteers' labour critical to fulfil the farm's daily tasks. A motivated, diverse group of around 20 rotating volunteers, made of members and non-members, has been regularly part of Pluk!'s workforce. These volunteers are able to take home some of the farm's produce, but they are especially motivated by the opportunities of joining a community of environmentally and health-conscious food growers and eaters, and spending time outdoors while locally making an impact.

The Pluk! community consists of a diverse group of individuals of different ages and socio-economic and political backgrounds, with a common appreciation for fresh, seasonal, locally grown produce and a desire to connect with earth and nature. Young and less young professionals, families with children and retirees, most of whom live within a 30-minute bike ride from the farm's location, have met in the past three years for monthly dinners, brunches and picnics, participated in cooking and food-preserving workshops and assembled a cookbook. Most recently, following the restrictions on physical activities caused by the COVID-19 pandemic, a committee was set up by the farmers, gathering representatives of the Pluk! community, including interns and volunteers, to maintain and continue growing the CSA's social capital. The committee members have already volunteered to assist with some of the non-farming tasks of the CSA, and brainstormed pricing solutions that would allow a better compensation for its farmers. Further discussions are also taking place to organise and implement side projects and community-building activities.

## 5. Towards a Post-Growth Food System

The two community-led initiatives presented in this chapter showcase how their community capacity can be leveraged to enable food prosumption practices, and specifically purchasing food from AFNs.

Although these initiatives do not subscribe per se to a post-growth agenda, they lay the groundwork for a more holistic approach to address questions such as the regionalisation of food, soil fertility decline, the development of circular food systems, and ultimately the transformation of conventional food supply chains. The

**FIGURE 12.1** Top: view of one of the fields cultivated by Pluk! CSA. Bottom: display of a portion of the weekly Pluk! CSA harvest with a map of the harvesting locations in the background

Source: photographs Pluk! CSA Groenten van West

different levels of community capacity that we recorded mean, however, that each initiative has a different impact and contribution to this approach.

In both cases, we found that, whether motivated by environmental, health or social concerns, these community-led initiatives are characterised by relatively high levels of social capital. Besides, their members are assembled and driven by a vivid awareness of the necessity to rethink their position within the current food supply chain, change their food consumption patterns and reduce their environmental footprint. Their organisational and institutional capacities present, however, challenges which hinder their chances to prosper within the current capitalist food system frameworks. In this system, the infrastructural capacities of these communities remain closely dependent on these initiatives' organisation and how they are integrated in the current regime, specifically, their ability to build partnerships, generate revenue and raise funds.

Next, we identify two aspects characteristic, respectively, of the organisational and institutional capacities of these community-led initiatives, and present recommendations to boost their ability to become a cornerstone of the transition towards a post-growth food system.

## 5.1 Inclusive Contractual Agreements: Sweat Equity as a Participatory Tool

As showcased by both initiatives, the levels and nature of expected individual engagement and contribution determine the ability of each community-led initiative to attract and retain members, and therefore to sustain and scale up. In-kind contributions are common within community organisational structures and, like in FoodCoopNoord, are often required. They allow for a greater inclusion and ensure a higher level of involvement and bonding among the community members. This, however, can create an access barrier for those unable to spare the time or effort to contribute, but who still adhere to the initiative's collective values. Alternatively, requesting only monetary contributions, such as in the case of Pluk! Groenten van West, on the one hand allows the CSA to include all those who can afford to pay its subscription fee, but on the other hand limits its ability to control the level of involvement of its members.

Regardless of their participatory frameworks, both FoodCoopNoord and Pluk! rely heavily on the voluntary involvement and dedication of their members to sustain their operations. It is also worth mentioning that much of this volunteering work is accomplished and led by women. This dominance of unpaid labour leads easily to frictions, namely a free-rider problem, and engenders uncertainty, as we found at FoodCoopNoord. In the case of Pluk!, a contractual agreement creates clarity by outlining the farmers' and the harvesters' responsibilities. A fair wage is, however, still not achievable if the product of the intense labour involved with farming in the CSA is valued based on the current market food prices.

We argue that the introduction of sweat equity as a rewarded contribution within the contractual agreement of community-led initiatives will put a value on the voluntary labour of dedicated members, and by extension will improve social inclusion by ensuring that those with little capital are also able to join. This can be done through internal rewards, such as an internal credit system, or by joining an established time-banking system. Furthermore, a minimum number of volunteering hours should be required of prospective members, not only as a community-building tool, but also to better institute prosumption practices within a post-growth economic system, challenging the existing patterns of overwork and overconsumption.

## 5.2 The Path to Institutionalisation: Integrated Food Policies and Neighbourhood Food Hubs

Both communities' organisational and institutional capacities are anchored in the existing growth vision of the economy and its market frameworks. In this context, the community-led initiatives presented in this chapter are reappropriating market strategies in a pragmatic approach to embed ethical and social values in the food value chain. The support these communities get from government entities is in line with the latter's current policies promoting sustainability, social innovation and building resilience in the face of economic crises and stagnation. This support is, however, not structural and remains subject to the political priorities of the municipal council, which challenges the ability of these initiatives to go mainstream and impact the food system at large.

To overcome this instability, we argue that integrated food policies should replace ever-changing municipal documents, address the burning questions pertaining to systemic change and establish, in a first step, prosumption as a fully operational model in parallel with the existing consumerist paradigm. A systemic long-term change would include, among other actions, a review of the European Common Agricultural Policy, capping production, embracing agro-ecology farming, and especially challenging strongly rooted growth narratives. On the ground, in the short term, the creation of dedicated neighbourhood hubs, in the midst of the centres of consumption that are cities, could play an important role in putting community-led initiatives on the map. Educational programs, information events, and the creation of meeting opportunities between citizens, local and regional farmers and AFNs would raise further awareness but especially would make the leap towards prosumption much more realistic and accessible.

In the path towards a post-growth food system, we argue that community-led food initiatives can play an important role in building the local capacity among urban dwellers to collectively engage in prosumption practices. These community-led initiatives are well-geared to offer their members the space to act and achieve concrete results at the local level. Despite challenges and criticism, and regardless of their philosophical and political backgrounds, they actively contribute to enabling a cultural shift that blurs the hard mental boundaries between production and consumption spaces, and to rebuilding connections between the urban and the rural.

## Notes

1 The "vertical" type of social capital is included within the "institutional capacity" indicator.
2 https://foodcoopnoord.nl/
3 https://cityplot.org/
4 A CSA typically consists of a community of individuals who pledge to a farm operation by making an upfront payment and receive, in exchange, a share of the farm's produce throughout the growing season. CSAs provide a short value chain for food, directly linking producers and consumers. This puts the relationship between the farmer and the community members at the center of the CSA – a relationship built on the principles of commitment, mutual support, trust and risk-sharing.
5 Demeter is a quality label for biodynamic agriculture and food. Demeter-certified farms and products comply with the International Demeter Biodynamic Standards, as well as applicable local organic regulations, in production, processing and final product packaging. In The Netherlands, the Demeter label is controlled and delivered by Stichting Demeter (www.demeter.net/).

## References

Bailey I, Hopkins R and Wilson G (2010) Some things old, some things new: The spatial representations and politics of change of the peak oil relocalisation movement. *Geoforum* 41(4): 595–605.

Bouma J, Boot P, Bredenoord H et al. (2020) *Balans van de Leefomgeving 2020. Burger in zicht, overheid aan zet*. Report. The Hague: Planbureau voor de Leefomgeving. Available from: www.pbl.nl/sites/default/files/downloads/pbl-2020-balans-van-de-leefomgeving-2020-4165.pdf (accessed 15 September 2020).

Brown G, Kraftl P, Pickerill J et al. (2012) Holding the future together: Towards a theorisation of the spaces and times of transition. *Journal of Marketing Research* 44(7): 289–302.

Callon, M (1998) *The Laws of the Markets*. Malden, MA: Blackwell.

Carroll JM (2012) *The Neighborhood in the Internet: Design Research Projects in Community Informatics*. New York: Routledge.

Centraal Bureau voor de Statistiek (CBS) (2019) *Bevolking 15 tot 75 jaar; opleidingsniveau, wijken en buurten*. The Hague/Heerlen: CBS.

Cohen AP (1985) *The Symbolic Construction of Community*. London: Routledge.

Cook IR and Swyngedouw E (2012) Cities, social cohesion and the environment: Towards a future research agenda. *Urban Studies* 49(9): 1959–1979.

Crang M and Thrift N (2000) *Thinking Space*. London: Routledge.

Cronon W (1991) *Nature's Metropolis: Chicago and the Great West*. New York: Norton.

Crow G and Allan G (1994) *Community Life: An Introduction to Local Social Relations*. New York: Harvester Wheatsheaf.

Cutcliffe SH (2010) Travels in and out of town: William Cronon's *Nature's Metropolis: Chicago and the Great West. Technology and Culture* 51(3): 728–737.

de Vries G, de Hoog J, Stellinga B et al. (2016) *Towards a Food Policy*. WRR Report no. 93. The Hague: The Netherlands Scientific Council for Government Policy. Available from: https://english.wrr.nl/publications/reports/2016/12/13/towards-a-food-policy (accessed 13 September 2020).

DeLind LB (2010) Are local food and the local food movement taking us where we want to go? Or are we hitching our wagons to the wrong stars? *Agriculture and Human Values* 28(2): 273–283.

Edwards F (2016) Alternative food networks. In: Thompson PB and Kaplan DM (eds), *Encyclopedia of Food and Agricultural Ethics*. Dordrecht: Springer.

Evans B, Joas M, Sundback S et al. (2005) *Governing Sustainable Cities*. London: Earthscan.

Gemeente Amsterdam (n.d.) Amsterdam Stadslandbouw. Available from: https://maps.amsterdam.nl/stadslandbouw/ (accessed 18 September 2020).

Gemeente Amsterdam (2019) Subsidie Stadslandbouw en Voedselinitiatieven. Available from: www.amsterdam.nl/veelgevraagd/?productid=%7B000808EA-6167-40D7-853E-6CFAC69DC6EB%7D (accessed 18 September 2020).

Gibson-Graham JK (2006) *A Postcapitalist Politics*. Minneapolis, MN: University of Minnesota Press.

Harvey D (1982) *The Limits to Capital*. Chicago, IL: The University of Chicago Press.

Healey P, de Magalhaes C, Madanipour A et al. (2003) Place, identity and local politics: Analysing initiatives in deliberative governance. In: Hajer M and Wagenaar H (eds), *Deliberative Policy Analysis: Understanding Governance in the Network Society*. Cambridge: Cambridge University Press.

MacKenzie DA, Muniesa F and Siu L (2007) *Do Economists Make Markets? On the Performativity of Economics*. Princeton, NJ: Princeton University Press.

Massey D (2005) *For Space*. London: SAGE.

McCarthy J (2005) Devolution in the woods: Community forestry as hybrid neoliberalism. *Environment and Planning A: Economy and Space* 37(6): 995–1014.

McClintock N (2010) Why farm the city? Theorizing urban agriculture through a lens of metabolic rift. *Cambridge Journal of Regions, Economy and Society* 3(2): 191–207.

Middlemiss L and Parrish BD (2010) Building capacity for low-carbon communities: The role of grassroots initiatives. *Energy Policy* 38(12): 7559–7566.

Mosconi G, Korn M, Reuter C et al. (2017) From Facebook to the neighbourhood: Infrastructuring of hybrid community engagement. *Computer Supported Cooperative Work* 26(4–6): 959–1003.

Mulugetta Y, Jackson, T and Van der Horst D (2010) Carbon reduction at community scale. *Energy Policy* 38(12): 7541–7545.

Peters M, Fudge S and Sinclair P (2010) Mobilising community action towards a low-carbon future: Opportunities and challenges for local government in the UK. *Energy Policy* 38(12): 7596–7603.

Rheingold H (1993) *The Virtual Community: Homesteading on the Electronic Frontier*. Boston, MA: Addison-Wesley.

Sibbing L, Candel J and Termeer K (2019) A comparative assessment of local municipal food policy integration in The Netherlands. *International Planning Studies* 26(1): 56–69.

van Kampen S (2020) *Lokale voedselgemeenschappen in Nederland: Inventarisatie en verkennend onderzoek*. Report, De schaal van Kampen. Available from: www.deschaalvankampen.nl/wp-content/uploads/2020/12/DSVK-Lokale-voedselgemeenschappen-in-Nederland1.pdf (accessed 20 January 2021).

Woolcock M and Narayan D (2000) Social capital: Implications for development theory, research, and policy. *World Bank Research Observer* 15(2): 225–250.

# PART 7
# Being

# 13
# BECOMING A POST-GROWTH PLANNER

Inner obstacles to changing roles

*Christian Lamker and Viola Schulze Dieckhoff*

## 1. Introduction

Post-growth thinking is increasingly being taken up by planning researchers in Germany (Brokow-Loga and Eckardt, 2020), wider Europe (Barry, 2020; Ferreira and von Schönfeld, 2020), and beyond (Nelson and Schneider, 2019). Scholars urge that humanity must stay within planetary boundaries and that people must shed their obsession with unfettered economic growth, with its damaging social, cultural, and ecological impacts. Most scholars insist on the necessity of strong actions against climate change and environmental crises. Some scholars go beyond matters of planetary impact, pointing towards the use of land and scarce resources, as well as to housing and mobility as questions of justice. A discursive momentum is building for developing planning roles and practices that are not based on an institutionalised growth paradigm. It is becoming conceivable that planners will emerge for whom growth is neither a starting point nor a goal. However, post-growth practices remain niche. Planners' capacity for imagining growth-independent spatial development depends on overcoming obstacles in their own mindsets, values, and worldviews. Moreover, knowledge about the challenges that planners face once they get in touch with post-growth ideas is thus far limited to a few singular projects and short-lived experiments.

Surprisingly little is known about what characterises "the planner" as an individual agent within transformation processes (Willson, 2020). Studies have uncovered where planners work, how they act, how they are educated, and which tools and instruments they apply in their daily practice. Much work is done to develop new courses of action for planners and to provide new kinds of information and evidence to feed into planning processes. However, there is an understudied aspect that appears like a black box in planning literature: the inner self of a planner and how the personality of planners impacts their professional roles and practices (Willson, 2020; Westin, 2014). This chapter, therefore, ponders two main questions. First, what hinders planners in imagining planning beyond growth? Second, what kinds of inner struggles do planners face when they imagine moving away from growth-dependent roles and practices?

The next section (section 2) explains the importance of understanding planners as individual beings with their own personal characteristics. The following methodological note (section 3) outlines transformative confrontations and actions with mostly German planning practitioners and planning researchers between 2017 and 2020. Section 4 shows nine reactions that surface amongst planners when they are confronted with post-growth ideas. Section 5 introduces four perspectives (desires, emotions, values, and sensemaking) that help to systematically understand the inner struggles and barriers that planners experience. These perspectives help to explain visible tensions in planning practice and theory, and with these, the potential for a transformation. Pinning post-growth planning discussions down to different types of reactions aims at enabling a shift away from the growth paradigm to rediscover the transformative potential of planning. Finally, section 6 concludes with potential avenues for overcoming these individual obstacles and enabling the emergence of post-growth planners in democratic societies.

## 2. Understanding planners to encourage post-growth planning

Planners generally, and those who work in public administrations in particular, collect and analyse information; develop and guide processes; use specific tools and instruments; and translate information into policies, strategies, and plans. Subsequent decisions, which are often both binding and publicly visible, are often taken without explicit reference to political agendas. However, although daily tasks can be routinised and left unquestioned, most are rarely neutral or objective. The assumption of political neutrality has already been challenged under the so-called communicative and argumentative turns. It is even more substantially challenged by recent turns to activism in planning research and practice (Mayer, 2020), as well as by an emerging focus on transformative actions and practices (Albrechts et al., 2020). It is now understood that the roles of planners have been constantly recreated and adapted, most notably with the shift to communicative planning ideals, strategic approaches, and governance processes (Healey, 2002, p. 1788; Othengrafen and Levin-Keitel, 2019, pp. 114 ff.). In line with this work, we recognise planning processes as political processes and planners as inevitably acting politically. We also recognise that the personal dimensions of every planner impact their professional actions (Willson, 2020, p. 46). To date, much research still circumvents questions about the nature of planners and the normative justifications for planning in a democratic society. This void obstructs productive engagement with detrimental structural forces, such as neoliberalism and economic growth.

Planning has been criticised for its inability to tackle either environmental problems like climate change and sustainability, or social problems like housing, mobility, and inequality. Clear long-term goals have been set but these often conflict with other policy targets. The German government has stipulated that net use of new land for settlements and infrastructure should be cut by more than half to less than 30 hectares per day until 2030 and, in the long run, to zero. However, planners find themselves at the complex interface between politics, science, citizens, and the development and implementation of integrated plans. Since the 1980s, a weak engagement with underlying values has enabled a neoliberal mentality to dominate planning (Barry, 2020, p. 123; Davoudi, 2016, pp. 617 f.). Some planners resolve this tension by engaging in politics alongside their professional work, whereas others leave planning to run for political office (Albrechts, 2020, pp. 6 f.). This schizophrenia between private and professional roles means underused creativity.

By pushing through this private/public divide, we aim to unlock planners' creative potential. Doubt remains about whether this is possible. Structural interpretations prevail, leaving a seemingly minor position for individual planners. This bias towards the economic system is often reproduced in post-growth debates (Barry, 2020). Davoudi (2016) resists this reductionist approach to planning, emphasising the importance of social and environmental values. It is important to recognise that each planner faces conscious or unconscious conflicts while engaging with basic dilemmas. As planning scholars, we need to understand the positions of planners before we can support them in transforming their roles. The challenge is to gain support for post-growth as a new normative direction without undermining professional positions, personal characteristics and values, and the democratic legitimacy of planning as such.

## 3. Methodological notes: towards transformative planning research

Ferreira and von Schönfeld (2020, p. 54) suggest that the economic growth narrative came to dominate public policy in general because, "it offered an ethically sound strategy to increase the wealth of all citizens without having to address the problem of inequality through redistributive policies (or a recurrence to exploitation)." Even thinking differently seems deeply challenging under such structural restraints, let alone acting differently. To begin with, conflicts and their productive potential need to be acknowledged and openly discussed. With this in mind, we engaged in what we call transformative confrontations. The starting point was a puzzle unfolding in a discussion amongst a group of about 15 young planners from academia and practice in the German state of North Rhine-Westphalia in September 2016. We felt uncomfortable with unquestioned truths within planning. Unlike most research projects, we did not develop an action plan, gain funding, and write dissemination plans. No support was deemed available for such ideas at the time. However, the group members were engaged in practice, in research, and/or in research–practice exchange groups such as within the German Academy for Territorial Development (ARL). It started with three workshops with young professionals and academics in 2017 to clarify the scope and questions of the new "post-growth planning", a term that we developed for these efforts in April 2017.

Our diverse engagements undertaken between 2017 and 2021 coalesced around the themes of confronting post-growth as an alternative future for planning and encouraging new, post-growth planners into being. The aim was twofold. First, to increase our own understanding of how post-growth and planning could be linked. We took confrontation as the first step towards transformation (Campbell, 2021, p. 6). Second, to trigger discussions around growth-independent planning roles and practices amongst planning theorists and practitioners. These developments would then enable the institutional embedding and capacity-building that are required for lasting transformative change (Wolfram, 2016, p. 126). Ultimately, the discursive confrontation with radical post-growth alternatives has the potential to become a "transformative confrontation" that also changes participants' ways of thinking. During events, we developed knowledge, reflected on routines, and experimented with thought alternatives, with the aim of triggering change and learning (see also Lamker and Schulze Dieckhoff, 2020).

The first three experimental workshops with young planners in 2017 were independently organised, with a small budget from the ARL for renting workshop rooms. All following actions were connected to workgroups, conferences, workshops, and other already existing planning events. These confrontations targeted, with few exceptions, public administration planners, applied planning researchers, and planning students from German-speaking countries. Besides smaller workshops, major events included a fishbowl with approximately 90 participants at the Dortmund Conference in 2018, a World Café session with approximately 50 planning researchers and practitioners from the state of North-Rhine Westphalia in Münster in November 2018, presentations at the Association of European Schools of Planning (AESOP) conference in Gothenburg in 2018 and Degrowth Vienna 2020, and the annual conference of the German Academy for Territorial Development (ARL) on post-growth and transformation in June 2019 with approximately 150 participants. We aimed to shift people's focus to planners and their potential to "experiment with and co-create the conditions for change that ultimately leads to a critical mass supporting post-growth" (Liegey and Nelson, 2020, pp. 93 f.).

## 4. Nine positions on post-growth in planning

Our experiences when confronting spatial planners with post-growth were mixed and partially unexpected. We observed a wide array of reactions from immediate opposition to full support. We identified nine positions that surfaced most clearly (see also Table 13.1). A dismissive "*We did that in the 1970s…!*" reaction (the out of fashion position) was common among planners close to retirement. Clearly, previous debates on the limits to growth amidst the oil crisis in the 1970s, as well as the rise of sustainability in the 1980s and 1990s made some planners confident that the major work is already complete. Talking about post-growth sounds like a personal offence and a denial of previous achievements. To our surprise, a high-ranking

German planning researcher denied the relevance of discussing planetary boundaries, literally because, "*There is the Moon and Mars…!*" (the unnecessary position). Technological solutions, including the potential to mine for resources on other planets, will render boundaries insignificant.

Older planning researchers often suggested, "*That's for young people and/or young academics…!*" (the exclusivity position). Post-growth was reduced to a side-debate amongst a group of young people that will ultimately learn how the real world works and subsequently drop such unrealistic thoughts. Similar arguments were commonly present in German political debates around the growing global climate movement in 2018/19. We did not manage to officially invite established municipal planning professionals to the first three workshops, because, "*We only do growth…!*" (the inappropriate position). One invitation to participate as a speaker and discussant was withdrawn because the planning department head did not allow engagement with post-growth agendas. Others participated privately without acknowledging their professional roles. Post-growth entails radical positions that seem valuable, but which are too detached from the usual work of planners. Although agreement about finite resources and the negative impacts of growth-dependent financial markets on land use and spatial development surfaced, the potential solutions were uncertain. Furthermore, some added that, "*We follow political decisions and mandates…!*" (the responsibility position). They explained that they do not see options available and that they are delegated mandates by their local or regional politicians.

A more positive set of reactions was most visible amongst younger planners. Interest grew quickly. This was most visible in the shift from niche workshops to conferences held by established planning and research bodies. First reactions included open questions like, "*What can we do with that…?*" (the uncertainty position). Against a general acceptance of post-growth thoughts, middle-aged participants struggled to see a specific role for planners when planetary boundaries, resource flows, and diverse indicators beyond GDP enter the debate. The uncertainty seems to be even larger for planning researchers than for practitioners. Interestingly, planners who were not interested in post-growth at all in 2017 and 2018 became active in emerging debates later. In a similar vein, others conveyed puzzlement, asking, "*What is the role of planners in that…?*" (the speculative position). A more enthusiastic position was captured in the question, "*How can we be a part of that…?*" (the inspirational position). This position was especially popular amongst young researchers, students, and spatial entrepreneurs. The potential to connect post-growth with spatial planning attracted a significant group of new actors (such as civil society initiatives, cooperatives, but also researchers from various disciplines such as arts, sociology, or economics) to join established planning conferences such as the annual ARL conference in 2019.

The most radical stance was offered by a retired regional planner, who openly stated: "*We need to smash the planning system and rebuild it up from scratch…!*" (the revolutionary position). He was upset with the experienced limitations on doing good planning and the dominant forces that pressured him in just one direction: providing

**TABLE 13.1** Nine positions adopted by planners on post-growth planning debates

| Position | Typical reaction to post-growth ideas | Potential for change |
| --- | --- | --- |
| Out of fashion | "We did that in the 1970s…!" | Low |
| Unnecessary | "There is the Moon and Mars…!" | Low |
| Exclusivity | "That's for young people and/or young academics…!" | Low |
| Inappropriate | "We only do growth…!" | Low to Medium |
| Responsibility | "We follow political decisions and mandates…!" | Low to Medium |
| Uncertainty | "What can we do with that…?" | Medium to High |
| Speculative | "What is the role of planners in that…?" | Medium to High |
| Inspirational | "How can we be a part of that…?" | High |
| Revolutionary | "We need to smash the planning system and rebuild it up from scratch…!" | High |

Source: authors

land and growth. Some practitioners agreed, but there was also harsh opposition from planning researchers.

Each of the nine typical reactions has a different potential for integrating post-growth thinking into planning (see Table 13.1). The first three positions unveil the broadest opposition to post-growth and therefore offer a low potential for more immediate changes. Further positions could be open to change but mainly defer the debate away from planning (such as to societal debates, political decision-making, legislation, formal tasks, and delegated duties). Others show an immediate engagement with post-growth but uncertainty as to the implications for doing good and legitimate planning. The last four positions appear to have the largest potential for change. However, as all these reactions are visible in contemporary planning in Germany, a deeper understanding of how and why they arise is helpful.

## 5. Becoming a post-growth planner: internal barriers versus opportunities for transformation

This section conceptualises post-growth planners as potential agents of post-growth transformation. Aiming to understand the inner struggles that planners face when they imagine moving away from growth-dependent roles and practices, we went through notes, recordings, communications, and interviews. This section draws on psychoanalysis, psychology, and philosophy literature exploring how perceptions are constructed to understand the perceptual forces upholding a reliance on growth. We focus on four barriers: desires, emotions, values, and sensemaking. We will discuss these separately, critically exploring the extent to which there is room for manoeuvre for reinterpreting these barriers as opportunities to move towards post-growth planning.

## 5.1 Desires

Using insights from psychoanalytical theory, we define desires as (often unconscious) drivers that guide individuals' thoughts, choices, narratives, and actions (Westin, 2014, pp. 32, 177). Planning research informed by psychoanalytical theory suggests that considering planners' desires can be a very effective approach to understand their professional choices (e.g. Gunder, 2011; Gunder and Wang, 2020; Hillier and Gunder, 2003). However, desires are not necessarily rational and do not necessarily present themselves as easily changeable. On the contrary, desires can become dangerous forces that lead to rationally unwanted behaviours, and they are open to being unconsciously instrumentalised and abused (Gunder, 2011, p. 201). Furthermore, engaging planners in debates explicitly referring to their desires is not a simple or necessarily constructive task, as it can be easily understood as unprofessional, personally intrusive, and even offensive. For this reason, we did not explicitly mention the personal desires of planners during our events – even though the debates often naturally flowed towards the topic in a veiled and unintentional way. In sum, identifying and overcoming barriers to post-growth, rooted in desires, can be a substantial challenge. However, deeply transformative potential can emerge from aligning planners' desires with the post-growth logic, and vice versa.

The German planning system puts a strong emphasis on formal institutions and legal processes that are predominantly controlled and operationalised by planners. However, planners themselves expressed concerns about the fading importance and decreasing recognition of their work in politics and society, which brings with it a decline in the resources they need to accomplish their legal duties. Their dwindling reputation also challenges both their willingness and their ability to support those aspects of post-growth thinking that emphasise collective action, civil society initiatives, and urban commons. They do not wish to give over what little control they have left to citizens. Planners desire to be influential; guardians of the public interest; and, therefore, in control of developments. These desires might represent some of the strongest and most resilient barriers against the post-growth logic.

Planning practice often entails performing numerous technical, procedural, and administrative tasks, and maintaining minimally harmonious relations between planning departments, citizens, private powers, and elected politicians. Due to these surface issues, many of the concerns of practitioners and researchers alike circle around planning instruments, methods, legal prescriptions, and processes (in line with findings of Othengrafen and Levin-Keitel, 2019, p. 121). Nevertheless, it was clear from the way planners expressed themselves during the events that, below this sometimes rather technocratic surface, most of them maintain a strong desire to do "good" and to altruistically serve the public interest in ways that express their unique personalities, knowledge, and skills. The personal desire to be more than a bureaucrat fulfilling a legal duty, subject to fluctuating political whims, was obvious on multiple occasions. This urge is an opportunity for triggering transformation towards post-growth planning. Indeed, if it became clear for planners that the post-growth logic is better aligned with the public interest than that of growth, the active endorsement of post-growth initiatives would be more likely. Planners adopting the revolutionary position might be particularly open to this, as might those holding the inappropriate and uncertainty positions. However, it is important to highlight the difficulty of identifying and defining the "public interest" (Gunder, 2016) and, consequently, the difficulty of anticipating the ways in which pursuing post-growth planning might either serve or harm it.

## 5.2 Emotions

Moving to psychology, we acknowledge rational thought and emotions are both dimensions of a person's logical thoughts (Fromm, 2010 [1968]). Consciously or unconsciously, emotions and emotional experiences guide actions. We contend, with Willson (2020, p. 28) and Baum (2015, p. 500), that incorporating emotional and personal dimensions is crucial to understanding why certain planning positions are favoured over others. Human decision making requires an emotional capacity (Tekeli, 2019, p. 233). Moreover, emotions are variations of desires (Thrift, 2004, p. 61) and understanding them supports sensitive, practical decision making. Although emotions can drive the radical changes post-growth agendas call for, they can also act as obstacles. Planners who position themselves against dominant economic (neoliberal) forces take responsibility but also a risk (Gunder and Hillier, 2007). Risk-averse emotions limit creativity and the potential to challenge and change the existing domain (Csikszentmihaly, 1996, p. 28; Kunzmann, 2004, p. 385). Anger, fear, and anxiety can further lead to paranoic characteristics that limit openness (Davy, 2019).

The German planning system emphasises the design and conduct of participatory processes, often in the early stages of planning and beyond legal requirements. Emphasising these processes demonstrates a belief in the power of discourse and argumentation but sets aside a deeper engagement with emotions, neglecting how motivation and agency are developed (Bögel and Upham, 2018, p. 133). In some settings, creating arenas for debate can solve tensions (Balducci, 2011). In other cases, debates stir emotions. Particularly in a polarised political climate, debates allow the "angry citizen" to enter the stage (Davy, 2019, p. 291). Emotions were overtly visible in our confrontations. A group of planners holding the out of fashion and unnecessary positions were personally offended by post-growth views. For them, radical thoughts devalue their hard work. Planners often feel, and this may well be true, that their efforts have led to major changes. They feel disrespected by basic criticisms of underlying planning values and their own previous or current practices.

On the one hand, these emotions seem to inhibit shifts towards post-growth planning. But on the other hand, they also show that planners want control and that they are not neutral towards normative directions. Planners taking the out of fashion position could be activated by acknowledging their achievements and demonstratively building upon their previous work. Those holding the unnecessary position may agree with some of the long-term goals of post-growth planning, such as climate neutrality, and could be open to debating the potential speed and balance of technological innovation and social and environmental concerns. An openness to talking about emotions seems most important for the inappropriate and responsibility positions. Planners occupying these positions feel uneasy with their professional roles, but fear negative emotions from politics and society if they step forward and propose alternatives.

## 5.3 Values

Values are fundamental to planning. The very definition of problems is shaped by whatever norms and values dominate in the time and place in which planners find themselves. Engaging with how people value space is central to how it is used and organised. This remains the case even when values are perceived to be absent. Drawing on the work of Jürgen Habermas, Savini (2019, p. 72) argues that "that sphere of moral values, has been colonized by the individual pursuit of growth, which substitutes pre-capitalist moral principles with the new foundational (amoral) principle of accumulative and individual economic success." In this case, what counts as good planning is defined by the assumption that value accumulation, growth, innovation, and progress are necessary.

The centrality of values may be hard to accept in Germany, and arguably also elsewhere, where planning is understood as a process of recognising and solving spatial problems (Diller and Oberding, 2017). For German authors in particular, planners are either the neutral moderators (in participatory processes aiming at consensus) or the objective technical-rational advisors of and within political processes. Values are underrepresented in favour of purportedly objective empirical methods and rational decision making. Talking about values is challenging and uncomfortable (Campbell, 2012, p. 392) and planners avoid discussing values openly (Xue, 2021, p. 14). In this context, integrating post-growth values in contexts where values of growth, consumerism, and capitalism are deeply rooted sounds impossible. If issues and roles of planning are going to change, finding and calibrating an ethical compass will be crucial (Hendler, 2002, p. 11). Nor are explicitly growth-oriented values the only blockage. Tensions also arise between post-growth values themselves, which may be at least preliminarily accepted by planners, and democratic legitimacy. In essence, public administration planners cannot be seen to present themselves as superior decision makers.

Looking into our confrontations, many planners saw their major task as the (temporary) allocation of scarce spatial resources, especially land, in the right way and by using professional planning instruments. Planners are eager to make and implement legally binding plans that suit the demands and contexts at hand. Legitimacy is derived from planning law and procedures; public participation; or the political decisions of councils and parliaments. For those holding the inappropriate and responsibility positions, the scope for engagement with values is narrow.

On the other hand, most planners are socialised in university environments that put a strong emphasis on spatial challenges from housing provision and affordability, to inequalities, to sustainability, environmental issues, and climate change. A transformative potential may arise for planners holding the uncertainty and speculative positions. They share broad post-growth values but lack a closer connection to the professional roles and practices associated with post-growth. Providing safe discussion environments, such as the transformative confrontations we held, could already serve as initial triggers.

## 5.4 Sensemaking

Spatial planning and the role of planners are shaped by processes in which planners make sense of their environment and their given tasks. Sensemaking is thus part of both the everyday work of planning (Metzger and Hillier, 2015, pp. 12 ff.) and the periodic need to reinvent planning. Decades of theorising planning have opened a folding fan of how it is framed – with diverse roles for planners related to each theoretical strand (Lamker, 2016, pp. 102 ff.). From this perspective, sensemaking processes are varied. However, the economy itself remains unquestioned as "an ordered machine that governs our lives" (Gibson-Graham et al., 2013, p. 1).

The challenge to implementing post-growth approaches to sensemaking is twofold. First, planners themselves perceive their profession as rather complex. They are already engaged in constant processes of sensemaking, but primarily in relation to digital transformation, sustainability, and climate change. Sensemaking is thus diverted away from more radical approaches. Second, just as with values, the foundation of planning is not perceived as a relevant discussion within planning. The norm is to promote the value of planning as such without putting forward specific normative directions (ARL, 2017, p. 24). Today, German planning research itself is in a process of redefining its relationship with politics, the public, and planning practice. Such efforts are worthy in terms of ensuring democratic legitimacy, but they have limits if planners retreat from developing alternative ideas, such as those provided by post-growth.

With the exception of the revolutionary position, planners in our confrontations understand themselves as nested within existing institutions and public administrations. They thus defer processes of sensemaking to structural forces. Interestingly, a study for the government of North Rhine-Westphalia positioned the future role of public administration as a counterpart to economic growth as early as the 1970s (Wagener, 1971, p. 8). This shift in sensemaking has not happened to date, though the speculative and inspirational positions clearly show openness to this direction. Quite to the contrary, after German reunification, the planning debate shifted even more towards European and global competitiveness, metropolitan cores, and economic growth agendas. With the adoption of the New Leipzig Charter in 2021 for European urban development policy, unlimited economic growth has lost its predominant role and growth-dependent planning may have sustained its first serious crack. This could enable planners holding the inappropriate and responsibility positions to rethink their roles and practices.

## 6. Conclusion

> The projection of alternative futures including serious roles for planners can exert its magic, can become performative, when others become persuaded and organize governance anew, allowing for a new planner to arise.
> (van Assche et al., 2017, p. 225)

Planning practice is already limited in its ability to find prompt spatial answers to accelerating crises. Spatial problems and their contexts are understood as complex, polarised, and ambiguous, with multiple overlapping uncertainties. However, a persistent desire to grow hinders the development of sustainable solutions to environmental and social crises. With an ambition to stay neutral, planners struggle to engage in value-laden, conflictual debates that touch upon basic understandings of their profession and themselves. They desire to be a meaningful profession, to deliver good results, and to communicate their profession's relevance well to politics and society. Planners' personal characteristics are pivotal to transformation but receive little attention in planning research. Changing in *any* normative direction from *within* planning, therefore, sounds unlikely and hard to achieve. The responsibility position is deeply anchored in the planner's self-understanding. Changing in a radically different, post-growth direction seems impossible at first sight. However, confrontations with post-growth show a large bandwidth of reactions that include support.

Becoming a "post-growth planner" and associated processes of making and taking new roles have become thinkable. On the ground, planners experience practical limitations in fulfilling growing demands for land, as well as seeing the impact of planning on the environment and our climate. As pleasing divergent demands gets harder, planners become more receptive to different approaches. Since 2018/19, leading planning networks and research institutions in Germany have put post-growth on their debate agendas. Policy documents and funding streams such as the New Leipzig Charter for urban development (finalised in 2020) have further shifted focus beyond GDP. Likewise, other disciplines such as health have begun to name and challenge "society's normal obsessions – efficiency, consumption, and growth" (*The Lancet*, 2020, p. 143). A discourse on values can be taken as a starting point for a paradigm shift and a reframing of responsibility in and of planning. Doing planning creatively sometimes means being "an urban or regional guerrilla", undermining "established bureaucratic and political agendas" (Kunzmann, 2004, p. 385). However, such an emphasis on individual planners does not detract from democratic legitimacy. It should not be misunderstood as instrumentalising planners for a post-growth agenda. Our aim is to show the enabling and transformative direction of post-growth ideas, which can help to revalorise core planning aims that have been lost to the focus on economic growth such as public interest and well-being.

To continue, we need to deepen our understanding of planners as human actors with personal characteristics and inner struggles. Planners can gain strong supportive agency and leadership in a post-growth transformation if we engage with desires, emotions, values, and perceptions.

Planners in public administration are and remain central actors in spatial development in both German and European contexts. However, the dependence on growth has a best-before date which is fast approaching. Open debate about appropriateness and responsibility remains crucial to reducing the uncertainty about what post-growth planning could mean and to using its transformative potential. To foster this debate, we summarised future directions for spatial planning in "six propositions of post-growth planning" (Lamker and Schulze Dieckhoff, 2019). The transformation of planning becomes conceivable if compassionate planners can act in the public interest, independently of dominant economic paradigms. Doing this will require courage, engagement, and reflection on personal values.

A critical debate on planning values can help planners to focus on doing good beyond growth. Future research should be open to the various ways planners react to post-growth, their different entry points and emotional states. Such conversations could be the start of a new planning system, based on compassion for the world with its social, cultural, and planetary boundaries.

## References

Albrechts L (2020) The challenge to make a difference. In: Albrechts L (ed) *Planners in Politics: Do they Make a Difference?* Camberley: Edward Elgar Publishing, pp. 2–9.

Albrechts L, Barbanente A and Monno V (2020) Practicing transformative planning: The territory-landscape plan as a catalyst for change. *City, Territory and Architecture* 7(1): 1–13.

ARL (Akademie für Raumforschung und Landesplanung) (2017) *Forschungskonzept 2017-2022*. Hannover: ARL.

Balducci A (2011) Strategic planning as exploration. *Town Planning Review* 82(5): 529–546.

Barry J (2020) Planning in and for a post-growth and post-carbon economy. In: Davoudi S, Cowell R and White I (eds) *The Routledge Companion to Environmental Planning*. Abingdon and New York: Routledge, pp. 120–129.

Baum HS (2015) Planning with half a mind: Why planners resist emotion. *Planning Theory & Practice* 16(4): 498–516.

Bögel PM and Upham P (2018) Role of psychology in sociotechnical transitions studies: A review and discussion in relation to consumption and technology acceptance. *Environmental Innovation and Societal Transitions* 28(September): 122–136.

Brokow-Loga A and Eckardt F (eds) (2020) *Postwachstumsstadt: Konturen einer solidarischen Stadtpolitik*. Munich: oekom verlag.

Campbell H (2012) 'Planning ethics' and rediscovering the idea of planning. *Planning Theory* 11(4): 379–399.

Campbell H (2021) Post-pandemic planning: Beyond 'stifling paradigms'. Achieving transformation requires grappling with the tiresome and low profile. *Planning Theory & Practice* 22(1): 3–7.

Csikszentmihalyi M (1996) *Creativity: The Psychology of Discovery and Invention*. New York: Harper Collins.

Davoudi S (2016) The value of planning and the values in planning. Viewpoint. *Town Planning Review* 87(6): 615–618.
Davy B (2019) Evil insurgency. A comment on the interface 'Strengthening planning's effectiveness in a hyper-polarized world'. *Planning Theory & Practice* 20(2): 290–297.
Diller C and Oberding S (2017) 'Probleme zuerst' – ein banaler, überholter imperativ in der raumplanung? *DisP – The Planning Review* 53(4): 55–70.
Ferreira A and von Schönfeld KC (2020) Interlacing planning and degrowth scholarship: A manifesto for an interdisciplinary alliance. Forum. *DisP – The Planning Review* 56(1): 53–64.
Fromm E (2010 [1968]) *The Revolution of Hope: Toward a Humanized Technology*. Riverdale, NY: American Mental Health Foundation Books.
Gibson-Graham JK, Cameron J and Healy S (2013) Reframing the economy, reframing ourselves. In: Gibson-Graham JK, Cameron J and Healy S (eds) *Take Back the Economy*. Minneapolis, MN: University of Minnesota Press, pp. 1–16.
Gunder M (2011) Fake it until you make it, and then… *Planning Theory* 10(3): 201–212.
Gunder M (2016) Planning's "failure" to ensure efficient market delivery: A Lacanian deconstruction of this neoliberal scapegoating fantasy. *European Planning Studies* 24(1): 21–38.
Gunder M and Hillier J (2007) Problematising responsibility in planning theory and practice: On seeing the middle of the string? *Progress in Planning* 68(2): 57–96.
Gunder M and Wang C (2020) *Lacan: Introducing Thinkers for Planners – A Narrative and Conversation*. Aesop Young Academics Booklet Project. www.aesop-planning.eu/uploads/lacan-introducing-thinkers-for-planners-a-narrative-and-conversation.pdf.
Healey P (2002) On creating the 'city' as a collective resource. *Urban Studies* 39(10): 1777–1792.
Hendler S (2002) It's the right thing to do – Or is it? Contemporary issues in planning ethics. *Plan Canada* 42(2): 9–11.
Hillier J and Gunder M (2003) Planning fantasies? An exploration of a potential Lacanian framework for understanding development assessment planning. *Planning Theory* 2(3): 225–248.
Kunzmann K (2004) Culture, creativity and spatial planning. *Town Planning Review* 75(4): 383–404.
Lamker CW (2016) *Unsicherheit und Komplexität in Planungsprozessen: Planungstheoretische Perspektiven auf Regionalplanung und Klimaanpassung*. Lemgo: Rohn.
Lamker CW and Schulze Dieckhoff V (2019) Sechs Thesen einer Postwachstumsplanung. Position paper, Post-growth Planning Collective. www.postwachstumsplanung.de.
Lamker CW and Schulze Dieckhoff V (2020) Postwachstum + Planung = Postwachstumsplanung?! Erfahrungen aus der Konfrontation zweier Diskurse. In: Brokow-Loga A and Eckardt F (eds) *Postwachstumsstadt: Konturen einer solidarischen Stadtpolitik*. Munich: oekom verlag, pp. 90–103.
Liegey V and Nelson A (2020) *Exploring Degrowth: A Critical Guide*. London: Pluto Press.
Mayer M (2020) What does it mean to be a (radical) urban scholar-activist, or activist scholar, today? *City* 24(1–2): 35–51.
Metzger J and Hillier J (2015) Connections: An introduction. In: Healey P, Hillier J and Metzger J (eds) *Connections: Exploring Contemporary Planning Theory and Practice with Patsy Healey*. Farnham: Ashgate, pp. 3–22.
Nelson A and Schneider F (eds) (2019) *Housing for Degrowth: Principles, Models, Challenges and Opportunities*. Abingdon; New York: Routledge.
Othengrafen F and Levin-Keitel M (2019) Planners between the chairs: How planners (do not) adapt to transformative practices. *Urban Planning* 4(4): 111–125.

Savini F (2019) Responsibility, polity, value: The (un)changing norms of planning practices. *Planning Theory* 18(1): 58–81.
Tekeli I (2019) Scientific knowledge and decision-making in planning: Understanding emotional aspects. In: Eraydın A and Frey K (eds) *Politics and Conflict in Governance and Planning: Theory and Practice*. New York: Routledge, pp. 227–242.
*The Lancet* (2020) No more normal. *The Lancet* 396(10245): 143.
Thrift N (2004) Intensities of feeling: Towards a spatial politics of affect. *Geografiska Annaler. Series B, Human Geography* 86(1): 57–78.
van Assche K, Beunen R and Duineveld M (2017) Witchcraft, oracle, and magic in the kingdom of planning: A reflection on planning theory and practice inspired by Ernest Alexander. *Planning Theory* 16(2): 223–226.
Wagener F (1971) *Information Planung und Führung in Regierung und Verwaltung: Untersuchung im Auftrage der Staatskanzlei des Landes Nordrhein-Westfalen*. Düsseldorf.
Westin S (2014) *The Paradoxes of Planning: A Psycho-Analytical Perspective*. New Directions in Planning Theory. Abingdon; New York: Ashgate.
Willson R (2020) *Reflective Planning Practice: Theory, Cases, and Methods*. London; New York: Routledge.
Wolfram M (2016) Conceptualizing urban transformative capacity: A framework for research and policy. *Cities* 51: 121–130.
Xue J (2021) Urban planning and degrowth: A missing dialogue. *Local Environment*: 1–19. DOI: 10.1080/13549839.2020.1867840.

# 14

# ONCE UPON A PLANET

Planning for Transition from Ego-Driven to Eco-Driven Economies

*Leonie Sandercock*

## 1. Introduction: From 'Dare to Know!' to 'How Dare You!'

In a 1930 essay titled 'Economic Possibilities for our Grandchildren' John Maynard Keynes speculated that by 2030 capital investment and technology would have raised living standards as much as eightfold, creating a society so rich that people would work less than 15 hours a week, devoting the rest of their time to 'non-economic' purposes. As striving for greater affluence faded, he predicted, 'the love of money as a possession… will be recognized for what it is, a somewhat disgusting morbidity' (Keynes 2010).

Yet here we are, nearly 100 years later, with most economic policy makers and politicians still committed to maximizing the rate of economic growth, and the majority of planning practice committed to serving that goal, underpinned by a techno-rational worldview that has dominated thinking, valuing, and acting since the Enlightenment. 'Dare to Know!' was the rousing and, for its time, radical call of the German philosopher Immanuel Kant in 1780, expressing unbounded faith in the liberatory potential of scientific and technical knowledge … the dark side of which, as we now know, has been humankind's assertion of the right to dominate nature for our own material ends for the past two centuries.

Once confined to the margins, the ecological critique of economic growth has been accumulating attention for several decades. At a UN climate change summit in September 2019, the teenage environmental activist Greta Thunberg declared: 'We are at the beginning of a mass extinction, and all you can talk about is money and fairy tales of eternal economic growth. How dare you!' (Cassidy 2020, 24).

Provoked by Thunberg, this chapter makes four interconnected arguments. At a meta-theoretical level, the argument is that planning theory and practice must undergo a paradigm shift from the techno-rational worldview that has dominated our field as it evolved from the Enlightenment frame of mind. A shift to more relational ways of being, knowing, and doing is necessary if we are to be the change agents whose work is relevant to today's most urgent global crises.

At a more grounded level, drawing on work with Indigenous communities in north west Canada, the lessons derived from Indigenous worldviews outline an ethic of care and relational accountability towards fellow humans, alongside an ethic of stewardship of their lands and waters, based on their understanding of the interconnectedness of all life forms. This worldview overlaps with an ecological perspective. Drawing further on this ecological perspective, the next theoretical argument is not for an end to growth (an ecological impossibility), but for a shift to *qualitative growth*. And finally, the argument returns to lessons learned at a more personal level through the work with Indigenous communities. As planners supporting this work, we find that the most important quality we bring to the work is a *way of being* that foregrounds relationships, trust, humility, deep listening, patience, and a beginner's mind.

## 2. Worldviews: From Possessive Individualism to Relationship and Interdependence

It is by now a well-rehearsed critique that the origins of contemporary planning dwell in both the Enlightenment project (Sandercock 1998, 2003) and the related European colonization project (Jacobs 1996; Jackson 1998; Sandercock 2003; Porter 2010, 2021; Roy 2021). I take these critiques as my starting point, as a given, rather than re-rehearsing them here. What I'm more interested in, as we try to imagine a 'post-growth future', is the worldview and attendant ontologies and social values underpinning these twinned or interdependent projects, their toxic and destructive impacts on both human community and Mother Earth, and the challenge of reordering our very ways of being and hierarchy of social values to ensure the survival of our one precious planet as well as meet the deep spiritual needs of human beings.

It was in the writings of Thomas Hobbes (1651) that the notion of what political theorist C.B. McPherson termed 'possessive individualism' as the moral basis of society was first made explicit.[1] Hobbes asked two questions: What is human nature? And how shall society be organized to accommodate this nature? Starting with this materialist model of human nature, Hobbes deduced the necessity of a market model of society, sidestepping the whole question of human bondedness, attachment, need for connection and belonging. This emerging worldview was linked with two equally powerful ideas: John Locke's view of land as Property that must not lie fallow but must be improved for human use; and the idea/l of progress or 'development' through the application of Reason, the vision of the political philosophers of the eighteenth century. Simply put, these emerging *beliefs* coalesced into a worldview that totally changed people's image of their place in the universe. 'From being servants of God, each contributing to the life of His Church on Earth, they became isolated competing agents… self-centered consumers of pleasure, the sole purpose of whose Reason was to further its own existence' (Clark 1989, 269).

Individualism, competitiveness, and materialism have been nurtured in us (children of the West), woven implicitly into the fabric of our worldview. And once accepted, this view creates the very kind of human behavior it assumes as inevitable. Our worldview becomes its own self-fulfilling prophecy, and we create systems to perpetuate it.

Over the past three centuries, the attributes of possessive individualism (materialism, independence, competition, property rights, individual conscience) that were at first designed to free people from oppressive social constraints have evolved into a bizarre concept of freedom that dominates twenty-first-century thinking in the West. The notion of individual freedom which began emerging at the end of the Middle Ages, as freedom from arbitrary control, has gradually been converted into the right to do whatever one pleases, nowhere more clear and more damaging than the current anti-mask movement in the midst of a global pandemic. This idea of absolute freedom, which has reached its most extreme expression in the materially richest country in the world, the USA, now signifies not just the absence of a few specified evils, but freedom from all culture and tradition, resulting in the isolation of the individual from all connection with others and from what has historically given life meaning: tradition, affection, personal and local ties, natural roots and sympathies.

It is tempting but too easy to blame all this on capitalism, as though it were a system out there over which we have no control. In fact, we are all part of this now-global system that fetishizes economic growth, and we help to reproduce it every day in all of our choices, unless we're one of the very few who've made the choice to live self-sufficiently, off-grid and outside the market economy.

Could there be a more toxic worldview than the one that has increasingly dominated the planet since the seventeenth century? Human nature has undergone a complete metamorphosis in Western experience from a culture-centered being to a self-centered being. Disconnected from others, people must independently invent their own life meaning while remaining seemingly helplessly trapped by social institutions devoid of moral direction. In seeking absolute freedom, we leave ourselves alienated from everything – from 'Nature' and from one another. With its central focus on growth and the consumption of material wealth, Western society, or rather the worldview that has emerged from the West and now pervades the rest (and I include here Russia and China, both equally intent on pursuing material wealth at all costs), is inexorably destroying both the environment and the soul or spirit of humanity. We have lost our capacity for mystery, wonder, awe, reverence. The self is the only sacred object that remains.

The foundational belief of the Enlightenment, that we can master all of Nature for our own ever-expanding 'needs', has turned out to be an illusion which has resulted in the destruction of the very life systems that support us, air, water, earth, without concern for the future, and is leading us to the brink of mass extinction, as Greta Thunberg warns us. Our survival as a species demands that we acknowledge the relational nature of our existence, that we are absolutely dependent on the connections that support our existence and make us whole. We must recognize, through a shift in our worldview, our utter dependence on and embeddedness in the natural world.

To adequately articulate this shift, we would need to redefine the secular, that is, all those institutions that organize the material and social foundations of life, as well as redefining the sacred. We could turn to the writings of such (Western) thinkers as Aldo Leopold's or Wendell Berry's work on the meaning of land; E.F. Schumacher's Buddhist economics; Fritjof Capra's systems view of life; ecological economists such as Paul Hawken, Amory Lovins, Herman Daly; James Lovelock's Gaia hypothesis; Mary Clark's exploration of the essentially cooperative nature of human nature; and the growing number of advocates of bio-regionalism. That sounds like a book project rather than a book chapter, so for this essay I will simply focus on what we in the field of planning scholarship and practice can do to address this crisis, and I will pay particular attention to the teachings of contemporary Indigenous scholar/planners and to current approaches to Comprehensive Community Planning being developed by Indigenous communities with whom we are working in the School of Community and Regional Planning in what is now known as British Columbia, the westernmost province of what is now known as Canada.

## 3. Working in Partnership: Being in Community

> Today we live in a globally interconnected world in which biological, psychological, social and environmental phenomena are all interdependent. To describe this world appropriately we need a new paradigm, a new vision of reality – a fundamental change in our thoughts, perceptions, and values. The beginnings of this change, or the shift from the mechanistic to the holistic conception of reality, are already visible… The gravity and global extent of our crisis indicates that the current changes are likely to result in a transformation of unprecedented dimension, a turning point for the planet as a whole.
> 
> *(Capra 1982, 29–30)*

> On every side we can now see people busily engaged in sawing off the branches on which they (along with many others) are sitting, intent only on getting those branches to market before the price of timber falls.
> 
> *(Midgley 1985, 135)*

> That land is a community is a basic concept of ecology, but that land is to be loved and respected is an extension of ethics. That land yields a cultural harvest is a fact long known, but latterly often forgotten.
> 
> *(Leopold 1949, viii)*

To register that physicist Fritjof Capra wrote these words in 1982 and philosopher Midgley in 1985, while Leopold's words go back to 1949, is to understand the increasing anger and impatience behind Greta Thunberg's protests. Her anger now pervades academia among students who see nothing but planning's complicity in environmental devastation and systemic racism. Students who want to be change agents are increasingly skeptical about the prospects of planning as a tool of social transformation. Our field is at a crossroads. Unless we address these global challenges with our students, we will lose their respect and trust; we will lose them.

So there has to be a paradigm shift from the techno-rational (Euclidian/Cartesian) worldview that has dominated thinking, valuing, and acting in our field since the Enlightenment, to more relational ways of being, thinking, and acting. I want to draw on my own experience in Indigenous community planning over the past 15 years to propose that we devote as much effort to *ways of being in the world* as we have in the past to *ways of knowing and ways of doing*. Another way of saying this is that we need to balance the inner and the outer, 'internalizing radical interdependence' in Patricia Wilson's wise words, because the conscious integration of these two enables the creativity, and risk-taking, and repair/healing work that we need to address the most pressing issues facing this one precious planet: such issues as the refugee/migration crisis; increasing social polarization; systemic racism; and impending socio-environmental catastrophe.

For heuristic purposes let's say there are three broad orientations in planning practice, three different kinds of job description, each with its own different skill sets, implicit politics, and ways of knowing and acting. There is the work of technical support: the back-room planner who works at her computer doing modeling or GIS, handling big data sets, forecasting, providing the numbers for the policy makers and politicians. There is the system-maintaining bureaucratic planner, fine-tuning program and service delivery and refining evaluation techniques to improve things at the margin, motivated more by efficiency than justice. And there is the planner as change agent: a catalyst and facilitator looking beyond technical problem solving and the efficiency of policies, programs, and delivery systems to addressing issues of social and environmental justice. It's this third orientation that I want to address, because this is the generative edge of our field.

If, as scientists argue, the world is continuing down a path to socio-environmental catastrophe, then surely we have to ask: how do we become more effective societal change agents? What are the attributes of planners as change agents? What is the job description? What are the underlying skills and sensibilities? What would it take to make our work truly transformative?

The kind of planning for transition that I want to advocate is, as I have already foreshadowed, an evolutionary shift: from the techno-rational Cartesian worldview (Sandercock 1998, 2003) to a more relational and holistic view of life. For the past 15 years I have been working with colleagues and students to support Indigenous communities in the north west of Canada, and two things stand out from this experience. The first is that, thanks to a new, community-driven approach, we are seeing significant transformation on the ground, one community at a time, each one inspiring another to embark on a holistic/comprehensive community planning process, the goals of which are self-determination and sovereignty. The second is that Indigenous worldviews share certain philosophical elements that have something to offer the global crises we're in the midst of: namely, an ethic of care and of relational accountability towards fellow humans (an emphasis on the 'we' and not the 'I'); and an understanding of the interconnectedness of all life forms on the planet, which leads to an ethic of stewardship of their lands and waters.

My work for over four decades has focused on social justice and sustainable community development. But my understanding of how to do that work has changed radically over the past two decades or so. In the 1990s part of my mission was to decentre the Enlightenment epistemology at the heart of planning and foreground an epistemology of multiplicity (Sandercock 1998, Chapter 3). *The evolution I now want to suggest is that in addition to focusing on different ways of knowing and doing, we need to make an inner or self-reflexive turn and focus more on ways of being.*

Ten years ago, I initiated a process of curriculum reform in our School of Community and Regional Planning, a process that various scholars across the settler societies of the New World (Jojola 2013; Matunga 2013, 2017; Porter 2017) refer to as the decolonizing and indigenizing of planning theory and practice. I initiated a community–university partnership in the design and delivery of a new Masters degree program in Indigenous Community Planning (ICP), approaching the Indigenous nation on whose unceded territory (i.e. stolen land) my university is located. The Musqueam Nation had, at that time, just completed their first *contemporary* Sustainable Community Development Plan, which subsequently won a UN Habitat award (I emphasize 'contemporary', because one of the things we learn from Musqueam and other First Nations in this program is that Indigenous communities have been doing their own planning for sustainable development, based on their own worldviews, laws, and traditional knowledges, since time immemorial).

I now co-teach, with various Musqueam knowledge holders, a core course within this program, entitled *Indigenous Community Planning: ways of being, knowing, and doing*. We spend half of our class time on Musqueam's reserve, listening to their elders talking about their worldview, their history and culture, and the devastating, near-genocidal impacts of colonization on their community.[2] Then, for half of the second year of the two-year program, students (Indigenous and non-Indigenous together) spend 400 hours working with an Indigenous community on their reserve, outside the metropolitan area, working in support of the goals established by that community through extensive community engagement processes, co-designed and co-facilitated by the students, with their community partner. Through this ongoing curriculum, we have now partnered with 18 Indigenous communities throughout the province, and what follows is the learning about social transformation the students and I have gleaned from this immersive experience.

The single most important learning for me on this journey is that the inner practice of community engagement is arguably more important than (although inseparable from) the outer practice: in other words, that the *way of being* that one embodies in community engagement and community building (literally *how* one shows up in community) is every bit as important as, if not more important than, the *ways of doing*. In fact, it is the *being skills* that make the *doing skills* possible. The being skills are about relational awareness, humility, patience, presence, intentionality, and courage.

To summarize what we've learned about working in partnership and *being in community* through the ICP program.

'Shut up and listen' would be the most common piece of advice we've received. Implicit in this advice is that planning cannot begin before trust is established, and trust will only be established if people feel heard, valued, and respected. Focus on building relationships, getting to know people. Social transformation moves at the pace of trust.

Trust the wisdom of the community. They will collectively find the answers: once they have a shared sense of purpose and a sense of safety, there's no limit to the creativity of communities. It's our job to nurture that creativity through creative forms of engagement.

Learn to work at the speed of the community, not at the speed of university or other institutional or funding deadlines. Learn to trust the process. Learn to improvise when things go sideways. And that implies an ability to always be in the moment and not leaping ahead to outcomes.

Let go of control. Let go of outcomes. Learn to thrive in uncertainty.

Learn to feel safe not knowing. Come with a Beginner's Mind.

Learn from your own mistakes. Own your mistakes and ask how to make amends.

Recognize your own blind spots. Know your own insecurities and defense mechanisms.

Develop the capacity to notice when the heart closes, when fear or judgement takes over. Always be fully present, 'with an open heart and an open mind' as the tag line of Musqueam's community plan reads. *Presence* is a much-underrated quality of being.

Learn to discern when and how to contribute your knowledge and expertise to the knowledge residing in the community. And when to step back, to let go.

And instead of focusing on what's wrong (the 'damage-centered' approach), focus on the community gifts and strengths, and that will tell you what's possible.[3]

All of these lessons speak to the importance, arguably the primacy, of both emotional and relational intelligence in planning work. Which connects with an emergent stream of thought in our field (Marris 1975; Baum 2015; Sandercock 2018; Willson 2018; Erfan 2017) arguing for a way of conceptualizing planning as the work of repair or healing: therapeutic planning, as I once labeled it (Sandercock 2003). Peter Marris's beautiful book *Loss and Change* (1975), written almost half a century ago,[4] made the case for acknowledging loss or grief as an inevitable part of the work we do as planners in managing change processes. All change, even change that's widely perceived as desirable, involves some loss, and unless we pay attention to that instead of sweeping it under the carpet, unless we're prepared to respect it as a legitimate response and work it through, we risk massive pushback.[5]

This emerging planner as change agent embodies self-awareness and relational awareness. This is an evolution that builds on the communicative and collaborative approaches developing since the 1970s. The works of Friedmann, Schon, Forester, Innes, Healey, and myself emphasized the importance of listening, and of dialogue. We challenged the dominant Enlightenment epistemology and proposed an epistemology of multiplicity, of multiple ways of knowing (Sandercock 1998). We added communicative and creative skills to the technical and design toolkits previously used by planners. And we also emphasized (thanks to Schon) the importance of reflection: reflection on action and reflection in action. The so-called communicative paradigm shift was an important shift in how some of us teach and practice *ways of knowing and ways of doing* in planning. But it did not turn the gaze inwards, to examine our ways of being in the world. That is the next step in the transformation of planners who aspire to be change agents.

So, now, to ground all this in one community: our ICP program worked in partnership with the (Skidegate) Haida community for four years on an extensive community engagement process, which led to their Comprehensive Community Plan, *Gud Ga Is*, which means, literally, 'coming together to talk' (Skidegate Indian Band, 2017). All of the qualities so far outlined were essential in doing this work together, and in the process we learned the Haida laws that have governed their planning since time immemorial:

> *Respect. All acts must be done with respect.*
> *Ask first. All acts must be done with consent.*
> *Everything depends on everything, all things are connected.*
> *Sharing of wealth.*
> *Only take what you need.*
> *Putting back into the ocean.*
> *When the tide is out there is food on the table / the table is set.*
> *The tide waits for no one.*
> *Time and tide wait for no one.*
> *The food is our medicine.*
> (Skidegate Indian Band 2017, 4; italics in original)

Indigenous elder and scholar, Umeek (E. Richard Atleo), a hereditary chief from the Nuu-chah-nuulth Nation on the west coast of Vancouver Island, has expressed a similar worldview in his book, *Principles of Tsawalk: An Indigenous Approach to Global Crisis* (2011).

'Tsawalk' translates as 'everything is one', just as the Haida say 'everything is connected'. According to the Nuu-chah-nuulth worldview, all living things (humans, plants, animals) form part of an integrated whole brought into harmony through constant negotiation and mutual respect. In this book, Umeek argues that contemporary environmental and political crises (and the related ongoing plight of Indigenous peoples) reflect a world out of balance, a world in which Western/ techno-rational approaches for sustainable living are not working. The global crisis is one of 'relational disharmony'. Likewise, Potawatomi scholar Robin Wall Kimmerer (2013), in her beautiful book *Braiding Sweetgrass*, embraces the notion that plants and animals are our oldest teachers. She brings these lenses of knowledge together to show that an awakening of a wider ecological consciousness requires the acknowledgement of our reciprocal relationship with the rest of the living world:

Berries are always present at our ceremonies. They join us in a wooden bowl. One big bowl and one big spoon, which are passed around the circle, so that each person can taste the sweetness, remember the gifts, and say thank you. They carry the lesson, passed to us by our ancestors, that the generosity of the land comes to us as one bowl, one spoon. We are all fed from the same bowl that Mother Earth has filled for us. It's not just about the berries, but also about the bowl. The gifts of the earth are to be shared, but gifts are not limitless. The generosity of the earth is not an invitation to take it all. Every bowl has a bottom. When it's empty, it's empty. And there is but one spoon, the same size for everyone.... The moral covenant of reciprocity calls us to honor our responsibilities for all we have been given, for all that we have taken. ... Whatever our gift, we are called to give it and to dance for the renewal of the world. In return for the privilege of breath.

*(Kimmerer 2013, 382–4)*

Māori scholar/planner Hirini Matunga describes Indigenous planning as 'as much an ethic and philosophy as it is a planning framework with a set of approaches and methods' (Matunga 2013, 31). He uses the image of a spiral to convey the conceptual basis of Indigenous planning. At the center of the spiral is *wairuatanga*, the state of being spiritual. Moving from this central anchor, around the spiral, he identifies next relationship and kinship, followed by the responsibilities and principles passed down from the ancestors to take care of the land and resources; respect given to visitors through sharing and caring; self-determination; unity; alignment; and transparency (Matunga et al. 2003). Elsewhere Matunga argues that Indigenous worldviews are essential for reconceptualizing human–environment relationships. Similar to Aldo Leopold's land ethic, the Māori worldview sees land as a community to which we belong and from which we are inseparable. In this worldview, furthermore, there is a hierarchy that positions humans below the natural environment, while seeing everything as connected. Māori *whakapapa* is a tradition of genealogy outlining not just kinship between humans but between humans and all living things and places and the spiritual realm (Matunga et al. 2020).

But now to connect all this work on the ground, by individual planners, community by community, to the bigger picture of paradigm or worldview shift, and see the connection between self and systems.

The processes of transition to more sustainable ways of living that our ICP program is a small part of in British Columbia are an approach that might be called a fractal theory of change: a strategy for building complex solutions through relatively small but holistic interventions and interactions. Community by community, Indigenous peoples living on reserves in British Columbia are transitioning to their own visions of self-determination, sovereignty, and sustainability. And the role of the planner is to support these goals. Changing the world one community at a time may seem like fiddling while Rome is burning, or rolling the Sisyphean boulder up an impossibly steep mountain. But in the context of what environmentalist Paul Hawken (2007) has called a 'blessed unrest', perhaps it is not such a fanciful theory of change. Hawken is referring to the coalescence and intertwining of hundreds of thousands of organizations worldwide into a 'movement' (without central leadership, command, or control) that has three basic roots: environmental activism, social justice initiatives, and Indigenous cultures' resistance to globalization. Although this phenomenon of 'blessed unrest' is primarily a grassroots movement of people from every culture and continent, it may also represent a natural self-organizing principle free of any hegemonic ideology. The philosophy suggested by 'blessed unrest' is that living systems are fundamentally cooperative: that life can only exist in cooperative, sharing relationships with other life. Self-organization: from the molecular to the cosmic. From the fishing net to the universe. A deeply relational/interconnected worldview.

## 4. Blessed Unrest: Connecting the Dots

My ecological economics literacy is basic, so I have avoided and will continue to avoid engaging with the detailed debates about the economic and institutional contours of a so-called post-growth world. I prefer to question the very concept of 'post-growth' and, drawing on an ecological perspective, talk instead about *qualitative growth* and what the field of planning has to contribute to this concept.

Granted, the perpetual growth myth promotes the impossible idea that indiscriminate economic growth is the cure for all the world's problems, when it is actually the disease that is at the root of our unsustainable global practices (see Brundtland et al. 2012, 41). The key challenge, then, is to shift from an economic system based on the notion of unlimited growth to one that is both ecologically sustainable and socially just:

> From the perspective of the systems view of life, 'no growth' cannot be the answer. Growth is a central characteristic of all life. A society, or economy, that does not grow will die sooner or later. Growth in nature, however, is not linear and unlimited. While certain parts of organisms, or ecosystems, grow, others decline, releasing and recycling their components, which become resources for new growth.
>
> *(Capra and Luisi 2014, 368)*

So let's define growth as that which enhances (rather than destroys) life – as generation and regeneration – and declare that what our planet most needs is more of that kind of growth.

This notion of 'growth which enhances life' – qualitative economic growth – can be sustained if it involves a dynamic balance between growth, decline, and recycling, and if it also includes the inner growth of learning and maturing, a spiritual growth (Capra and Luisi 2014). So now we circle back to section 3, to the resurgent practice of Indigenous community planning, with its emphasis on relationships between people and between people and land, and an internalized awareness of the necessary interdependence of these, as expressed in Indigenous worldviews.

Why is this *way of being* a part of the causal chain of socio-ecological transformation? It is in the work of Otto Scharmer that the causal connection between the inner and the outer, between ways of being and social transformation, has perhaps been best articulated among non-Indigenous scholar/activists. He talks about the need to shift from 'ego-system to eco-system economies' (Scharmer and Kaufer 2013). The two insightful propositions that undergird his 'Theory U' (2007) are 'form follows consciousness' and 'As within, so without'. Theory U is a *way of being and doing* in organizational, civic, and community life. It foregrounds the feminine qualities of soulfulness, love, and nurturing. Scharmer explains that real change starts with the source of the attention we give to the world and then manifests itself through relationship and action. Each thought and every step we take embodies explicitly what we want to create. Deepening our own inner capacity to let go of our ingrained sense of a separate self and recognizing our indivisible interconnectedness is the only way to sense the needs of the whole. Large-scale systems change for healing the whole starts with the individual and collective capacity to perceive, know, and care about the dynamic, evolving whole of which we are all a part.

Scharmer's own theoretical trajectory was in turn influenced by the spiritual traditions of Buddhism (practices of inner peace), Daoist and Confucian philosophies of being and change, and the German phenomenological focus on individual consciousness (Wilson 2019, 185). His major contribution has been to link all of these to groups, organizations, and larger living systems: linking the micro, meso, macro, and mundo (global) scales. In this chapter, I have aimed similarly to make the connections between the micro (ways of being), the meso (Indigenous/community planning), and the macro/mundo (ecological perspective from cities to Mother Earth).

Building and nurturing community lies at the core of ecological sustainability, and building and nurturing community lies at the heart of community planning, whether that community planning is serving to support resurgent Indigenous communities on their path to self-sufficiency and self-determination, or working in the multi-ethnic, multi-racial neighbourhoods of cities, addressing systemic racism and other forms of discrimination, and encouraging strangers to become neighbours (see Sandercock and Attili 2006). A community planning that has as its heart a practice of kindness (Forester 2021), loving attachment (Porter, Sandercock, and Umemoto 2012), caring for each other and the air, lands, and waters, requires a shift of attention in our field that *connects* ways of knowing and acting to *ways of being, as part of the broader ecological paradigm shift embracing connectedness, relationship, and interdependence.*

## Notes

1 Hobbes was not alone. Descartes, Spinoza, Adam Smith, Freud, Camus, and many more revered thinkers believed that self-interest was the fundamental human trait and prime mover of human action.
2 Under the Indian Act of 1876, and still extant today, Indigenous peoples were dispossessed of their former sovereign territories, mostly without any treaties being signed, and forced

to live on tiny parcels of land, disconnecting them from their territory and traditional way of life and forcing them to become dependent on the state. These tiny parcels of land are known to this day as 'reserves' – lands reserved for Indians – and are arguably the most blatant example of spatial, social, and economic apartheid in modern history.
3 I am struck by the congruence between these 'lessons' and those drawn by Patricia Wilson from her work in communities in the global South, as described in Wilson (2019).
4 And based on Peter's work not only in working-class communities in London but also with squatter settlements in Africa, the most important *neglected* book in our field.
5 Arguably this emotional process is at the root of the populist shift to the right across Europe as well as the New World. People are grieving the loss, as they perceive it, of something precious, a way of life that is passing/has passed, so they seek to blame those they see as responsible, whether elites or immigrants or both. And arguably loss and grief will be all the more prominent as more and more neighbourhoods are torn down for redevelopment, as we lose social networks, whole ecosystems or species, and languages (2019 is the International Year of Indigenous Languages). As these processes become increasingly part of our physical and emotional landscapes, in planning for transition planners will need to learn how to hold space for people to grieve these losses. And possibly also to hold the space for anger and rage.

## References

Baum, H. 2015. 'Planning with Half a Mind. Why Planners Resist Emotion', *Planning Theory & Practice*, 16, 4: 498–516.
Brundtland, G.H. et al. 2012. *Environment and Development Challenges: The Imperative to Act.* (New York: UNEP Report).
Capra, F. 1982. 'A New Vision of Reality', *New Age*, February, pp. 29–32.
Capra, F. and P.L. Luisi. 2014. *The Systems View of Life: A Unifying Vision* (Cambridge: Cambridge University Press).
Cassidy, J. 2020. 'Steady State', *New Yorker*, 10 February, pp. 24–27.
Clark, Mary E. 1989. *Ariadne's Thread: The Search for New Modes of Thinking* (New York: St. Martin's Press).
Erfan, A. 2017. 'Confronting Collective Traumas: An Exploration of Therapeutic Planning', *Planning Theory & Practice*, 18, 1: 34–50.
Forester, J. 2021. 'Our Curious Silence about Kindness in Planning: Challenges of Addressing Vulnerability and Suffering', *Planning Theory*, 20, 1: 63–83.
Hawken, P. 2007. *Blessed Unrest. How the Largest Social Movement in History is Restoring Grace, Justice, and Beauty to the World* (New York: Viking).
Hobbes, T. 1651. *Leviathan*.
Jackson, S. 1998. Geographies of Co-existence: Native Title, Cultural Difference and the Decolonization of Planning in Northern Australia. Unpublished PhD, School of Earth Sciences, Macquarie University, Sydney.
Jacobs, J. 1996. *Edge of Empire. Postcolonialism and the City* (London: Routledge).
Jojola, T. 2013. 'Indigenous Planning: Towards a Seven Generations Model' in R. Walker, T. Jojola and D. Natcher. Eds. *Reclaiming Indigenous Planning.* (Montreal, QC: McGill-Queens University Press).
Keynes, J.M. 2010 [1931]. (2010) 'Economic Possibilities for our Grandchildren' in *Essays in Persuasion* (London: Palgrave Macmillan).
Kimmerer, R.W. 2013. *Braiding Sweetgrass. Indigenous Wisdom, Scientific Knowledge, and the Teachings of Plants* (Minneapolis, MN: Milkweed Editions).

Leopold, A. 1949. *A Sand County Almanac* (London: Oxford University Press).
Marris, P. 1975. *Loss and Change* (London: Routledge Kegan Paul).
Matunga, H. 2013. 'Theorizing Indigenous Planning' in R. Walker, T. Jojola and D. Natcher. Eds. *Reclaiming Indigenous Planning* (Montreal, QC: McGill-Queens University Press).
Matunga, H. 2017. 'A Revolutionary Pedagogy of/for Indigenous Planning', *Planning Theory & Practice*, 18, 4: 640–644.
Matunga, H. et al. 2003. *The Values Associated with Maori-Centred Tourism*. Tourism Recreation Research Centre, Report 35, Lincoln University.
Matunga, H. et al. 2020. 'From Exploitive to Regenerative Tourism: Tino rangatiratanga and Tourism in Aotearoa New Zealand', *MAI Journal: A New Zealand Journal of Indigenous Scholarship*, 9, 3: 295–308.
Midgley, M. 1985. *Evolution as Religion* (London: Methuen).
Porter, L. 2010. *Unlearning the Colonial Cultures of Planning* (Burlington, VT: Ashgate).
Porter, L. 2017. 'What is the Work of Non-Indigenous People in the Service of a Decolonizing Agenda?', *Planning Theory & Practice*, 18, 4: 650–653.
Porter, L. 2021. 'Against World-Killing Silence', *Planning Theory & Practice*, 22, 1: 111–115.
Porter, L., L. Sandercock and K. Umemoto. 2012. 'What's Love Got to Do with It? Illuminations on Loving Attachment in Planning', *Planning Theory & Practice*, 13, 4: 593–630.
Roy, A. 2021. 'Planning on Stolen Land', *Planning Theory & Practice*, 22, 1: 116–121.
Sandercock, L. 1998. *Towards Cosmopolis: Planning for Multicultural Cities* (London: Wiley).
Sandercock, L. 2003. *Cosmopolis 2: Mongrel Cities of the 21st Century* (London: Continuum).
Sandercock, L. 2018. 'Finding My Way: Emotions and Ethics in Community-Based Action Research with Indigenous Communities' in J. Christensen, C. Cox and L. Szabo-Jones. Eds. *Activating the Heart: Storytelling, Knowledge Sharing and Relationship* (Waterloo, ON: Wilfred Laurier University Press).
Sandercock, L. and G. Attili. 2006. *Where Strangers become Neighbours*. 50-minute documentary (Montreal, QC: National Film Board).
Scharmer, C. Otto. 2007. *Theory U: Leading from the Future as it Emerges* (Cambridge, MA: Society for Organizational Learning).
Scharmer, C. Otto and K. Kaufer. 2013. *Leading from the Emerging Future: From Ego-System to Eco-System Economies* (San Francisco, CA: Berrett-Koehler).
Skidegate Indian Band. 2017. *Gud Ga Is* (Skidegate Comprehensive Community Plan, 2012–17).
Umeek (E. Richard Atleo). 2011. *Principles of Tsawalk. An Indigenous Approach to Global Crisis* (Vancouver, BC: UBC Press).
Willson, Richard. 2018. *A Guide for the Idealist* (New York: Routledge).
Wilson, Patricia. 2019. *The Heart of Community Engagement* (New York: Routledge).

# PART 8
# Envisioning

# 15
# A MANIFESTO FOR POST-GROWTH PLANNING

With their eyes set on a post-growth world, planners and policymakers, people and organisations shall promote:

## For dwelling

- Approaches to dwelling that cease being environmentally destructive and sources of lifelong financial debt for isolated individuals and fragmented communities.
- Non-commodified ways of dwelling in which housing becomes a catalyst for human flourishing, community building, and democratic engagement.
- Residential buildings that foster a symbiosis between humans and natural ecosystems through the implementation of regenerative and participatory design, and through the reduction of resource consumption and energy use.

## For moving

- Integrated approaches to transport, land use, and patterns of activity in which mobility ceases to be provided by environmentally destructive machines that constrain human beings and predetermine what or whom they need or aspire to reach.
- Patterns of land use and activity that allow people to access healthy food, care, meaningful social engagement, and work in their vicinity, thereby reducing their dependence on mobility.
- Transport systems that prioritise ecological and social sustainability, as well as slow mobility and physically active travelling.

## For governing

- Approaches to urban governance that cease to fetishise private property as an inevitable right and are no longer dominated by standardised State bureaucracies.
- Approaches to governance that are oriented towards fulfilling essential needs, namely social care, health, meaningful social engagement, and human well-being.
- Institutions that pursue autonomy and democracy in communities in an inclusive and just manner, and enable the commoning of resources and services.

## For regulating

- Planning regulations that cease to facilitate land development and ever-increasing land values as the key solutions to urban problems.
- Planning regulations that set constitutional limits to the ecological impacts of human activities and promote ecological regeneration.
- Planning laws that recognise the social value of land and real-estate, above and beyond its economic value, and enable the social and spatial redistribution of resources and wealth.

## For nurturing

- Urban metabolisms that cease to be ravenous recipients of resources and predatory fabricators of carbon emissions, pollution, and waste.
- Approaches to territorial planning that balance and synergise the mutual prosperity of urban, rural, and natural areas.
- Resource provision practices that actively foster human health and ecological regeneration, while doing as much as possible to engage local communities in the design, governance, and maintenance of their own bio-physical sustenance.

## For being

- A societal ethic no longer dominated by competitive collaboration and individualism, extractivism and anthropocentrism.
- A professional ethic of mutual understanding, trust, and compassion, which places the regeneration and protection of ecosystems at the centre of a new generation of professional deontologies.
- Education systems for planners and associated professions that focus on developing deep listening abilities and respectful mentalities so that graduated professionals are prepared to truly engage with all people and communities that are affected by planning and urban management decisions.

# 16
# A GLOSSARY OF AND FOR POST-GROWTH PLANNING

## Autonomous housing

A form of housing commons that is maintained through dispersed and disputable property rights. Commoning is a political practice of keeping housing out of the speculative real-estate market, which leads to the overaccumulation of properties. It involves a community of dwellers collectivizing property. Together, they manage, own, and organize the estate on which they live by way of intense democratic engagement and solidarity. In current growth-dependent economies, the challenge facing autonomous housing is that of maintaining autonomy against the constant threats of state co-optation, commodification, and internal enclaving. The dispersal and disputability of property rights is a condition for the protection of housing commons against these risks.

## Being skills

Being skills are the capacities and attitudes of planners that make planning action possible. Being skills are embodied in 'ways of being' and 'worldviews', the most inner and self-reflexive position of planners themselves within communities and the values that those planners use to make sense of places. As planners, if we aspire to be part of the solution to current global crises rather than continuing to be part of the problem, we need to move away from the techno-rational worldview that has dominated thinking in our field since the Enlightenment. Learning from Indigenous communities and from their worldviews, we come to understand that the inner work of community engagement and community building is as important as, arguably more important than, the outer practice, the act of doing planning itself (although inseparable from it). *How* one shows up in community might be called the 'being skills', and it is these being skills that make the doing skills (that is, acting)

DOI: 10.4324/9781003160984-24

possible. The most crucial of these being skills are relational awareness, humility, patience, presence, deep listening, letting go of control, improvisation, a beginner's mind, trusting the wisdom of the community, moving at the speed of relationship, starting from where the community is at, and building trust. Social transformation moves at the pace of trust.

## Beyond the growth node

Planning has long been associated with managing urban growth and associated urban development. Such development often occurs within and around growth nodes, such as cities that are building their local economies upon clusters of industries, particularly service and knowledge-based industry. Yet there are many areas in all countries that lie beyond the spread of the beneficial effects of such growth nodes. In these areas, there are weak economic demand for urban development, low property prices, and higher than average unemployment. Such areas 'beyond the growth node' pose a difficulty for planning that is oriented to managing and regulating urban development pressures and using these pressures to deliver community gains. Planning positively beyond the growth node remains a challenge but there are suggestions that alternative models of planning here, involving more diverse landownership, may provide lessons for post-growth planning more generally.

## Clumsy mobility solutions

Transport-related policies, plans, or initiatives that can be accepted and willingly promoted by individuals and social groups with radically different understandings about the world, namely in terms of the values, knowledge, stakeholders, processes, and substantive measures they consider appropriate to shape transport-related decisions. These solutions manage to articulate and synthesize the key aspirations held by all concerned. They are labelled 'clumsy' due to their low inner-consistency and lack of streamlined properties, which are expectable features of mobility solutions developed by individuals and groups with consensual and homogeneous views among themselves. This lack of consistency is the source of the flexibility, adaptive capacity, and resourcefulness of clumsy mobility solutions. In practice, they can be achieved in two alternative, but complementary, ways. The first is integrative: each mobility solution satisfies the aspirations and requirements of all concerned. The second is combinative: even though each solution in itself satisfies the aspirations of only some, a range of very diverse solutions is promoted in parallel so that, at the aggregate and systemic level, all concerned will have their key expectations met and major contributions integrated. The process of developing and implementing clumsy mobility solutions is open, responsive, continuous, and dynamic: when new perspectives and strong criticisms emerge, solutions assessed as suitable until that point are revised while alternative ones are (re)considered.

## Cost-shifting

A process that occurs any time (economic) agents, by implementing their activities, generate social costs, i.e. costs that can be monetized or not, and that affect directly or indirectly third persons or the environment. Unless forced, economic agents that generate such costs generally do nothing to avoid, minimize, or compensate (if it may be possible) them. Social costs are extra-economic in the sense that they are not the result of market transactions; however, to be considered as such they need to be avoidable. The agent could avoid generating them but prefers to ignore it. According to Kapp, scholars and policy makers should not deal with social costs simply or only with economic calculation; on the contrary for him dealing with systemic cost-shifting implies institutional reforms and implementation of social norms that prevent this phenomenon from being so pervasive. A major shortcoming of the notion of cost-shifting from a classical economics standpoint resides exactly in the fact that it cannot be solved simply and only with market transactions and monetization.

## Eco-collaborative housing

Collaborative housing communities that follow environmentally sustainable household and community-level practices; innovate with ownership, financial, and governance arrangements; and build and retrofit their housing with low-carbon and environmentally sustainable facilities. Collaborative housing includes a range of collective housing types: cohousing, land trusts, self-build projects, housing cooperatives, ecovillages, communes, political squats, and shared (or 'joint') households. Household members act as a community, cogoverning and sharing spaces, amenities, and facilities. It is common for certain spaces and facilities to be shared with their wider neighbourhood. The collaborative characteristic of such communities extends beyond internal members to partnerships and interrelations with government agencies, private sector actors (especially construction industry and professionals), and neighbours. Eco-collaborative household members often engage in self-provisioning with respect to food gardening and maker workshops, including re-use, repair, sharing and caring practices, and low-carbon transport sharing. Such multi-household communities are ideally placed to install and operate efficient and cost-saving collective systems including for energy provision, water supply, grey water and black water management, Internet access, and shared use of cars and white goods.

## Emerging and necessary commons

*Emerging commons* are goods that are functional to the direct exercise of social, economic, and political rights, used in non-exclusive forms and through a collective governance that distributes rights between an open community of commoners in a non-rivalistic and cooperative way. The legislative context must enable their special governance regime, encouraging and guaranteeing the establishment of collective civic management and popular assembly bodies, which constitute a new horizon of democratic self-government. Examples are ex-urban or rural places refunctionalized as spaces for the claiming and exercise of rights and of collective fulfilment.

*Necessary commons* are goods that are functional to the exercise of fundamental rights. Their public ownership must be preserved. Where they are private, they should be subject to collective use, through easement or else exceptions should be made or licences and/or patents granted to allow for them to be established for non-commercial purposes. In order to guarantee and reinforce their 'common' dimension, international treaties and laws must recognize participatory governance, which includes those for whom those goods are indispensable via their representatives, associations, groups, or public and private institutions. They might be tangible, intangible, or knowledge commons. Examples include water resources, vaccines, and all life-saving drugs.

## Food prosumption practices

Prosumption is an interrelated process of consumption and production with associated social, economic, institutional, and political connotations. When focusing on food prosumption practices, we refer to food-related practices that enable citizens to actively participate in the food supply chain. These citizens are not passive consumers anymore, they shape innovative food production and consumption practices which shorten supply chains and embed ethical and social values in market exchanges. By performing these practices, they connect with local community networks of like-minded people, develop their knowledge of the food system, and are empowered to become part of the food value chain. Prosumption is a political construct whereas consumption is an economic one. Food prosumption practices challenge current understandings of what is normal when it comes to producing, purchasing, and consuming food, therefore contributing to a paradigm shift. This shift offers an opportunity to radically reconfigure power relations between the rural and the urban in a more democratic, just, and inclusive way.

## Post-growth planner

A spatial planner who perceives growth neither as a necessary starting point to planning nor as a goal that should be achieved by means of planning. She or he works on change but does not set economic growth (especially in GDP terms) or competition among public entities (especially for population and for economic numbers) as a goal. Post-growth planners aim to enhance the quality of life for a diversity of people, but not with more of the same growth solutions. They act within available resources (including land) and planetary boundaries through a multiplicity of roles to enable a good life for all, with not always the same winning.

To achieve this, critical post-growth planners engage and motivate to take honest, just, and democratic decisions.

## Post-growth planning law

The legal framework of planning that is built on post-growth principles, norms, and values. By setting out the ground rules for managing land use, this law builds a planning system and provides planning tools that can facilitate planning practices contributing to societal post-growth transformation. Concretely, post-growth planning law needs to build on an ontology of finity that recognizes the existence of environmental limits. Respect for the environment lays the foundation for other concerns. Post-growth planning law formulates clear substantive values including redistributive justice and respect for environmental limits that concretize the overarching goal of sustainable development. Effective tools facilitating the achievement of these substantive goals need to be designed and offered by the law. Furthermore, post-growth planning law builds on an understanding of property rights as a social function that addresses the use value of land rather than the exchange value. Lastly, this law builds a planning system that distributes more equally the power among planning authorities at different levels, embedding democratic decision-making mechanisms within a hierarchical planning system.

## Post-mobile society

A society in which mobility is an option rather than a need. In a post-mobile society people can meet their needs and thrive in the environment where they are. Well-being and welfare in a post-mobile society are decoupled from intensive, high-carbon (long-distance) mobility. Post-growth society is likely to incorporate some elements of a post-mobile society.

## (Re)production (social reproduction)

(Re)production means to 'bring forth' (produce) something 'back to the original place; again, anew, once more' (re-). (Re)production is the sphere of social cooperation that has a bodily, cognitive, affective, emotional, relational preoccupation with the *production of human beings by means of human beings*. It means that human beings *are both* the means and the end of production, opening to the *possibility that cooperative processes are designed in such a way as to favour* coincidence between means and ends. The problematic of (re)production opens an autonomous space of collective reflection for the social forms necessary to articulate in a socially just way human beings as the means and end of social endeavour. The sphere of (re)production also includes a correspondent preoccupation with maintaining the ecological precondition of human existence, for us and for future generations, as our necessary and vital entanglement to all that is living in general reflects on the need that the balancing of means and ends, their mutual adjustment processes, also involves our relation to the living.

## The rural/urban divide

The concept of the rural/urban divide both illuminates and obscures. It illuminates a certain disconnection between urban and rural livelihoods in terms of economic, social, cultural, and political realities. Regarding the topic of feeding the city, the concept quite successfully captures the cultural rift between urban consumers and the mostly rural places, practices, humans, and non-humans that produce their food. It represents the simplified categories that we use to understand and shape the world, the *imaginary* boundary we have drawn between the city and the countryside. Importantly, the concept is so good at capturing 'realities' because it has been performing them for quite some time. As much a socially constructed purification as the binary between humans and nature, the notion of a rural/urban divide obscures the fundamental hybridity of rural and urban lives as manifested in the abundance of material and cultural relations that inextricably link cities and countrysides. And by doing so, by obscuring the fact that cities were made and are sustained by rural resources and labour, the concept contributes towards concealing the ongoing exploitation and subjugation of the rural under the urban that was effected by the onset of capitalist urbanization and cannot be disentangled from the history of environmental destruction that was set off simultaneously.

# INDEX

*Note*: **Bold** page numbers indicate tables, *italic* numbers indicate figures.

absolute freedom 205
abstract hope xviii
accelerating worldview of mobility 87
accessibility-by-proximity 83, 86
aesthetic approaches to nature 20–21
agencies, planning 11
aggregate indicators of wealth 6
agrowth *see* post-growth thinking
aim of this book xix
alternative food networks (AFNs) 175, 178–184, *182*
Amsterdam: alternative food networks (AFNs) 178–184, *182*; de Nieuwe Meent housing cooperative 37, 41–46; FoodCoopNoord 178–179; food scene 175–176; Pluk! CSA Groenten van West 180–181, *182*
Ashby's law 101, 102
Atacama Indigenous group 26–27
austere principles 84
autonomous housing 35–36; de Nieuwe Meent housing cooperative, Amsterdam 37, 41–45, *44*, 45–46; meaning 221; rights and 36–37, 38; *see also* housing commons

Barcelona, Glòries Park 24–25
being, in manifesto for post-growth planning 220

being skills 204, 208; in community 206–212; Indigenous peoples 207–213; meaning 221–222
beyond the growth node 137–138; Cambridge 131–132; disentangling planning from growth 5–6; influence of growth-dependent planning 131–134; Malmö, Sweden 132–136; meaning 222; planning and growth 4–5, 129; regional implications of growth node reliance 134–137; reliance on growth by planning 129–134; Skåne region, Sweden 134; uneven distribution of growth *130*, 130–131
blueprints, standardised, avoiding 15
*buen vivir see* post-growth thinking

Calcutta 164–165
Cambridge 131–132
Cambridgeshire 134–137
capitalism: negation of xvii; questioning of assumptions about xvii–xviii; and the urban/rural divide 160–161
Catalonia, Spain 25–26
centralization of power 145–146
change agents, planners as 207, 209
Chile, lithium mining in 26–27
China, Tianjin eco-city 22–24
cities: capitalism and the urban/rural divide 160–161; commons, governing cities as 102, 106, 109–110; compact cities

**228** Index

162; and country, relationship between 173–174; ecologically sustainable 161–164; empowerment of operational nodes 103; entrepreneurial approach to governance 4; environmental degradation 4; as growth machines 3; holons/holon structure 103, 104; land productivity, pursuit of 4; radical urban scholarship 163–164; rural-inclusive planning 164–167; socio-ecological prosperity of 13; *Territorios Campesinos Agroalimentarios* movement, Colombia 167–168; viable system model (VSM) 102–109, *105, 107*; *see also* urban/rural divide
clumsy solutions 88; mobility 80, 89–91, 222 (*see also* mobility)
cognitive commoning 98
collaborative housing 223
collective ownership of housing 9
colonisation, growth-oriented 6–7
commissioning rights 38, 42, 43
commons/commoning: cognitive commoning 98; eco-collaborative housing 50, 54–55, 58–60; emerging 223–224; governance 117; governing cities as commons 102, 106, 109–110; hacking the law 117–120, 121; legal framework 117; necessary 224; practices of, governance and 11; urban commons 116–117; *see also* housing commons
community capacity 177–178
community engagement and building 221–222
Community Land Trusts (CLTs) 137–138, 139
community-led food initiatives 174–175, 177–184
community mining 27
community planning, Indigenous 207–213
compact cities 162
complexity: governance and 100; variety of responses, need for 100–101; viability and 100–101
concrete hope xviii, xix
connections 205–206
cooperative housing 9
co-optation, housing commons and 36, 46
cost-shifting: by businesses and individuals 21; Catalonia, Spain 25–26; consequences of 21–22; cultural 23; examples 21; Glòries Park, Barcelona, Spain 24–25; greening and 21–22, 27; Green New Deal (GND) initiatives 20, 23; lithium mining 26–27; long-distance 26; meaning 223; measuring 22; minimisation of in planning 27–28; Nature-Based Solutions (NBS) 20–21, 23; participation of local people in green initiatives 28; regional 22–24; renewable energy planning 25–26; short-distance 24–25; social costs 22; Tianjin eco-city, China 22–24
country and cities: relationship between 173–174; *see also* rural/urban divide
Covid-19 pandemic: eco-collaborative housing 60–61; mobility and 66, 68–76
cybernetics 100–101, 103

decentralization principle 152–153
decision-making, democratic 40–41, 53
de-commodified housing 9
de-growth concept xviii; aims 19; critique of resource exploitation 19; underpinnings 19; *see also* post-growth thinking
democracy, law and 146
democratic decision-making: eco-collaborative housing 53; housing commons 40–41
DemoDev 50
de Nieuwe Meent housing cooperative, Amsterdam 37, 41–45, *44*, 45–46
dense urbanism 162
desires 195–196
diverse economies agenda 165
dwelling: manifesto for post-growth planning 219; opportunities for post-growth transformation 9–10; planning and 9–10; *see also* housing

East Cambridgeshire District Council 137–138
eco-collaborative housing: best practice in 49–50; commons/commoning 50, 54–55, 58–60; COVID-19 pandemic 60–61; democratic decision-making 53; enabling mechanisms 50–51; features of 49; finance 54; interpersonal relations 53–54; Kalkbreite housing cooperative, Zürich 55, 57–59; Kraftwerk1, Zürich 55, 57–58; Lilac (low impact living affordable community) 52–55; meaning 223; mutualism 50, 53–54, 56–58; rights 58; solidarity 56–58; state legislation, power and politics 50, 52–53, 55–56, 60; Zürich 55–56; *see also* housing commons
eco-housing 9
ecologically sustainable cities: proposals for 159; rural, role of 161–164;

rural-inclusive planning 164–167; *Territorios Campesinos Agroalimentarios* movement, Colombia 167
economic growth, mobility and 65–66, 81–82
economic language and ways of thinking 6–7
education, in manifesto for post-growth planning 220
emergence 100
emergent messy governance 99–100
emerging commons 119, 121, 122, 223–224
emotions 196–197
empowerment of operational nodes 103
entrepreneurial approach to governance 4
environmental degradation, cities and 4
ethics: law 145; manifesto for post-growth planning 220; professional ethic of planning 14
European Commission, lithium mining in Chile and 26–27
European Green Deal 20
extractive practices, cities as sustained by 4

feminist urban scholarship 162, 164–165
finity 145
FoodCoopNoord, Amsterdam 178–179
food prosumption practices: alternative food networks (AFNs) 175, 178–184; Amsterdam's food scene 175–176; community capacity 177–178, 183–184; community-led initiatives 174–175, 177–184; FoodCoopNoord, Amsterdam 178–179; integrated food policies 184; meaning 224; neighbourhood food hubs 184; Pluk! CSA Groenten van West, Amsterdam 180–181, *182*; rural/urban relationship 174; sweat equity 183–184; volunteering 183–184
freedom 204–205

gentrification 24–25
Germany 191
global/liquid societies 78n1
global urban/rural divide 160
Glòries Park, Barcelona, Spain 24–25
glossary for post-growth planning 15, 221–226
good life, the *see* post-growth thinking
governance: commons 117; commons, governing cities as 102, 106, 109–110; complexity and 100; as coordination within complexity 100; diffuse and participatory model, need for 101–102;

emergent messy governance 99–100; empowerment of operational nodes 103; entrepreneurial approach to 4; good 115–116; holons/holon structure 103, 104; local 114–115; manifesto for post-growth planning 220; meta-management 103–104, 109; political power, critiques of 112–113; post-growth 11; public/private relations 113–116; (re)production and 97–99; stakeholders 114–115; style of 113–116; subsidiarity principle 116; variety of responses, need for 100–101; viability and 100–101; viable system model (VSM) 102–109, *105*, *107*
green aesthetics 20–21
green economics *see* post-growth thinking
green-grabbing 23
greening: cost-shifting and 21–22, 27; European Green Deal 20; Green New Deal (GND) initiatives 20, 23; Nature-Based Solutions (NBS) 20–21, 23; trend of 20
Green New Deal (GND) initiatives 20
green sacrifice zones 25–26
growth: beyond growth nodes 137–138; Cambridge 131–132; disentangling planning from 5–6; influence of growth-dependent planning 131–134; link with planning 4–5; Malmö, Sweden 132–136; planning as originating in 129; questioning of assumptions about xvii–xviii; regional implications of growth node reliance 134–137; reliance on growth by planning 129–134; Skåne region, Sweden 134, 135–136; uneven distribution of *130*, 130–131
growth nodes 222

hacking the law 117–120, 121
hedonistic principles 84
holons/holon structure 103, 104
hope xviii–xix
housing: Cambridge 133; Malmö 133; *see also* eco-collaborative housing; housing commons
housing commons: admission and unit allocation 42–43; autonomous 221; autonomy and 35–36, 39; commissioning rights 38, 42, 43; commoning 221; compass of rights 36–37; co-optation 36, 46; degrowth, commoning and 35, 36; democratic decision-making 40–41; de Nieuwe Meent, Amsterdam 37, 41–45, *44*, 45–46; dispersion of rights

39–40; disputability of rights 40–41, 46; eco-collaborative 223; inclusion rights 38–39, 42–43; income rights 39, 44–45; institutional architecture of 37–41; management rights 38, 43–44; manifesto for post-growth planning 219; marginalisation 46; opportunities for post-growth transformation 9–10; rights 36–37, 38–40, 42–45; risks faced by 36, 46; trade-off between energy and expertise 40–41; as transitional practice towards degrowth 45–46

inclusion rights 38–39, 42–43
income rights 39, 44–45
indicators of wealth 6
Indigenous peoples: Atacama Indigenous group 26–27; community planning 207–213; political ecologies 14
individualism 204–205
infrastructural capacity 177–178
institutional capacity 178
institutions, post-growth 11
interdependence, widening conception of 122
interpersonal relations 53–54
Italy: Civil Code 119; Naples 118, 121–122; natural resources, governance of 121; subsidiarity principle 116

justice 145

Kalkbreite housing cooperative 55, 57–59
Kraftwerk1 housing cooperative, Zürich 57–58

land productivity, pursuit of 4
land use in manifesto for post-growth planning 219
law: commons/commoning 117; decentralization principle 152–153; democracy 146; eco-collaborative housing 53; ethics 145; finity 145; foundations for post-growth law 144–146, **147**; hacking the law 117–120, 121; justice 145; manifesto for post-growth planning 220; municipal planning 149–150; national planning 148; non-materialistic quality of life 146; ontology of a stratified world 145; Planning and Building Act 2008, Norway 147–153; post-growth and 144; post-growth planning law 153–154, 225; property rights as foundation of planning law 151–152; redistribution 145–146; regional planning 149; substantive norms 152
Leeds, Lilac (low impact living affordable community) 52–55
left-wing politics compared to post-growth thinking 7–8
legal frameworks: commons/commoning 117; decentralization principle 152–153; democracy 146; ethics 145; finity 145; foundations for post-growth law 144–146, **147**; hacking the law 117–120, 121; justice 145; municipal planning 149–150; national planning 148; non-materialistic quality of life 146; ontology of a stratified world 145; Planning and Building Act 2008, Norway 147–153; post-growth and 144; post-growth planning law 153–154, 225; property rights as foundation of planning law 151–152; redistribution 145–146; regional planning 149; substantive norms 152
Lilac (low impact living affordable community) 52–55
liquid/global societies 78n1
lithium mining, cost-shifting and 26–27
local people and contexts: community capacity 177–178; community engagement and building 221–222; Community Land Trusts (CLTs) 137–138, 139; community-led food initiatives 174–175, 177–184; community planning, Indigenous 207–213; engagement with 15, 221–222; lithium mining 26–27; participation of locals in green initiatives 28; Tianjin eco-city, China 23
local/stagnant societies 66–67, **67**; mobility, Covid-19 pandemic and 68–76

Malmö, Sweden 132–136
management rights 38, 43–44
manifesto for post-growth planning 15, 219–220
Māori worldview 211
marginalisation, housing commons and 36, 46
marketisation, housing commons and 36
measures of wealth 6
metabolic rift 160–161
meta-management 103–104, 109
migration, rural to urban 3
mobility: accelerating worldview 87; accelerators 88; access 67, **67**, 69–71;

accessibility-by-proximity 83, 86; alternative narratives 82–83; ambivalence 76–77; appropriation and meaning 67, **67**, 73–74; Cambridge 134; clumsy mobility solutions 89–90, 222; competence 67, **67**, 71–73; congestion 81; Covid-19 pandemic 66, 68–76; dependence on, promotion of 10; dependence on and disruption of 82; discovery and opening 76–77; diversity in responses to lack of, need for 77; dominant pro-growth narrative 81–82; economic growth and 65–66; environmental impacts 82; explorers 89; innovations 82; integration of worldviews 90–91; local/stagnant societies 66–67, **67**; Malmö, Sweden 134–135; manifesto for post-growth planning 219; materials 67, **67**, 74–75; negative impacts of improving 82; participators 89; planning and 10–11; post-growth approach 10–11; post mobility growth world 77; rebels 88–89; Skåne region, Sweden 135; sustainable mobility paradigm 65–66; time traveling, value of 84–86; trade-offs between faraway and nearby 77; typology of worldviews 86–89, *88*; values of current narrative 80; virtual mobility 82–83, 86; well-being of individuals and 66, 76–78; working from home, experiences of 68; worldviews on, integrating 80
Multi-Level Perspective (MLP) 66
mutualism 50, 53–54, 56–58

Naples, Italy 118, 121–122
nature, cities and 12–13; *see also* rural/urban divide
Nature-Based Solutions (NBS) 20–21; Glòries Park, Barcelona, Spain 24–25; Tianjin eco-city, China 23
necessary commons 224
neo-liberalism 112, 113
Netherlands: alternative food networks (AFNs), Amsterdam 178–184, *182*; de Nieuwe Meent housing cooperative, Amsterdam 37, 41–45, *44*; FoodCoopNoord, Amsterdam 178–179; food scene in Amsterdam 175–176; Pluk! CSA Groenten van West, Amsterdam 180–181, *182*
nodes, growth 222
non-materialistic quality of life 146
Norway, Planning and Building Act 2008 147–153

nurturing: manifesto for post-growth planning 220; post-growth 12–13

obesity 83
ontology of a stratified world 145
operational nodes, empowerment of 103
organisational capacity 178
orientations in planning practice 207
ownership model of property 45

Parc de les Glòries, Barcelona, Spain 24–25
pesticides, cost-shifting and 21
planners, post-growth: desires 195–196; economic systems, bias towards 191; emotions 196–197; internal barriers 194–199; meaning 224–225; opportunities 195–199; political, processes of as 190; positions on post-growth in planning 192–194, **194**, 199; private/professional roles 191; research into post-growth planning 189; sensemaking 198–199; transformative planning, research into 191–192; values 197–198
planning: disentangling from growth 5–6; link with growth 4–5
Planning and Building Act 2008, Norway: decentralization principle 152–153; ideological underpinnings 151–153; municipal planning 149–150; national planning 148; process, primacy of 152; property rights as foundation of 151–152; purpose of 147–148; regional planning 149; substantive norms 152; sustainable development as purpose of 147–148, 152
Pluk! CSA Groenten van West, Amsterdam 180–181, *182*
political power, critiques of 112–113
possessive individualism 204–205
post-colonial urban scholarship 162, 164–165
post-growth: concept xviii; law and 144
post-growth planners: desires 195–196; economic systems, bias towards 191; emotions 196–197; internal barriers 194–199; meaning 224–225; opportunities 195–199; political, processes of as 190; positions on post-growth in planning 192–194, **194**, 199; private/professional roles 191; research into post-growth planning 189; sensemaking 198–199; transformative

planning, research into 191–192; values 197–198
post-growth planning law: commons/commoning 117; decentralization principle 152–153; democracy 146; eco-collaborative housing 53; ethics 145; finity 145; foundations for post-growth law 144–146, **147**; hacking the law 117–120, 121; justice 145; manifesto for post-growth planning 220; meaning 225; municipal planning 149–150; national planning 148; non-materialistic quality of life 146; ontology of a stratified world 145; Planning and Building Act 2008, Norway 147–153; post-growth and 144; post-growth planning law 153–154, 225; property rights as foundation of planning law 151–152; redistribution 145–146; regional planning 149; substantive norms 152
post-growth thinking: aggregate indicators of wealth 6; alternative vocabulary for 7; early 8; economic language and ways of thinking 6–7; lack of for planning 8; left-wing politics compared 7–8; name of field 6; need for planning 8–9
post-mobile society: access 67, **67**, 69–71; appropriation and meaning 67, **67**, 73–74; competence 67, **67**, 71–73; COVID-19 as trigger for 68–76; diversity in responses to lack of mobility, need for 77; materials 67, **67**, 74–75; meaning 225; trade-offs between faraway and nearby 77; well-being, mobility and 76–78
power centralization 145–146
*The Principle of Hope* (Bloch) xviii
professional ethic of planning 14
property regime approach 38–39
property rights as foundation of planning law 151–152
prosumption *see* food prosumption practices

qualitative growth 212–213
quality of life 146

radical urban scholarship 163–164
reality, questioning of assumptions about xvii
redistribution 145–146
regional implications of growth node reliance 134–137
regulations: Cambridge/Cambridgeshire 131–132, 134–137; Malmö, Sweden 132–136; manifesto for post-growth planning 220; post-growth 11–12; self-regulation of housing 9; *see also* law
relational worldview 205–206, 207–212
renewable energy planning, cost-shifting and 25–26
(re)production: applied to human beings 98; cognitive commoning 98; emergent messy governance 99–100; governance and 97–99; governing cities as commons 102, 109–110; as layered and transversal 98–99; meaning 98, 225–226; operations in a city 106; viable system model (VSM) 102–109, *105*, *107*
resource provision in manifesto for post-growth planning 220
rights: eco-collaborative housing 58; housing commons 36–37, 38–40, 42–45
Rodotà Commission 118–119
rural/urban divide: capitalism and 160–161; food provision and 173–174; global 160; meaning 226; questioning 13; radical urban scholarship 163–164; rural-inclusive planning 164–167; *Territorios Campesinos Agroalimentarios* movement, Colombia 167–168; urban sustainability studies, ideas from 161–164

second-order governance 103–104
self-building of housing 9
self-organisation within systems 100
self-regulation of housing 9
sensemaking 198–199
Skåne region, Sweden 134, 135–136
social acceleration 84
social capital 177
social costs 223; cost-shifting 22
social justice, Tianjin eco-city, China 23
social reproduction: cognitive commoning 98; emergent messy governance 99–100; governance and 97–99; governing cities as commons 102, 109–110; as layered and transversal 98–99; meaning 98, 225–226; viable system model (VSM) 102–109, *105*, *107*
socio-ecological prosperity of urban areas 13
solidarity 56–58
Spain: Catalonia 25–26; Glòries Park, Barcelona 24–25
stagnant/local societies 66–67, **67**; mobility, Covid-19 pandemic and 68–76
stakeholders 114–115
standardised blueprints, avoiding 15

states: eco-collaborative housing 50, 52–53, 55–56, 60; new forms of post-growth 11
steady-state economics *see* post-growth thinking
stratified world, ontology of a 145
subsidiarity principle 116
sustainable mobility paradigm 65–66, 81
sweat equity 183–184
Sweden: Malmö 132–136; subsidised premises for SMEs 138
Switzerland: Kalkbreite housing cooperative, Zürich 55, 57–59; Kraftwerk1 housing cooperative, Zürich 57–58

*Territorios Campesinos Agroalimentarios* movement, Colombia 167–168
Theory U 213
Tianjin eco-city, China 22–24
time traveling, value of 84–86
transport: accelerating worldview 87; accelerators 88; access 67, **67**, 69–71; accessibility-by-proximity 83, 86; ambivalence 76–77; appropriation and meaning 67, **67**, 73–74; Cambridge 134; clumsy mobility solutions 89–90, 222; competence 67, **67**, 71–73; congestion 81; Covid-19 pandemic 66, 68–76; dependence on, promotion of 10; discovery and opening 76–77; diversity in responses to lack of, need for 77; dominant pro-growth narrative 81–82; economic growth and 65–66; environmental impacts 82; innovations 82; integration of worldviews 90–91; local/stagnant societies 66–67, **67**; Malmö, Sweden 134–135; manifesto for post-growth planning 219; materials 67, **67**, 74–75; negative impacts of improving 82; participators 89; planning and 10–11; post-growth approach 10–11; post mobility growth world 77; rebels 88–89; Skåne region, Sweden 135; sustainable mobility paradigm 65–66; time traveling, value of 84–86; trade-offs between faraway and nearby 77; typology of worldviews 86–89, *88*; values of current narrative 80; virtual mobility 82–83, 86; well-being of individuals and 66, 76–78;

working from home, experiences of 68; worldviews on, integrating 80

uneconomic growth 81
United Kingdom: Cambridge 131–132; Cambridgeshire 134–137; Lilac (low impact living affordable community), Leeds 52–55
urban activism, early 8
urban areas: entrepreneurial approach to governance 4; environmental degradation 4; as growth machines 3; land productivity, pursuit of 4; socio-ecological prosperity of 13; *see also* cities
urban commons 116–117
urbanisation, wealth creation and 3
urban/rural divide 173–174, 226; capitalism and 160–161; global 160; questioning 13; radical urban scholarship 163–164; rural-inclusive planning 164–167; *Territorios Campesinos Agroalimentarios* movement, Colombia 167–168; urban sustainability studies, ideas from 161–164
urban sustainability: capitalism and the urban/rural divide 160–161; ideas from studies on 161–164; rural-inclusive planning 164–167
urban symbiotic practices 13

value of time traveled 84–86
values 197–198
viable system model (VSM) 102–109, *105*, *107*
virtual mobility 82–83, 86

waste dumping, cost-shifting and 21
wealth, aggregate indicators of 6
well-being: defined 66; mobility and 66, 76–78
willful planning xix
wishful planning xix
working from home, experiences of 68
worldviews: Māori 211; possessive individualism 204–205; post-growth 14; relational 205–206, 207–212; transport-related 86–89, *88*

Zürich: Kalkbreite housing cooperative 55, 57–59; Kraftwerk1 housing cooperative 57–58

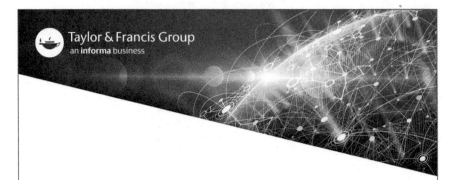